Praise for *50 Ways to Leave Your 40s*

"Dipping into this treasure trove of a book makes me want to go back in time so I can leave my forties again. *50 Ways to Leave Your 40s* offers so many creative ideas, so much thoughtful information, and so darn much fun, I'm sure I'd do it more gracefully, healthfully, and happily the second time. Congratulations and thanks to Sheila Key and Peggy Spencer for giving all of us a life-affirming map to follow, no matter what our age."

— Judy Reeves, author of *A Writer's Book of Days*
and *Writing Alone, Writing Together*

"Sheila Key and Peggy Spencer know that a new decade of life is the beginning, not the end, of something great. With generous helpings of wisdom and wit, *50 Ways to Leave Your 40s* is a recipe for joy during what comes next."

— David Niven, PhD, author of *The 100 Simple Secrets of Happy People*
and *The 100 Simple Secrets of the Best Half of Life*

D0107162

50 Ways to
Leave Your 40s

50 Ways to Leave Your 40s

Living It Up in Life's Second Half

SHEILA KEY & PEGGY SPENCER, MD

New World Library
Novato, California

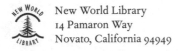

New World Library
14 Pamaron Way
Novato, California 94949

The material in this book is intended for educational purposes only. No expressed or implied guarantee as to the effects of the use of the recommendations can be given nor liability taken. The authors' experiences used as examples throughout this book are true, although identifying details such as name and location have been changed in some cases to protect the privacy of others.

Permissions acknowledgments appear on page 282.
Text design by Tona Pearce Myers

Library of Congress Cataloging-in-Publication Data
Key, Sheila.
50 ways to leave your 40s : living it up in life's second half / Sheila Key and Peggy Spencer.
   p. cm.
Includes bibliographical references.
ISBN 978-1-57731-545-2 (pbk. : alk. paper)
1. Middle age—Psychological aspects. 2. Middle-aged persons—Psychology. 3. Middle-aged persons—Conduct of life. I. Spencer, Peggy. II. Title. III. Title: Fifty ways to leave your forties.
BF724.6.K49 2008
155.6'6—dc22   2007049235

First printing, March 2008
ISBN: 978-1-57731-545-2

Printed in the United States on 50% postconsumer-waste recycled paper.

New World Library is a proud member of the Green Press Initiative.

10 9 8 7 6 5 4 3 2 1

To Richard, my heart, and Maya and Sayre, my jewels
— S. K.

To the memory of Steven M. Spencer
— P. S.

Contents

PART 1: BODY

PART 2: MIND

PART 3: SOUL

PART 4: HEART

"Doc in the Box" Contents

BODY

MIND

SOUL

SOUL

Stop! Hey, What's That Sound?

Tick-tock, y'all! Hear that? Tick-tock.

You're thinking of a clock, no doubt, and you're right. For what else is a birthday — *any* birthday — if not a measure of the passing time?

But the Big Five-oh? That really *is* big. Like Welcome-to-Life's-Second-Half big — which is to say, gigantic. Momentous. Pivotal!

Shh, listen! Is it the ticking clock that sounds throughout these pages, or is it your beating heart? Either way, this book grooves to the rhythm. With a title spun from an old Paul Simon hit, and me (a radio DJ from back in the day) calling the tune, *Fifty Ways to Leave Your Forties* was bound to pound out a jammin' beat.

Did I say "pound"? Oh yeah, this book was also bound to be a chunky little thing, packing that other kind of pound. For your most momentous, pivotal, *gigantic* Five-oh, Dr. Peg and I wanted merely to give you the world. I'd have called down the sun, moon, and stars, too, but Peg, in her doctorly wisdom, prevailed on me to make this a book that "people our age" could actually lift! So we kept everything short but still packed a lot in. For you, dear reader, all for you!

So. Ready to lift? Who needs barbells to do a few muscle-building reps, when you could just pick up a second copy of *Fifty Ways* (ostensibly for a friend) and have a chunky little number in both hands. Use 'em or lose 'em, as they say. That's another of the beats sounding throughout this book, and I hardly need to explain why.

We midlifers get pulled in lots of directions. We do and do and do for our kids, our parents, our bosses. Many of us move from one sitting position to another, all day, every day, eating junk or nothing at all. And if ever we do get a little time to ourselves, about the only thing we can manage is to shlump in front of a mind-numbing TV show with a stiff drink in hand. It's no way to live — like I need to tell *you*.

Calling all couch potatoes! This "big-oh" birthday rolls you right up to a crossroads. You can either start taking better care of yourself, or — do you *really* want to roll? — you can resign yourself to the inevitable wheelchair. Sorry if that harshes your mellow, but it's the God's honest truth. It's also the reason Peg and I fitted each of the fifty Ways in the book with one of our "Cool Moves." Call them exercises if you must, but I think you'll find many of these activities to be like no other exercises you've ever done, especially the ones adapted from Dahn yoga, a holistic wellness program of ancient Korean origin that remains relatively unknown in the States. Our fondest wish is that you'll go for all the gusto in life's second half. That you'll follow your heart, expand your mind, feed your soul, be all that you can be! And for feats such as these, dear one, you're really going to want a body that's physically up to the challenge.

Can't wait to get started? Then go! *Go!* In the immortal words of E.T., I'll be right here.

So! How to give you the world for your birthday? For starters, we divided the fifty Ways into the four realms of Body, Mind, Soul, and Heart. In that order, the realms correlate with the four directions (North, East, South, and West), the four seasons (Winter, Spring, Summer, and Fall), and the four sacred elements (Earth, Air, Fire, and Water). Now, is that cosmic, or what?

Seriously, *cosmic* is one word for it. *Holistic* is another, and this is a drum I beat with enthusiasm, for holism thrums with tidings of great hope: *You are not alone. We are all connected. The Whole is greater than the sum of its parts.* Besides, most holistic traditions originated in the East, and I wouldn't dream of giving you only half a world.

Even Peg, a Western doctor by training, has her toes tapping in both camps, as you'll discover in the "Doc in the Box" sections, which she researched and wrote for each Way. Her subjects range from the mainstream of allopathic (Western) medicine to the edgier modalities of what is often called "complementary care" or "integrative medicine." Ah, but our Peg is no pushover. If you think she'll just up and embrace every alternative therapy in the book, well, as the Mods banged out back in '66, "you've got another think coming."

In addition to "Cool Moves" for fitness, and "Doc in the Box" for medical advice, each Way chimes with ideas for further exploration: "Scribbles & Doodles" to get you into your journal and "Things to Try at Least Once" to get you out of your rut.

Mostly, though, what Peg and I hope you'll hear among these pages is the irrepressible rustling of joy — joy enough to make you bust out laughing, sure, and the kind that comes from improving your mental outlook and physical habits, even just a little. But also the simple joy of having lived this long, of being able to look back over five full decades and forward to who-knows-how-many more; not to mention (though you know I will, at least once or twice) the joy of living more mindfully in the ever-present Now, and that most liberating and cleansing of all joys, the one born of forgiveness.

It ain't over till it's over. Pay no mind to the fat lady in your life's "green room." So she's practicing her scales, so what? For now, the beat goes on.

Happy birthday, by the way. Wanna dance?

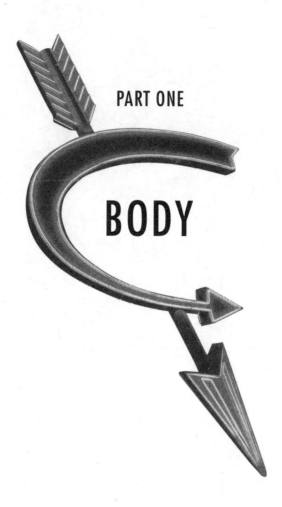

PART ONE

BODY

WAY 1   Just Keep Breathing

Breathing is like an entire book distilled into one sentence.

— Deepak Chopra, *Golf for Enlightenment*

*H*ere's the minimalist's approach to leaving your forties: in, out, repeat. If you're not the kind to fuss over birthdays — if you just can't be bothered with anything more taxing than taking a breath — then this is the Way for you. Just keep breathing.

There's nothing to it! Newborn babies can do it with their eyes closed. So what's the big deal, right?

Well . . . there's breathing, and then there's *breathing*. Just ask the midwife, the athlete, the asthmatic. Ask the opera singer or the auctioneer. Ask anyone who does yoga or meditates. There are *lots* of ways to breathe.

Oh, for Sighing Out Loud!

Voicing your exhalation with a deep, audible sigh helps relax the body from head to tail. Try it. It's the fastest, easiest, most accessible stress reducer there is — cheaper than Valium, and with fewer negative side effects.

3

SCRIBBLES & DOODLES
Breathe through Your Pen

Close your eyes. Breathe normally, and relax for a few moments. Open your eyes and begin to write, keeping your pen point moving at all times, until you've filled three pages. What to write? Finish these two sentences in alternating sequence: "When I inhale..." and "When I exhale..." Write whatever comes. No editing or overthinking allowed! Just keep finishing the sentences. Repetition is okay. After you finish, read your writing aloud (give *breath* to your words!), and mark any passage that brings emotions to the surface. Write a few minutes more about the experience. Any surprises? There are no wrong answers.

Breath comes instinctively as that good, old sigh of relief — *shuh-wheew!* — after a real scare (or, say, a particularly dreaded birthday). But for ordinary, everyday stress — the background noise of life — *just keep breathing*. Evenly. Mindfully. Keep the O_2 coming, and the CO_2 going. And continued for as long as possible.

The Body-Mind Bridge

You may think of breathing as merely a nose-mouth-and-lung thing, but, in fact, the oxygen exchange of respiration occurs within every cell of your body. Breathing is one of the body's autonomic functions, doing its thing whether or not you're thinking about it. But unlike other autonomic functions — the beating of the heart, digestion, and such — breathing is within your conscious control. And *that*, my friend, is the key to the kingdom!

Through breath, you can use your body to relax your mind. Through breath, you can use your *mind* to relax your *body*. According to some Eastern traditions, the breath does more than exchange oxygen for carbon dioxide at the cellular level. It also drives the circulation of chi, the essential life-force energy, throughout the body. Consider the words *spirit*, *aspire*, and *inspiration*: all are close cousins of *respiration*. By breathing more consciously, you will breathe more fully, thus drawing into your body's every nook and cranny the spirit of life itself.

You Don't Know the Half of It!

Ever been in an exercise class where the teacher reminds everyone to breathe? People laugh, as if to say, "Oh, yeah, I forgot." But chances are they only forgot step two: breathing out.

"When we focus on the breath, we tend to think of inhaling more deeply, but not exhaling more deeply," observes body-centered psychotherapist (and friend) Bhanu Joy Harrison, LISW. She adds that this is consistent with our tendency to value work more than rest: "As we get on toward our fifties, we try to *hold on* so much — to our bodies, our minds, our sense of control. But it is the *letting-go* — the exhalation — that makes room for what comes next."

Bottom line: Waste no time "waiting to exhale."

Quit Holding Out and Draw Another Breath

Once you're hip to the ins and outs of your own breath, you may discover something that millions of meditators know: observing your breath keeps you centered and present, "in the Now." And, as wise ones have been pointing out for ages, there is no better place — in fact, no *other* place — to find spiritual enlightenment. Guess that's why it rates a capital N.

 COOL MOVES

Breathe Here Now (Breath-Counting Meditation)

"*Sit quietly and observe the breath.*" That's typical meditation guidance for the beginner. But if you've tried it, you know that, even if you can manage to sit *comfortably* for ten minutes or more, getting your chatty brain to shut up can be a real struggle. Next time, try this. Sit comfortably with your spine tall and your head ever so slightly bowed. Close your eyes, and take several deep breaths. Then let the breath come naturally. The depth and rhythm of your breaths may vary, but aim for slow and quiet. Count each exhalation, up to five, then begin a new cycle. Never count higher than five, and count only exhalations. You will know your attention has wandered when you find you've counted past five. Continue for ten minutes or longer.

 DOC IN THE BOX: *The Good, the Bad, and the Ugly (Bad Breath)*

We have all known, or been, someone with (stage whisper) *halitosis*. Even if you don't have it, you might fear that you do, and that would make you a *halitophobe*. That's a real diagnosis! I'm making fun here, but it's really no joking matter. Bad breath is off-putting and embarrassing.

The word *halitosis* means "foul breath" in Latin, but it wasn't a diagnosis until Listerine popularized it in company ads in the early 1900s. Some halitosis is caused by illness, such as a gum infection, and will resolve once the illness is treated. Most is caused by (cue creepy music) an alien invasion: bacteria. I mean the nasty kind, with five o'clock shadows and mismatched socks. These grungy outcasts don't even breathe oxygen. That's why your breath is worse in the morning; they've been partying in your closed mouth all night. First they root through the alleys between your teeth, munching on stuck chunks of proteinaceous leftovers. Then they kick back in the Lowlife Lounge at the back of your tongue, slurping postnasal mucus and having a contest to see who can emit the most noxious gases. Charming, eh?

If that doesn't get you to floss, then you're a hopeless *halitophile*. (Okay, that one's not a real diagnosis.)

It's not always easy to know if you have halitosis. Our noses are acclimated to our own odors; it's hard to smell yourself, in other words. If you think you might have bad breath, ask someone you trust. If they confirm your worst fears, include the following alien-busters in your daily routine.

Floss, floss, floss. Drink plenty of water, and eat high-fiber foods. Gargle with mouthwash. Brush your tongue as well as your teeth, or get a tongue scraper and demolish the Lowlife Lounge. Once you've cleaned up the neighborhood, the air will be sweet again!

〰️ THINGS TO TRY AT LEAST ONCE

☐ *Breathe like a baby.* Let your belly rise with the in-breath and fall with the out-breath. Now see if you can make this motion as automatic as breathing itself.

☐ *Breathe like a dragon.* Pranayama's Breath of Fire is one of the innumerable breathing techniques out there designed to enhance your well-being. You may suck at all of them (to use a respiratory term), at least at first, but they're worth a try, even if only for the head rush!

☐ *Never quit quitting.* Smokes, that is. You can't expect to "just keep breathing" if you don't have any lungs.

☐ *Take singing lessons.* A good voice teacher will help you harness the power of your breath.

☐ *Blow the dust off.* Has an important *something* been dormant for too long? The musical instrument under the bed, for example, or your love of long, slow needlework? If so, then breathe life back into it.

Love Thy Body as Thyself

Enjoy your body. Use it every way you can. Don't be afraid of it or what other people think of it. It's the greatest instrument you'll ever own.

— Mary Schmich, *Chicago Tribune*, "commencement address" column

It may be sagging, balding, aching, graying, and wrinkling. But honey, it's the only one you've got. Be it ever so humble, there's no place like home, and in this life, your body is *it*! We're talking valuable real estate here, the permanent address not just of your physical parts but also of every thought in your mind and every emotion in your heart. There's no trading up from *this* "home, sweet home," so mind the upkeep, would'ja?

Do You Love Me? Will You Love Me Forever?

Your body's no dummy. It wants tender loving care *daily*, not just a once-in-a-blue-moon spa treatment (though no doubt your body wants that, too). True love is constant, for better or worse, in sickness and in health. You may not recall the "I do's," since this was a marriage made in utero, but believe you me, the "till death do you part" clause is absolute. So please — do your darnedest to keep the love alive.

"You Talkin' to Me?"

If you get nothing else from this chapter, please get this: Stop trash-talking your bod! If you want to talk *to* or *about* your long-suffering parts, fine, but remember: you'd be up a creek without them.

Be especially mindful in the presence of youngsters, whose developing sense of their bodies will be colored by what you say about yours. A sore knee is not a "bad" knee; try "tender" instead. Big legs are strong; why label them "fat"?

Let us give our bodies some well-deserved credit, shall we? If yours is still in the race after this many hard-driven laps around the track, then *that's one fine piece of machinery you've got there*!

Welcome to the Age of Acceptance

Perhaps the best way to show your body love is simply to accept it — its size, its looks, its limitations. Holly, an on-and-off dieter since her teens, finally gave up the "losing" proposition in her forties. "I finally learned to ignore what I call 'the mean parent in my head,'" she emailed. "I'm now on the 'eat-what-I-want-when-I-want-to' diet. I decided, 'I'm forty-eight, I've had a child, and who said I have to look like an athlete, anyway?'"

For Tuko, it wasn't her weight that was bothering her. It was her knees. She'd become decidedly active in midlife, beginning with the rollerblades she gave herself as a fortieth birthday gift.

SCRIBBLES & DOODLES
"What I Like about You . . . You Really Know How to Dance"

Set a timer for five minutes and, as fast as you can, complete this sentence over and over: "My body can . . ." Think of as many different endings as possible, and keep it positive. Repetition is okay. After the bell goes ding, read your list *out loud*. Hear that drumbeat? "My body can . . . My body can . . ." Your deepest self will hear and heed this empowering chant. Read what you've written again (and again) the next time your body could use some encouragement.

But after moving to Hawaii at age forty-seven, playing beach volleyball with people half her age helped her find her limits. "I'd wake up the next day barely able to walk!" she recalled. "So now, instead of four games in a row, I'm playing a game and a half, max."

You Are More Than the Sum of Your Parts

For all its importance, the flesh-and-bone temple that houses your soul is *not* the be-all and end-all of life. Think of Christopher "Superman" Reeve after his riding accident or Stephen *A Brief History of Time* Hawking after his diagnosis of Lou Gehrig's disease. Think of Helen Keller, Franklin Roosevelt, and *anyone you know* with extraordinary physical limitations. Despite their loss of physical capability, these individuals continue (in many cases, even after their death) to have a positive influence in the world. You — with your body — can, too.

COOL MOVES
Those Three Little Words

Your body hears everything you say about it, even the wicked opinions you express only to yourself. Hate your hips, you say? Then I hope you're saving up for new ones! (Fact: hip replacements, numbering 234,000 in 2004, are the fifth most common surgery performed in the United States.) Here's a better idea: Do as they teach in Dahn yoga (aka Dahnhak), a modernized version of an ancient Korean holistic-health program. While standing, clap your hard-working hips

DOC IN THE BOX: *Love It or Change It? (Plastic Surgery)*

"Love thy body," we say. Well, what if you don't? What if you look in the mirror and pine for days gone by and a body gone bye-bye? What if you don't want basset hound eyelids, a "turtle" neck, or a sumo belly? What if you liked having your breasts *above* your beltline?

If you don't love it, why not just "fix it"? A nip here, a tuck there, and voilà! The new you.

I hear what you're thinking. "Well, why not? It's not as if it could kill me!" Well, think again. It is surgery, after all. And any surgery comes with risks, such as bleeding, infection, and blood clots. With general anesthesia, you add the possibilities of brain damage, paralysis, and death (oh, that). Cosmetic surgery adds yet more risks, such as skin necrosis, asymmetry, slow healing, and "unsatisfactory results." Remember your cousin who didn't like the shape of her new nose after all? Then there's my patient "Karla," who showed me the "unsatisfactory result" of her boob job, which could best be described as cockeyed. One faced northeast, the other southwest. She was on her way back to the surgeon, in tears, for a brutal fix under anesthesia.

Still want that nip and tuck?

There is no fountain of youth. Rearranging slabs of flesh and skin will not reverse the aging process. If you don't love thy body, could you at least accept it? Next time you look in your "mirror, mirror on the wall," ask yourself this: Wouldn't it be a lot less expensive and risky to lift your attitude instead of your face?

In my professional opinion, the best kind of face lift is absolutely free — of cost, risk, and pain. Smile! Show us those laugh lines. See that? Beeeeyoootiful!

repeatedly with your cupped palms and shout, "I love my sexy hips!" Pat (*hard!*) all around your hips — front, back, sides — and keep telling them how much they mean to you. (If you're not chanting, at least exhale through your mouth, and think loving thoughts!) Choose any part — *every* part — and express your love for it, out loud and often, while patting or rubbing it (thus stimulating circulation) with your "healing hands." Don't forget your *beautiful* face and your *powerful* brain.

〰️ THINGS TO TRY AT LEAST ONCE

☐ *See your doctor.* This is a "thing to try at least once" *every year.*

☐ *Use* Arnica montana. Known as wolfsbane in days of old, this yellow daisylike flowering herb, the essence of which is available in a topical ointment or oral pill, relieves muscle aches and bruises.

☐ *Compose a love poem to your body.* Gush rhapsodically ("How do I love thee? Let me count the ways") about every last little thing you'd do to demonstrate your love for your bod.

☐ *Treat yourself to a professional massage.* It's nice to be kneaded. And speaking of kneading, if "dough" is an issue, find a massage school, many of which offer reduced rates to give students plenty of warm bodies on which to practice. Or buy a how-to book, and practice massage yourself or with a partner.

Don't Let Gravity Get You Down

Build me straight, O worthy Master!
Staunch and strong, a goodly vessel.

— Henry Wadsworth Longfellow, *The Building of the Ship*

*O*h, the temptation to wallow in cynical humor about gravity's ill effects on our supple selves! Growing jowls — or going from a bra size of 36C to 36-long — that sort of thing. But this book's aim is decidedly upward, so let us consider how to live in harmony with that ever-present g-force, and even to turn it to our advantage.

This Old House: The Body as Architecture

Bodies, like buildings, must obey the laws of physics. This I know only too well because, for twenty-nine years, I was the "leaning tower of Sheila." Due to an uncorrected lazy eye, I unwittingly cocked my head to one side, so as to point my stronger eye at the world. This in turn threw my spine out of whack. By the time I'd corrected both my eyesight and posture through a vision reeducation program, the damage had been done. Nearly two decades later, I still struggle with musculoskeletal problems stemming from those crooked early years.

The moral of this story (to quote everyone's mother): "Stand up straight, dear!" Dividing your weight evenly between your two feet is the proper place to start. Here are more ways to "be at one" with gravity:

Reel it in. Keep your head over your shoulders, where it belongs, and tuck your chin slightly. Just this one postural correction works wonders.

Bag the shoulder bag. Fanny packs and backpacks are okay, but only if they are *always* centered on the body. For larger loads — briefcase-toters, listen up! — take a lesson from flight attendants, and pull it on wheels.

Keep it symmetrical. Break the leg-crossing habit (a low footrest can help). And *please* stop jamming that phone between shoulder and ear. Consider a hands-free adapter required equipment.

Face it head-on. Square up to the table, and place your task front and center, close to your body. This goes for even fleeting moves such as refilling cups and signing guest books.

Be ergonomically correct. At your desktop computer or laptop, adjust your chair, screen, and keyboard to satisfy this checklist: spine tall, chin tucked, gaze fixed slightly downward, shoulders relaxed, upper arms hanging straight down, elbows at a 90-degree angle, wrists straight, knees level with (or slightly higher than) hips, feet on low footrest. This checklist goes for mouse clicking as well as for keyboarding. Laptop tip: No slumping! Sit your tailbone wayyy back in your chair, and place a hard "hotdog" pillow behind your lower back. Better, yes?

Rock on. Avoid standing with the bulk of your weight on one hip. Instead, shift rhythmically from foot to foot. This stimulates circulation in your hip joints and promotes blood return to the brain, preventing the infamous "soldier's faint."

Let 'em dangle. Your hands, I mean. Don't wear your shoulders for earrings! Notice which muscles are truly needed for the job, and consciously relax all the rest. "Let go of what's not working" is good advice on the yoga mat and in life.

The Upside of Gravity

Ask any astronaut: we owe our very strength to gravity. (Before they were tasked with heavy-duty exercise as a regular part of their responsibilities, spacemen's bodies shed significant amounts of bone density and muscle mass during extensive stays in a weightless environment.) Weight is gravity's handiwork, and *weight-bearing exercise* is practically synonymous with *strength training*.

If you're thinking, "Not for me, the bodybuilder's physique," that's fine. But if you're trying to beg off weight training entirely, let me appeal to your fraying nerves, with the words of Dr. Henry S. Lodge, coauthor (with Chris Crowley) of *Younger Next Year*: "Generally, we aren't aware of nerve decay as we get older, but it's the main reason our joints wear out, our muscles get sloppy and our

SCRIBBLES & DOODLES
Defy Gravity, Defy the Grave

Write about "the gravity of the situation." What situation? You decide, just as long as it's grave enough to have gravity! Is something getting you down? Well, don't just wallow six feet under. Push up a few daisies, as it were. Find the growth opportunity available to you in this dark hole. Out of decay rises new life.

DOC IN THE BOX: *Two Ways to Straighten Up (Rolfing and Alexander Technique)*

When it first came to the United States from its native Germany, Rolfing rapidly gained a devoted following, although there were those who used words like *steamrollering* to describe the experience. You'll be relieved to know that according to the Rolf Institute, Rolfing, formally called Structural Integration Technique, has lightened up over the years. Think of the technique as a kind of deep-tissue massage.

Dr. Ida P. Rolf developed her holistic system of soft-tissue manipulation and movement education in the middle of the last century. By organizing the whole body in gravity, the Rolfer's manipulations are designed to refine the body's patterns of movement, making them more efficient and economical, thus conserving energy and reducing wear and tear. According to the Rolf Institute's official website (www.rolf.org), such structural improvements, besides bringing a new level of comfort to the body, can also reduce chronic stress and enhance neurological functioning. All that, and not a steamroller in sight!

Still, if the idea of deep-tissue manipulation rubs you the wrong way, you might be interested in the subtler Alexander Technique.

Early last century, an Austrian actor named Frederick Alexander lost his voice. The doctors couldn't fix it, so Alexander decided to try to cure himself. Surrounding himself with mirrors, and carefully observing his movements and speech efforts, he discovered that his vocalization changed significantly depending on his stance. In a mere(!) nine years of practice, his perseverance was rewarded with the return of his full, rich voice.

The Alexander Technique has been called a process of *unlearning*. You've seen the straight back of a walking toddler. That is the natural, healthy, low-stress position that we lose, to our detriment, after years of hard living and endless sitting. The Alexander Technique teaches the body, through gentle correction by suggestion or touch, how to regain "primary control" and return to natural, fluid movements in harmony with gravity. Learn more at www.alexandertech.org.

ability to be physically alert and powerful begins to fade. And *it is reversible with strength training*" (emphasis mine).

In other words, there's a lot more riding on those barbells than the promise of a buff bod. *Pumping iron helps keep you young.* Now *there's* a gift I bet you didn't expect to get from gravity!

COOL MOVES

Do a Balancing Act

Place two bathroom scales side by side and calibrate them so that they both weigh you the same. Stand with one foot on each and, without peeking, distribute your weight equally between them. Now peek: Do the scales confirm your sense of balance? If not, shift your weight until the two readings match. Take heed: this is what balance feels like. *Memorize it!*

THINGS TO TRY AT LEAST ONCE

❑ *Bone up*. Pump iron, get enough calcium, and visit www.nof.org, the official website of the National Osteoporosis Foundation, to learn all you can about bone health.

❑ *Straighten up!* Modalities that help correct alignment problems abound. Try Googling "chiropractic," "Reiki," "osteopathy," and "myofascial trigger-point therapy," or even just "spinal alignment."

❑ *Invert yourself*. Whether by donning inversion boots, reclining on a slant board, practicing inverted yoga postures, or simply lying on your back with your legs up the wall, the practice of turning gravity on its head (or on *your* head) offers benefits ranging from roses in your cheeks to better mental functioning. It also rests the heart, relieves an aching back or feet, and takes the pressure off varicose veins. Warning: Do not invert if you're pregnant.

❏ *Try ben-wa balls.* Ladies, especially if you've had babies, stick this pair of marbles where the sun don't shine (vagina, not rectum), and you'll be on your way to a stronger pelvic floor (read: better bladder control and sexual enjoyment). (See also "Kegel! Kegel! Kegel!" on page 92.)

Get Your Motor Runnin'

There was the fire, snapping and crackling and promising life with every dancing flame.

— Jack London, *To Build a Fire*

*R*acy machines are the quintessential midlife toys, but they're not the only way to hum! Consider the motor inside you. As you notch 50,000 miles on the ol' girl (or guy), how's she running? Does she start right up in the morning?

This Way helps you to look under the hood and ask, How can I stoke my "internal combustion"? How can I zoom into life's middle laps with maximum horsepower and smooth-running endurance? We look both East and West for answers.

Coffee, Tea, or Chi!

I happen to love coffee — I love caffeine in general — so I'm not about to diss a good, hot jolt of joe in the morning or a cup of real tea in the afternoon. But with supermarket shelves growing crowded with high-octane "energy drinks," aimed at amping up a populace already riddled with substances of both the upper and downer variety, it really must be said: a tankful of stimulants will not get you very far.

Food is the true metabolic fuel. (We'll get to that in Way 9.) But forget *input* for now. Let's talk *output*. Let's talk about the proverbial "fire in the belly" and how you can stoke it to maximize your "machine's" performance. Let me begin by describing the Eastern view of what makes the human body's motor hum.

The Original Biofuel

We'll be talking about chi a lot in this book. Variously spelled (sometimes as *qi* or *ki*) and pronounced (usually as "chee," sometimes as "key"), depending on the Asian language used, chi is the essential energy of life. For robust, good health, chi must flow. That's Eastern medicine in a nutshell. Circulation is health. Stagnation is death. (This may strike you as a little over the top, but listen! Over-the-top stuff gets remembered better.) Go ahead, read it out loud (that helps, too).

Circulation is health. Stagnation is death.

Bus Stop, Bus Go, Press Here, Chi Flow!

Chi circulates throughout the body by way of a dozen primary and eight secondary energy channels called meridians. These are akin to

SCRIBBLES & DOODLES
Basic "Auto" Mechanics

The prefix *auto* means "self." Think about something you've wanted to do but haven't been able to get started. Then take a good look under your hood. What seems to be the trouble? Out of gas? Are the spark plugs shot? Maybe it's flooded! Whatever the metaphor, ask yourself what it would take to get that baby running — jump-start? tune-up? tow? — and, again, define what the metaphorical solutions mean. Keep tinkering. You'll get that baby up and humming.

bus routes, along which are located hundreds of points akin to bus stops. By stimulating these points (through acupressure, acupuncture, massage, or another modality), a person helps the chi on or off the bus. Stagnation breaks up and disperses, chi flows freely, and well-being is restored. It's a bit more complex than that, involving yin and yang, fire and water energies, and more. But by and large it's all about chi flow.

Perhaps most vexing to Western minds is the fact that, unlike the conduits of the circulatory and nervous systems (and, to be clear, unlike actual bus routes and bus stops), energy meridians and points are not physical structures. A surgeon could poke around inside somebody all day and never actually find any of them. Ilchi Lee explains, in his book *Brain Respiration*: "Meridians consist of pathways along which energy flows in highest density. Energy does not travel through a fixed, predetermined highway system, but forms a network of roads by the act of passing."

Fire in the Belly

The "batteries" of the meridian system are called *dahn-jons*, in Dahnhak terms (which is to say, in Korean). Located in the head, chest, belly, hands, and feet, not only do these seven energy centers "power the grid," sparking the chi to move, but just like other rechargeable batteries, they also accumulate and store energy for later use.

The granddaddy of all *dahn-jons* is centered in the lower abdomen, about two to three inches below and behind the navel. In the Eastern view of body-as-car, that fire in your belly, that granddaddy of all *dahn-jons*, is the motor. Ready to get yours running?

COOL MOVES

Stoke the Fire (Dahn-jon Tapping)

Stand with your feet parallel and shoulder-width apart. Keep your knees soft, and bounce slightly in rhythm to your tapping. Clap your cupped palms in unison on your lower abdomen, counting two claps as one rep. Keep your gaze slightly downward and your neck and shoulders relaxed, and exhale through your open mouth. Do a few hundred, five to ten minutes' worth. *Tap it like you mean it!*

Variation: With soft fists (wrap fingers loosely around thumbs), tap the pinkie side of your fists on your lower abdomen as if it were a drum,

---

 DOC IN THE BOX: *Bump Up Your Idle (Metabolism)*

When you take your foot off the gas pedal, your car's engine runs on idle for a moment, until you turn the ignition off. Then the engine rests. Your body is different. Your engine is always running. There is no rest until the Eternal Rest! Even when you're asleep, stock-still in dreamland, your motor is burning calories.

We all have different idle speeds. In cars it's called RPM. In bodies it's called BMR, or basal metabolic rate. This is your idling speed, the rate at which your body burns calories at rest. Your BMR depends partly on your genetics, and you're stuck with that. But it also depends on your body composition. The more muscle you have relative to fat, the higher your idle speed. Muscle burns more calories at rest than fat does. It makes sense, really. It takes more energy to be a lean, mean muscle than a sloppy slab of fat.

Now, we all know that our overall metabolism slows down with age. It gets easier to gain weight and harder to lose it. However, as you see here, there's an extra bonus to shaping up. As you exercise more, replacing fat with muscle, you will burn more calories *even in your sleep!* Doesn't that fuel your motivation to exercise? Give yourself a high-octane gift for your fiftieth birthday: build some muscle and adjust that idle up!

alternating hands with each beat. Either variation can be done seated or standing, though standing naturally removes a major kink from the meridians. Take that fire in your belly for long "drives" of ten to thirty minutes, to relieve headaches, calm anxiety, cool hot flashes, and generally keep your energy system running smoothly. Finish by rubbing your belly in a clockwise direction (look down at your body and *be* the clock!).

THINGS TO TRY AT LEAST ONCE

❑ *Reduce your use!* Next time you're jonesing for java, try a glass of water or a short, brisk walk first. Caffeine gives you a short-term boost, but on the energy front, its net effect is negative. If a hot beverage is a cherished treat, try herbal tea instead.

❑ *Burn, baby, burn.* Focus throughout the day on the *dahn-jon* energy center in your lower belly. Feel it as the driver of your body's energy system.

❑ *Rent a little red Corvette* (or the muscle car of your dreams) for a drive up the coast or a joyride around town.

❑ *Rev up an Easy Rider party*. Rent the movie, sing along to that good ol' Steppenwolf classic "Born to Be Wild," and reminisce about your own wild travels. Or hey, haul out your "hog," and head out on the highway!

5 S-t-r-e-t-c-h I-t O-u-t

A mind that is stretched by a new experience can never go back to its old dimensions.

— Oliver Wendell Holmes (1808–1894)

*H*ave you been noticing your muscles more often lately? I know I have! No doubt these "rubber bands" that hoist the bones have wanted proper care all along, but by fifty they fairly demand it. Many of us hit the gym in pursuit of stronger muscles. But what good are strong muscles if they're tied up in knots? Seriously, if you're trying to strengthen muscles that are locked in spasm, you're wasting your time and misplacing your effort.

Loosen Up

Nature gave muscle fibers exactly one job to do — tighten — a job they sometimes do too well, frankly. Getting them to relax? That's your job, and they don't always make it easy for you. With my own spinal weirdness and long years of treatment, I was quite stunned to learn that unhealthy muscles can practically *live* in spasm. They never let go of their clench, unless their loving, caring owner takes the time — *lots* of regular, daily time — to coax the muscle fibers back into proper place, shape, and mobility.

Circulation is health, remember? It delivers the goods and carts off the trash. If you don't move enough, your body's various circulations (blood, lymph, chi) can't reach every cell and capillary. Stagnation sets in. Oh, have I mentioned? *Stagnation is death!*

So stretch *all* your parts, would you please? Or, as in the old tooth-flossing joke, only the ones you want to keep!

R-e-h-a-b-i-t-u-a-t-e

Chances are you already know how to stretch out all your muscles. The how-to's of proper stretching are posted in any gym worth its salt. But what you might not know (until you read Dr. Peg's explanation of muscle anatomy and function) is how important it is to hold your stretches for a l-o-o-o-n-g time. Ours is a rush-rush world, so even if you do know that you should hold stretches for thirty seconds or longer, you may still speed through them. Don't.

Rehabituate your muscles through long, slow, regular stretching, and you'll start feeling younger, more agile, and unbelievably comfortable in your own skin. Here, to occupy your mind during those long, slow, *delicious* stretches, is a little word poem to use as a mantra (sorry,

SCRIBBLES & DOODLES
Super (Stretchy) Hero!

Enter the world of make-believe, if you dare! That dreadful mishap with your spandex undies yesterday unleashed strange doings in your DNA. Suddenly, this morning you're a superhero. *Elasti-Gal!* Or maybe *Bungee Boy!* What on earth to do? Imagine: if you could stretch as far and as flexibly as you wanted (literally and/or figuratively), what feats would you accomplish? Think *big*, or should I say, *long*-term!

the word *rehabituate* contains no *M* for *muscles*, so they became hemp-fibers): ***Release-Elastic-Hempfibers.-Allow-Bones,-Initially-True,-Unimpeded-Access-To-Efficiency***. Don't miss Peg's variation of this slow-stretching Word to the Muscles.

Make It Last

Another kind of "stretching it out" feels wonderful and should be sustained for a good, long while. It's the proverbial "party going on around here" that Kool & the Gang sang about. You know the one I mean? "A celebration to last throughout the year!"

You only turn fifty once. S-t-r-e-t-c-h I-t O-u-t! Savor it. Turn it into the Energizer Bunny of birthday celebrations. Just think: with fifty-two weeks in the year, you could do a special weekly something *fifty* different times this year — go see a play or exhibition, jot in a journal, get out for a "nature day," *nap* — and still have two whole weeks left over for a little vacation!

 COOL MOVES

Squeeze in a Stretch

In a busy life, clocking thirty minutes of mat time can be a stretch, all right! Plan B calls for doing what you can in the wee moments between appointments. Try these:

- *Star gazer:* Sitting in a low-backed chair, interlace your fingers behind your head, and lean back as far as you can (being careful not to tip, of course). Hold for thirty seconds.

DOC IN THE BOX: *"My, Oh, Myofilament!"* *(Muscle Stretching)*

What is stretching, exactly? Is it really possible to increase our flexibility? If so, how? To understand, we have to go back to Anatomy 101 for just five minutes. Stay awake!

Your muscles are made of bundles of bundles, like a telephone cable. The smallest "phone wire" is called a *myofilament.* A mere fraction of the width of a human hair, and coming in a variety of lengths, these tiny threads are responsible for all your strength. When you "make a muscle," the myofilaments slide alongside each other, stacking up to effectively shorten (and thicken) the muscle. When you stretch, they slide the other way, unstacking and lengthening the muscle. Picture raw spaghetti sliding in and out of the package.

If a muscle stretches too far, it will tear. Your body, in its wisdom, has a stopgap for this. Each muscle houses an internal monitor, the muscle spindle, which detects the amount of stretch going on. When the stretch gets to its limit, the spindle sends a signal for the muscle to contract, thus preventing an overstretch injury. However, if you hold a stretch long enough, the spindle will get "habituated," or accustomed to the new muscle length, and send fewer signals to contract. If you do this over and over, you can retrain your spindles to allow a greater muscle stretch.

Another monitor, the Golgi tendon organ, lives in the tendon, the tissue that attaches muscle to bone. It is less sensitive than the spindle, meaning that it takes more stretch to activate it. It also has a different response: when the Golgi is activated, the muscle actually lengthens. That sudden "give way" feeling you got if you ever lost at arm wrestling was Golgi in action. Golgi is why, after you hold a stretch for thirty seconds, you'll find you can stretch farther.

Knowing this, Sheila offered her Word to the Muscles poem above to use as a nice, slow stretching mantra that, at the same time, affirms the muscles' ability to rehabituate. As promised, here's my variation. If you'll give three long beats to every word — or repeat the mantra three times slowly during each stretch — that should do the trick: *Relax-Entangled-Hempfibers,-Allow-Bundles,-Initially-Tight,-Unimpeded-Access-To-Elongation.*

Last word: warm muscles stretch better. Start with a brisk three-minute walk before stretching.

- *Toe gazer:* Don't try this right after lunch. Push your chair back from the desk, and fold your body forward, letting your head and arms dangle. Feel the stretch in your spine. Hold for thirty seconds.

- *Shy turtle:* Keeping your shoulders down and relaxed, pull your chin (or chins!) back toward your spine. Don't tip the head back; keep your chin tucked. Hold for a slow count of three, then release. Repeat five times.

- *Gyrohead:* Let your head drop forward, with chin toward chest. Roll your head from side to side, slowly, going no farther than ear-to-shoulder in each direction (ear won't touch shoulder). Repeat ten times. On the final few reps, when your head is all the way to one side or the other, place that side's hand on your head, and let the weight of your arm deepen the stretch.

- *Twister:* While seated in a chair, grab the right armrest or right side edge of the chair seat with both hands. Pull gently to effect a spinal twist in that direction, while maintaining an upright posture. Hold for thirty seconds. Repeat on the left side.

〰️ THINGS TO TRY AT LEAST ONCE

- ❏ *Take a Pilates class.* "Reform" your muscles, lengthen your spine, and strengthen the all-important core. Find out what everyone's been talking about!

- ❏ *Stretch your boundaries.* Go out of your way to do something new and different. Read a provocative book. Make a cake from scratch. Bring home a big lump of clay, and see what happens.

- ❏ *Eat Slow Food.* Stretch out your mealtime. Put your fork down between bites. Broaden your palate by continually trying new foods. Value quality (culinary artistry) over quantity (fast, cheap "filler"). Explore local growers' markets, and click on www.slowfood.com to learn more about the larger concept — the socioeconomics of Slow Food.

❑ *Survey the horizon.* See those decades s-t-r-e-t-c-h-i-n-g both behind and before you? Take stock, notice progress, look ahead, set goals. What is your intention for the decade of your fifties?

WAY 6   Run for Your Life

A good set of feet can take you anywhere, doesn't require a parking place, can go up and down stairs, usually comes as standard equipment on a human body, isn't likely to be stolen and is allowed on a variety of surfaces in all 50 states.

— Kent Judkins, *Time* magazine

*N*ow that we're all warm and limber from the previous two Ways, it's time to get moving. "Run!" this chapter implores, but really any type of aerobic exercise will do. The importance of working up a good, *longish* sweat several times a week cannot be overstated.

If you've never had much of an exercise habit, or if, like me, you tend to be on-again but mostly off-again, let me do as Chris Crowley and Henry S. Lodge, MD (authors of *Younger Next Year*), did for me. Let me scare the holy bejeezus out of you.

Run! Your arteries are hardening! Your bones are becoming brittle! Your muscle mass is dwindling. For heaven's sake, *run*! If you want to live (and live well), *run*. Or at least move fast and keep moving!

Where's the Fire?

Oh, it all sounds like such hard work, doesn't it (she whined)? But listen! I want to emphasize this. You don't have to run miles or pedal a bike to nowhere or do any of those "exercise"-type things. Indeed, if you've never been particularly athletic, then age fifty is probably not the time to *take up* running. Never say never, of course, but my best suggestion would be to work up a daily sweat while engaging in a passion. Dance. Swim. Chase after grandkids. Or just *walk*. Get out into the world and discover previously unknown beauty in your midst.

More and more and more, if you have someplace to go, walk there.

Clip on a pedometer, and just you wait (no, don't! go now!): you'll park farther away, you'll take the stairs, you'll go the long way around — just to rack up more steps. The average office worker walks fewer than five thousand steps a day. Double that — ten thousand steps a day! — and you'll be well down the road to better health.

Walking Back to Wellsville

A deadly car crash left Janine with a broken pelvis and a traumatic brain injury. During her month in a medically induced coma, her family wondered whether she would ever walk again. Meanwhile, across town, her old college chum Lynne, a longtime distance runner, was experiencing a crash of a different sort.

"In a matter of weeks, I went from running twelve miles a day to barely being able to lift my legs," Lynne recalled. Turns out, it was leukemia. Lynne heard about Janine's accident and tried to call her but didn't hear back before her own diagnosis eclipsed everything else.

"And a couple days into my treatment, in walks Janine, like a miracle!" Lynne said. "The last I knew, she was in the hospital. Now here she was — walking! — without any cane or crutches, like nothing had even happened to her."

Talk about motivation! As soon as Lynne got out of the hospital, she and Janine got busy walking together every day. Soon, they joined the Leukemia & Lymphoma Society's Team-in-Training program. By now they can't even count how many fund-raising marathons they've walked, or even run!

SCRIBBLES & DOODLES
A Walk through Time
(Walking Meditation)

Walk around the block *counterclockwise* while mentally taking yourself back through the years of your life. When you return home, sit and contemplate the nothingness that was you before you were born, and write about the walking-meditation experience so far. Then up again to walk around the block — *clockwise* this time — while mentally moving forward through the ages and stages of your life. On arriving home once more, complete your writing about this walk through time.

Big and Hairy and Audacious — Oh, My!

Stephanie's motivation to take up marathoning was a Los Angeles Unified School District program called "Students Run L.A.," which trains (mostly) at-risk kids to complete a 26.2-mile race. As you might guess, running is not the real lesson.

"What these kids learn," Stephanie explained, "is that they can accomplish really big things in their lives — what in graduate school we used to call a 'Big, Hairy, Audacious Goal' — if they really set their minds to it. This program is completely voluntary, and I thought, if these kids can show up here after school to take on something so huge . . . then the least I can do is help them."

In the process, of course, Stephanie helped herself, too, and learned all the lessons that marathoning teaches: How to increase your endurance through training. How to pace yourself for the long haul. How to keep your eyes on the prize, even when your energy's flagging.

"Now, no matter what my latest B-HAG," Steph says, abbreviating the hairy audaciousness of her many big entrepreneurial ventures, "I say, 'Okay, what's the goal, and what's my training schedule?'"

And with that, she's off and running again!

 DOC IN THE BOX: *Tender Loving Foot Care*

The feet are the unsung heroes of most aerobic workouts, and sore, aching feet are one of the most frequent excuses people give for not getting enough exercise. But most foot problems are treatable, many of them at home. So no more excuses! Take care of your feet, and they'll take care of you. Here are some home remedies for the most common feet ailments:

- *Cracked soles.* Do you have yellow, dry, cracking heels? The culprit is usually a fungal infection. Try this. After you shower, go after that thick, cracking skin with your weapon of choice — pumice stone, file, even a razor (careful!). Then, when you've removed most of the dead, calloused stuff, apply an antifungal cream or tea tree oil (melaleuca), and rub it in well. Do this every time you shower, and you can say good-bye to cracked feet!

- *Stinky feet.* Also due to the fungus among us. Keep your feet clean and dry, changing socks frequently. Don't go barefoot at the public gym or changing room. Slather on the antifungal cream daily or even a few times a day. And, hard as it may be, dig every stinky shoe out of your closet, throw it away, and start fresh.

- *Blisters.* Use petroleum jelly or any thick ointment to grease up the areas of your feet most likely to develop blisters. Wear acrylic socks. Their layered construction will absorb the friction so your tootsies won't have to. Or wear two pairs of socks, especially for a long hike. The thinner pair goes inside. If you start to get a "hot spot" (a place that's red and sore but not yet a blister), take the pressure off it right away by applying moleskin.

- *Tender toe tips.* Keeping your toenails short will keep your toes more comfortable in those running or walking shoes. Be sure to cut them straight across, not on a curve, to avoid the dreaded ingrown nail.

- *Middle-age spread.* Recheck your shoe size yearly; it tends to increase with age. Wear flat, wide, comfortable shoes to avoid Achilles tendon shrinkage, bunions, and foot pain.

Last word: podiatrist. Remember, the foot bone is connected to the everything-else bone, so treat those dogs well. Don't put up with foot pain. See the specialist.

COOL MOVES

Tap Your Toes, Move Big Chi

This Dahnhak exercise is a new angle on moving the feet (faster! faster!) to elevate the heart rate, though its true aim is to unblock the energy meridians in the hip area. Do this at bedtime to quiet the brain, cool the fires of hot flashes, help overcome insomnia, and relieve restless legs syndrome. Lie on the floor (or in bed) with your legs straight and your feet together, resting your hands on your lower abdomen. Begin rolling your legs rhythmically outward and inward from the hips, moving your toes apart and together, alternately tapping the pinky toes on the floor and the big toes together. If you can't manage the entire range of motion, just do the best you can. Keep your heels together throughout the exercise, and move faster and faster for greater benefit. Begin with one hundred repetitions and build up to five hundred or more. As you complete your count, slowly stop the motion. Relax, open your mouth, breathe naturally, and enjoy the sensation of once-stagnant energy flowing out through the soles of your feet.

THINGS TO TRY AT LEAST ONCE

- ❏ *Zip it up.* While walking, consciously engage the abdominal muscles. Think of your core musculature (including the pelvic floor) as a girdle, and keep it zipped — not clenched, but snug.

- ❏ *Go the distance.* Run a marathon. Walk a half-marathon. Sign the whole family up for a Fun Run. Set your sights on a goal within your fitness range, and train for the big day. Dress comfortably (no brand-new shoes!), wear a hat, apply sunscreen liberally every two hours, and stay hydrated.

❏ *Walk the labyrinth*. Find one of these beautiful circular paths, many of them replicas of the famous labyrinth at Chartres Cathedral in France, and enjoy a walking meditation. Google "labyrinth locator" to find one near you — or buy a portable one, on canvas. Such a product actually exists.

❏ *Try reflexology*. According to practitioners of this modality, the feet mirror the body, containing energy connections to every bodily structure, and by manipulating the foot, you (or a professional reflexologist) can effect healing throughout. Detailed "foot maps" are widely available, but who needs a map when you can simply let the tender spots tell you, "Yes, massage here"? Be careful not to go too deep too fast, though. Drink lots of water after a reflexology treatment, and come back to tender spots again tomorrow.

7 Pause

To sit with a dog on a hillside on a glorious afternoon is to be back in Eden, where doing nothing was not boring — it was peace.

— Milan Kundera

Calgon, take me away!
— TV commercial, ca. 1970

*S*top! Whoa! Time out! In honor of the momentousness of your Big Five-oh passage, permit me to declare *now* the Perfect Time to Pause. For how long — a few breaths, a long weekend, a summer off, a sabbatical year — is for you to decide. Forget power lunching. Let's talk power *resting*.

What's the worst that could happen? Would your friends and family disown you if you skipped today's shower and shave? Would civil society crumble if you stayed in your jammies all day? Would your house fall off the planet if you postponed this weekend's home-maintenance project in favor of a movie-watching marathon? No, no, and no, am I right? So just do it! Or rather, just don't do it! Don't do anything — and keep it up (er, down) for as long as possible.

Pop Quiz! The Nuttin'-Doin' Downtime Endurance Test (aka D-TET)

In case you're one of those type A's who needs a darned good reason to indulge in even the least amount of downtime, let us call this a test. The object of the test is to do nothing. That's it. Simply pause . . . for as long as you can. "You are a human being," as the gurus say, "not a human doing." So just be.

Think not of laziness or wasted time. Just be. With single-minded determination, just be. Ready? Go!

Stoplight: The Pause That Refreshes

I know, I know. Stuff piles up if you leave it too long. But even momentary pauses refresh the spirit. Which is why I like to think of stoplights as both reminders and opportunities to "just chill." Think about it: giving pause is what stoplights do for a living, and they're not about to . . . *stop!* So we might as well turn them to our own advantage, wouldn't you agree?

Next time you're stopped at a red light, instead of stressing about how late you're going to be, instead of zoning out, just pause and be mindful of yourself in this moment. Notice your breath, and smile lightly. Release your shoulders. Let your jaw go slack. "Shift and lift" yourself into proper posture. Breathe easily, and let your mind relax. Allow all the red lights in your path to call you back to your True Self, the you who dwells ever in the here and now. Then may each green light find you more centered and at peace, ready to resume your movement in traffic.

SCRIBBLES & DOODLES
"Sit! Stay!"

It's nice to be out in nature for this one. And while it can be tremendously enjoyable to write while in the great outdoors, writing is not the same as pausing, so this exercise asks you to keep your pen stowed until you return from your outing. Find a comfortable place, and just sit there, eyes open, and be present, from moment to moment, for a half hour or longer. Allow your thoughts to drift by. There's no need to attach to any of them. Feel your breath move in and out. Notice everything: sights, sounds, smells, the textures of things. Just be. That's all. Return to your journal, and write about your experience, in glorious sensory detail.

COOL MOVES

Press Pause

Dahn yoga teaches momentary breath-holding as a way to nudge stagnant energy that is blocking the free flow of chi. One such pause goes like this.

With your feet hip-width apart, inhale deeply while raising clasped hands high over head, turning palms toward the ceiling as you straighten the elbows. Hold your breath and, keeping your body facing forward, bend sideways at the hips, as far as you can. Focus on your pain points and *prrresss* your held breath against the stagnant energy trapped there. "Here," pain says, pointing at the blockage, "open up this area here." After several long moments, exhale exuberantly — *pheeeeeeeew!* — to drive out the blockage, as you return to an upright position. Repeat in the opposite direction.

THINGS TO TRY AT LEAST ONCE

☐ *Monotask*. Multitasking is all fine and good, but when *la vida* starts feeling too *loca*, focus decidedly on just one thing, and put everything else on pause.

☐ *Get down with your bad self*. Aching? Flagging? Find a nice, open spot on the nearest carpeted floor, and lie down for ten minutes. Let gravity pull on you from that angle for a while. Put a pillow beneath your knees if that's more comfortable. Get up slowly by first bending your knees and turning to one side.

DOC IN THE BOX: *Oh,* That *Kind of Pause!* (Menopause and "Manopause")

In my medical training, I was taught that menopause, while not exactly an illness, was still a sad state of affairs. It was a *failure* of a woman's ovaries, resulting in a *lack* of hormones that medical science needed to *replace*. Women got decrepit, dry, and brittle, poor things, and it was up to Medicine to come to the rescue, to bring rain to the desert. Madison Avenue and Big Pharma have added their own bold colors to this mirage.

In fact, passage from our fertile years to our golden years is a normal, natural phase. Like any life change, it can be smooth or rough, joyful or painful. The word *menopause* literally means "cessation [*pause*] of menstrual periods [*meno*]," but it's not like turning off a faucet, nor is it only about bleeding. It's a multisystem process that can last for several years. And it's not all bad. No more tampons! No more pregnancy worry. No more PMS.

Having said that, I readily admit that this "natural process" can be distracting, uncomfortable, and a downright nuisance. You might be bothered by physical symptoms (dry skin, weight gain, "power surges"), emotional fluctuations (we call them "mood swings," but they can be more like that amusement ride where you get catapulted up two hundred feet and, one second later, yanked back to ground level), and/or mental changes (uh, I forgot what I was going to say here!).

If you have "change-of-life" symptoms that are getting in your way, by all means get some help. Both the Western and Eastern traditions offer ways to smooth this transition for you. Hormone replacement therapy (HRT) is by no means the only option. And don't forget to use contraception if you're in a heterosexual relationship, until the transition is complete. We've all known someone who had (or was) a change-of-life baby.

Oh, I almost forgot (must be my hormones): What about the guys? Is there anything to this rumor of "manopause"? Or are they just trying to keep up with the Joneses? This is a controversial topic. Male hormones do decline gradually with age. Again, it is a normal, expected change. Some men experience symptoms that interfere with their functioning, such as depression, sexual difficulties, and even night sweats. And as with menopause, there is help to be had, from both East and West. Let the golden years shine!

❑ *Stare at the wall.* Ah, the tabula rasa, the blank slate! Georgia O'Keeffe was known to sit for hours, contemplating a blank, white wall before starting her next painting.

❑ *Give new meaning to HRT.* Hallelujah, Retail Therapy! Menopause has its upside. Stuff your ugly, old undies into the rag
   bag, and go blow some dough on a bunch of pretty new ones!

W A Y 8 Play Ball!

None are so old as those who have outlived enthusiasm.
— Henry David Thoreau (1817–1862)

*D*on't you just love the TV ads that are broadcast during big sport-ing events? All over the world, people are "playing the game" or "going for the gold," as they say on the telly. Office jocks feign free throws into wastebaskets. Street kids kick around an empty milk jug. The baseball diamond in a pickup game magically links Latin America and Japan by way of St. Louis.

To play ball is almost elemental. Like electrons around a nucleus, like planets around the sun, balls in motion are nature's way. Got game? If so, it promises good fun with friends, a healthy break from the seri-ous stuff, and — if you turn off the TV — a good romp out in the fresh air and sunshine.

So Many Balls, So Little Time

Let me be clear: we are talking all kinds of balls here — yup, even that euphemistic kind! Dr. Peg will get into men's health matters *down there*,

41

while I wander far afield, so to speak, way beyond playing ball, as in team sports. Indeed, *ball* is not this Way's only key word. There's also *play!*

So what kind of ball are you into? Ever play seven-up as a kid? That was my game — just me, the ball, and a wall! My lazy eye got between the ball and every bat or racket I ever swung, but the solo game of seven-up worked for me, even after I upgraded to a superball and the size of my game grew to gigantic proportions.

"Dad? Wanna Go Outside, Toss around the Hoberman?"

Ever heard of Hoberman's Sphere? Maybe you've seen one of these cool, kinetic, educational toys and not known what it's called. Think *polyhedral* and picture a brightly colored, hinged-plastic skeleton of a ball that pulls open from "about yea big" to "ginormous." Hoberman's, in my humble opinion, is the coolest species of ball on the planet, and should you ever be lucky enough to own one, my guess is you'll draw a crowd wherever you play with it. Naturally, everyone else will want to play, too.

Do You Have the Balls?

If not ball, then play *something*. Anything! Just be sure to get your daily dose of fun. Babies and very young children do almost all their learning through play, and these days, it's all over the news how important play is — and not just for kids.

Also, since I'm talking ballsy, let me play umpire a moment and call you right up to the plate. Aw'right, so what's that metaphorical ball you've been wanting to smack out of the park? Think fast! Because . . . *hey batta-batta-batta, hey, batta-batta.* You're up!

COOL MOVES
They Bounce, You Balance

Have you ever tried using a big exercise ball in place of your office chair? *So good!* It's soft and bouncy, it makes you sit up straight, and — here's the best part — it works your core! Because it's unstable, the ball-as-chair requires *you* to be the stable one, and to do that, you must engage the deep muscles. And keep them engaged. As "balance challenges" go, this is a mild one, yet there's not a ball sitter among us who hasn't slipped off. So *be careful*. Beyond seated hip circles and such, and just plain bouncing as the gentlest of low-impact aerobics, the ball offers no end to body-building fun. To learn "ball work" for every major muscle group, and some more robust ways to be aerobic with the ball (round ball square dancing, anyone?), consult the illustrated how-to poster that comes with purchase, or scout around for an especially inspired "balls class."

SCRIBBLES & DOODLES
Spheres of Influence

From the hugest planets to the tiniest subatomic particles, spheres are nature's preferred form. Imagine that the important people in your life are electrons orbiting the nucleus that is you. Then get out your colored pencils or crayons, and draw a picture of your spheres of influence. Who's in the inner circle? Who hails from a galaxy far, far away? How are they all connected to each other and to you? Have any of them been "Plutoed" lately (i.e., demoted to subplanet status)? How many degrees of separation are there between you and Kevin Bacon? This is all in fun, so *have a ball!*

THINGS TO TRY AT LEAST ONCE

❑ *Have a ball on your fiftieth.* Here's a different spin on the word *ball*. Rent a hall. Go for engraved invitations, Oscar-worthy attire,

DOC IN THE BOX: *The Pesky Prostate*

While you're seated at your desk on that big exercise ball (see "Cool Moves"), can you men name the gland you're sitting on? Yep, the prostate, producer of seminal fluid. You probably never even thought twice about this little guy in the past. Most men are much more interested in its two pendulous neighbors, the testicles, or, you know, Big Daddy himself! So why worry about the prostate now? Because, for the mature man, this walnut-sized gland can sprout problems as big as a mighty oak. The most common of these are BPH, cancer, and infection.

BPH stands for benign prostatic hypertrophy. (*Hypertrophy* means "growth," and the emphasis is on the second syllable.) The prostate surrounds the urethra, so as it enlarges, it puts the squeeze on. If you're having trouble starting or stopping your stream, or if you're having to urinate more frequently than usual, you may have BPH.

Cancer of the prostate is the second cause of cancer death in men over forty-five, after lung cancer. It can be silent (presenting no symptoms), or it can present the same symptoms as BPH, plus possibly blood in the urine or semen, and back pain. Infection can cause pain with urination or ejaculation, blood in the urine, and achy "pendulous neighbors."

How best to care for your prostate? In a nutshell: Bend over, eat tomatoes, and have a lot of sex. Not all at the same time! Yearly rectal exams are no fun, I know, but they help your doctor find cancer early or distinguish BPH from cancer, so grin and, well, *bare* it. It only takes a minute. While you're at the clinic, ask about a PSA (prostate-specific antigen) blood test.

Research suggests that cooked tomatoes may help prevent prostate cancer, so time to go Italian, *signore!* Check www.nccam.nih.gov for the latest research on other foods, herbs, and more.

And finally, take a roll in the hay! Men who ejaculate more may have a decreased risk of prostate cancer. And you thought sex was only for fun!

an orchestra, the works! Or go all *Saturday Night Fever* and hang a glittering disco ball.

❏ *Get a game night going.* Here's a different spin on the word *play.* Invite some friends over to square off around your favorite board, card, or parlor game. Serve cheese balls, melon balls, highballs, and/or rum balls.

❑ *Stuff two balls in a sock.* Got back pain? Try rolling against two tennis balls tied firmly inside a sock, either on the floor or against a wall, with one ball on either side of your spine. Or position the pair where they feel the best, and just lie on them.

❑ *Step up to the plate.* Volunteer for a good cause, something you believe in. Give of yourself: your time, your energy, your expertise.

Eat, Drink & Be Wary

Our lives are not in the lap of the gods, but in the lap of our cooks.
— Lin Yutang, *The Importance of Living*

We were talking about coffee a few chapters back and how I, for one, am not about to give it up. But I did finally dump the fake creamer I used to pour into my coffee. You know the stuff? That sweet liquid that comes in different flavors? It's totally fake. There's absolutely nothing in it of any nutritional value!

Name Your Poison

The world is full of crap being sold as food, and it is up to each of us — alas! — to resist the temptations. Ah, but human nature is such that we *won't* always resist, and the crap-makers know it. They're counting on it! Yes, we each bear personal responsibility for what we put in our mouths, but this much is equally true: I could not stuff my face with Cheetos if no such thing existed.

Day by day, more weird foodstuffs come to market, and their nutrition labels get you only so far. There's no mention of residual pesticides or bovine growth hormone, for instance, or whether the food was genetically modified.

But read what does make the list. Can you say "polysyllabic nomenclature"? Imagine the chemical formula for some of that stuff! Gad, the molecular structure must look like something you get when you piece together every last Tinker Toy in the can. I know it's microscopic but . . . we're supposed to swallow that? This is precisely my problem with nondairy creamer. It may taste all sweet and yummy, but it's still some strange laboratory output disguised as a food product.

Moderation in All Things

Did you hear about that guy who developed what they now call "popcorn lung" after he ate an average of two bags of microwave popcorn every day for a couple of decades? Now he's got what is technically termed bronchiolitis obliterans, which was probably caused by the popcorn-flavoring chemical diacetyl. Okay, people like this provide an important public service. Seriously. Now, owing at least in part to this guy's lawsuit, the manufacturers of microwave popcorn are going to have to use something other than the dangerous diacetyl. Also, the rest of us are reminded of the wisdom of moderation in all things. Graze not deep, but wide. Not only is variety the spice of life; it can also help you avoid outright toxicity from eating too much of any one thing.

Besides exercising moderation and aiming for variety, here are the best tips I can offer:

• Shop the store's perimeter, where the whole foods are (avoid the aisles, with their cans and boxes full of who-knows-what-all).

- Go organic where meats are concerned, especially organ meats.

- Educate yourself about the nutrition labels on food packages, and get in the habit of comparison shopping.

- Grow your own and/or shop at farmers' markets.

Want to go an extra mile and do your good deed for the day (not to mention for posterity)? Call one of those 800-numbers you see on packages of "food" products, and let them know what you think about fake and artificially flavored whatzit posing as food. Agribusiness will keep feeding us crap as long as we keep buying it.

Oh, the Comforts of Home (Cooking)!

I wag my finger like a schoolmarm about all the fake stuff passing for food these days, mostly in the hope that we can all save room for the naturally occurring no-nos, the kind we tend to imbibe quite knowingly and willfully. Like *real* cream in your *caffeinated* coffee, homemade chocolate-chip cookies, and the occasional hard liquor!

My dear mom baked bread every Wednesday when I was a kid. *White* bread, thank you very much. Caramel rolls, too. And old Mrs. Stuart, beloved "Sturty" to us eight Key kids, made "g'doot" for us whenever she babysat. It's actually spelled *gröt*, but it's still Norwegian for rice pudding, and when it was served up hot and topped with butter, sugar, and cinnamon, there wasn't a chance in the world that anyone would mistake it for health food.

Oh, but those white, refined treats would cure whatever ailed you! They put the "mmmm" in comfort. Still do, and here's my point. We may have all kinds of reasons, four or five decades on, for eating healthier fare than we did in our youth. But the foods we come from, those time-honored bringers of comfort, deserve a place at the table, at least on special occasions. Call them guilty pleasures if you must, just as long as you put the emphasis on *pleasure*!

COOL MOVES

Intestinal Exercise

"I don't recall ever exercising my intestines before," I thought to myself, that first day at Dahn yoga. To Westerners, this exercise "works the abs and pelvic floor." Dahn practitioners do it to "warm" the intestines and stimulate the major energy center of the body, the *dahn-jon*, housed right there in the gut. Stimulating the intestines promotes the flow of chi throughout the body's meridians.

Stand, sit, or lie on your back with your feet hip-width apart and your hands on your lower tummy. Rhythmically pull in your abdominal muscles, as if to touch your belly button to your spine, then release. Squeeze your rectal muscles at the same time. Keep going: squeeze, release, squeeze, release. Momentarily pat or rub your body anywhere tightness occurs. Exhale through your open mouth. Don't overdo it, since digestive discomfort can result. Start with fifty reps, and work up to three hundred.

SCRIBBLES & DOODLES
You Are What You Eat

In food terms, who were you yesterday? Draw a "foodie" self-portrait. Were you a French-Fry-Crested Burger-Butt Bird? Or a Protein-Shaking Cheetah with Power-Bar Legs? Maybe Three Squares with Gravy? Remember, this is you *yesterday*. Today is a whole new day, and you can be a whole new you. With that in mind, design the You Are What You Eat of tomorrow, incorporating the healthiest possible food choices. Perhaps broccoli hair, fish breasts, almond eyes, a carrot nose, and whole-grain buns? Now you're cookin'! Foods of every color flatter the healthy palate, so for this New You portrait, go full-spectrum.

End by rubbing your lower abdomen in a clockwise direction (right rib to left rib, down and around).

 DOC IN THE BOX: *Where's the Beef (Been)? (The E. Coli Story)*

Once upon a time, there was a little coli named E. He lived down in Cow Gut, with his brothers and sisters, on a big factory farm with lots of other cows and colis. For a time they lived in harmony, and all was well. But E.'s cow was a skinny cow, and a skinny cow makes small hamburgers, which means small moneybags for the people who own the cows. So the people fed the cow a special ingredient called Antibiotic. In fact, since there were so many skinny cows, the people just put Antibiotic into the drinking water, so all the cows got some. Antibiotic made the cows grow big and fat, fat enough to make lots of big, fat hamburgers. Big hamburgers meant big moneybags. And the people were happy.

Now, alas for the colis, Antibiotic was poison to them. Most of them died. But E. and a few hardy others survived and formed the Antibiotic Resistance. Members of the AR could not be killed by this new poison. They had Special Qualities. They grew up strong and mean, stronger and meaner than the average coli.

One legion of the Resistance left the cow (through the usual route) and spread out over the pasture. When the rain came, some of the tough Resistant colis washed down the hill to the nearby spinach farm, where they took refuge on the spinach plants. When the spinach was harvested, the microscopic legion went along and soon established a new post in Human Gut.

Another legion of the Resistance stayed in Cow Gut. When the time came, the cow was butchered, and E. and his mates were gathered up into Ground Beef. Some of the Ground Beef was thoroughly cooked, which utterly decimated the Resistance. But some of the Ground Beef was undercooked, allowing the Resistant colis to survive. This lucky battalion passed into Human Gut as well, where they joined forces with the Super-Resistant spinach contingent.

Finding their new host deliciously undefended, E. coli and his fellow members of the Antibiotic Resistance tore down the walls of Human Gut and ran amok in the countryside, causing a state of Widespread Infection. No poison sprayed or swallowed into Human Gut could vanquish Widespread Infection. Human Doctor tried, but all the toughest Antibiotics had been used in Cow Gut, and you *know* what happened there. E. and his buddies, with their Special Qualities, were nigh on invincible. They just laughed in the face of Human Doctor's feeble attempts and proceeded to destroy their host.

The moral of this story? You tell me. All I know is, when it comes to meat, I'm buying it drug-free and cooking it well-done.

〰️ THINGS TO TRY AT LEAST ONCE

❑ *Order the Roy G. Biv Special.* Green salad is so...monochromatic! More colors = more vitamins. Fill your bowl with an entire rainbow's worth of veggies, the brighter the better. Choose dark-green lettuce over pale iceberg, for example, and yellow corn over white. Remember: fruits are good in salads, too. And there's a cheese that's bleu!

❑ *Go for the whole enchilada.* Challenge yourself to cook whole-food meals in which not a single ingredient comes from a can or a box.

❑ *Bypass fast food for a week.* If this sounds too hard, start by watching Morgan Spurlock's documentary *Supersize Me*, or reading Eric Schlosser's *Fast Food Nation*. Then try for a month!

❑ *Sample the smorgasbord.* For old time's sake, stage a Comfort Foods of Yore potluck. Have everyone bring their favorite food from childhood, be it mac and cheese from a box, beanie weenies, bologna and Miracle Whip on white bread, tuna casserole, quivering Jell-O "salad," whatever! Maybe stir up some Tang or "just add water" to that cocoa mix with dehydrated marshmallows....

Take a Load Off Fanny

Every increased possession loads us with new weariness.
— John Ruskin (1819–1900)

*A*t first glance, you're thinking this Way is about weight loss, right? Well, it is — though not just the bathroom-scale variety. Body weight is an issue we'd be remiss to skip, especially as it can be such a bad mamma-jamma in midlife. Even Skinny Minnies may balk at their relative bulk after forty. Seems ill-timed, too, that the pounds should pile on *just* as ye olde parts are feeling a little achy-breaky with age.

So, yes, if you really should lose a few — or even a few dozen — please know that Dr. Peg and I are right there with you in spirit, doing what we can to work our own butts off, too.

Then again, none of us should regard our caboose as life's only load!

Give It Away, Give It Away Now

Permit me to generalize. Many of us spent our twenties getting careers and committed relationships established, our thirties accumulating stuff (also kids and *their* stuff), and our forties coming to realize what a hassle it is to manage it all. By fifty, look around! Your baby birds (if you had any) may be flying off, but is the nest anywhere near empty?

This Way calls for a *purge*! Go through every nook and cranny. Clean out your house, office, car, computer, filing cabinets, address book, dresser drawers, jewelry boxes, storage cabinets, garage, attic, everything. *Clean out your life!* How gratifying to move into life's second half without a ton of dead weight from the first!

Precious Thing, Perfect Gift

Ever heard of a potlatch? Not to be confused with a potluck, a potlatch is also a kind of party, but instead of everyone bringing a dish to share, at a potlatch the host ceremoniously bestows gifts on his or her guests. The practice originated with several Native American tribes of the Pacific Northwest, in whose languages *potlatch* (or a very similar word) meant "to throw or distribute."

Sounds like fun, doesn't it? What a cool way to "throw out" the precious, sentimental artifacts you've held on to long enough!

COOL MOVES
Brush It Off

Pent-up energy that has settled to a stop within your body is like a beaver dam on a stream. Dislodge some of the plugs, and get your "chi river" flowing again with this Dahn yoga exercise.

Stand with your feet parallel and hip-width apart. Relax your body.

DOC IN THE BOX: *Crash and Burn (Weight Loss)*

Obesity is a huge and growing problem, causing adult-onset diabetes and contributing to heart disease, joint pain, and many, many other health problems. If you really need to take a load off your fanny, remember that the basic formula for weight loss is in fact quite simple. You have to burn more calories than you eat. Period. No fancy pill, frozen meal, or television show can do this metabolic math for you. It's all you, babe.

If you have ever tried a crash diet, you know they don't work, at least not for the long haul. Why? The answer lies in evolution. We are programmed for alternating between feast and famine. Back in the day, when it was feast season, we put on weight and kept it on, storing up for famine time. When winter settled in, the food supply dwindled, and our bodies slowed down, trying to conserve energy. Muscle takes more energy to maintain than fat, so when we starve (or hibernate), our body hangs on to the fat for as long as it can but quickly jettisons the high-cost muscle. In Way 4, I explained how a body composition of high fat and low muscle makes for a slower metabolic rate. A slower metabolic rate makes it more likely that you'll *gain* weight, not lose it. So don't starve. Don't hibernate, either — get that rear in gear and *move it*!

We're also programmed to be eaters of meat, whole grains, and fresh fruits and vegetables. Our evolving bodies haven't caught up to the modern way of life. The average American diet, overpacked with simple carbohydrates, processed food, and artificial ingredients, is wreaking havoc on our elegantly designed metabolisms. Diabetes, obesity, digestive problems: we're creating these epidemics for ourselves. A caveman metabolism doesn't know what to do with a drive-through meal of simple carbs and fried fats, except to rejoice in the feast and pack it away for the famine, as flab. So now that supersized meal just becomes more load for the fanny. If that is not your plan, pile on the protein and healthy complex carbs, and resist the junk.

By far the best way to lose weight is to take the long view and make gradual changes. Slowly decrease your caloric intake, and slowly increase your activity level. Give yourself time to adjust to each new level before you make another change. It took you years to put on this unwanted weight, and it won't melt off in a few weeks or months. But keep to the basic formula, and it *will* come off, and stay off. You can do it!

Curl your hands into not-quite-fists. With the backs of your fingers, rhythmically brush down the sides of your body, from armpits to hips, lightly bouncing your knees as you do. Keep your body soft. Let your arms drop fully with each stroke, and imagine flicking spent energy off your fingertips. Begin with fifty reps, and work up to a hundred, or two hundred. When you finish, let your arms hang at your sides, deeply relax your body, breathe through your mouth, and enjoy the tingle of stirred-up energy, no longer stagnant, *streaming* out your fingertips.

THINGS TO TRY AT LEAST ONCE

❑ *Throw a potlatch party.* Shower your friends with gifts from among your own possessions. Imbue a common thing with special meaning, and let that be part of the gift.

❑ *Quit the warehouse club.* If you're like me, you're not saving money there anyway, only buying more stuff than you really need. Scale down, and shop local merchants and growers instead. You'll keep your grocery dollars in your own town and open up loads of storage space in the bargain.

❑ *Reduce, reuse, recycle.* Eschew buying new! Take a load off the planet.

❑ *Learn about the Freegans.* Maybe even join their efforts to reclaim perfectly usable stuff that's been discarded. www.freegan.info.

❑ *Downsize.* If the nest is empty, take a load off your pocketbook by getting into a smaller mortgage.

SCRIBBLES & DOODLES
Load? What Load?

Create a detailed vision of yourself with the load gone — whether in terms of body weight, the material sphere, a troubling situation, or anything else. Project yourself into a new reality, and describe everything you can discern with your senses — how fantastic you look, how agile you feel, how much happier your feet are, how much your lab results have improved, how easy it is to find stuff in your uncluttered home, how joyful you are! Bookmark this page in your journal — or print it out and post it — so you can inspire yourself with repeated readings.

11 "Fung" and "Shway" to Free Your Chi

Are you in right relation? Where is your water?
— Elders of the Hopi Nation

*Q*uick! Point north. That, according to feng shui, is the best place to put your water — your aquarium, your coffeemaker. It's supposed to keep your career prospects flowing. My own tabletop fountain shares a shelf with family portraits in the north end of my office, and it's a thirsty little bugger. I top it off almost daily. Mindful of the smiling young faces pictured nearby, I tend to the task prayerfully. "My career is not just about me," I pray. "When it flows, it feeds a family." I pour the water as if refilling a cup for the muse. The burbling sound always soothes.

Birds Gotta Fly, Fish Gotta Swim

Flow is a good place to start any discussion of feng shui (pronounced "fung shway" and meaning, literally, "wind water"). Flow is what this ancient Chinese art of placement is all about. *Chi* flow. Yes, the same life energy that circulates within the human body (see Way 4) is present throughout nature — throughout the cosmos, some say — and, for best results, *chi's gotta flow!*

Now, even if you don't believe a word of it — that feng shui can change your life by aligning your material sphere with nature so the chi flows most auspiciously in your midst — you may love it on looks alone. Elegant, uncluttered, everything in simple balance, the room *alive* with subtle energy — what's not to love?

From Little Fixes to Grand Design

While the particulars of this art are many, its tools are the simple stuff of nature: the four (actually eight) directions; the basic elements (of the Orient) — water, earth, wood, fire, and metal — and the colors of the changing seasons. While a whole industry has sprung up to support you in this, feng-shui-yourselfers need not feel daunted. Google the term or pick up a book on the subject, and you could be improving your home's feng shui by sundown. Sometimes all it takes to transform a stagnant aspect of your life is to reposition your favorite reading chair or paint one wall of your bedroom a different color.

You can start this very moment, if you want, with any of the quick fixes in our "Things to Try" list below. Or you could think big and design your entire next home according to feng shui principles.

SCRIBBLES & DOODLES
"And Everything in Its Place"

What is *your* place in life's second half? Are you in alignment — with your loved ones, your work life, your spiritual beliefs? Is it possible that, in order to be fully aligned, a rearrangement may be necessary? If so, start small. Decide which imbalance to address first, and seek out an appropriate feng shui solution for just "that wall."

COOL MOVES

Look Near, Look Far

The "fung" and "shway" of this Way's title always make me think of "to" and "fro." Here's an eye exercise to match the pattern.

Stand or sit, holding a sewing needle in each hand. Place the point of one needle into the hole of the other, and then vice versa; doing so will force your eyes to focus on fine details at very close range. Close your eyes, inhale deeply, and as you exhale, open your eyes with your focus out to the distant horizon. Blink a few times. Breathe. Repeat all steps: Needle in one hole, needle in the other, close eyes, deep breath, and exhale as you open to the distance. Do ten reps. Adopt the habit of moving your focus from near to far and back again on a regular, *flowing* basis. Helpful hint: On the wall beyond your computer screen, hang a piece of art (say, a landscape) you can look into. Either that, or position your computer so that, when glancing up, you look out a window or across the room.

THINGS TO TRY AT LEAST ONCE

- ❑ *Tidy up a bit*. Clutter is the Anti–feng shui, and dirt is so very inauspicious!

- ❑ *Stir the chi*. Hang a crystal. Its many facets, twisting in the air, will serve to gently break up severe and heavy chi lines, such as those created by ceiling beams.

- ❑ *Reflect it back*. A blazing fireplace is cozy, but don't let the room's chi escape up the chimney! Hang a mirror above the fireplace.

DOC IN THE BOX: *"Are You in Right Relation?" (Hakomi)*

I happen to believe that everyone would benefit from regular psychotherapy. I know I have. Different strokes for different folks, though, and I went through several types before Lady Luck visited me a few years ago with the gift of Hakomi. This one is *it* for me, and I'm thrilled to have the chance to introduce you.

As feng shui is to the external arrangement of objects, Hakomi is to the internal arrangement of beliefs. Hakomi is a Hopi Indian word meaning "How do you stand in relation to these many realms?" The Hakomi Institute offers a modern translation: "Who are you?" You think you know? You might be surprised.

As children, we learned by trial and error, through experience and observation. We toddled and babbled, then walked and talked. We developed beliefs about how the world is and ways of interacting with it that worked for us. These deeply held beliefs, formed by a child's mind, became part of what Hakomi calls "core material," that inner stuff that guides us at a subconscious level.

Our core beliefs may serve us well when we are children, and our goals and needs are those of a child. But adult life is a job for adult tools, and the deeply ingrained habits and beliefs of childhood can actually hinder the blossoming of our inner selves as adults. Hakomi is all about changing our core beliefs and behaviors for our benefit.

Hakomi draws on concepts and techniques from a variety of traditions, from Buddhism to Neurolinguistic Programming. The foundation of Hakomi, as with any therapy technique, is the establishment of a safe, respectful client-therapist relationship. In that setting, the client practices careful observation of current life experiences, including body awareness, in a way that leads to the discovery of core material. Once unhelpful core beliefs are unearthed, the client can consciously modify them, thereby enhancing growth and wholeness.

In short, you listen carefully to your body and heart to inform your mind and make deep and lasting changes in your psyche. Hakomi is a gentle yet profoundly powerful way to transform and heal. Learn more at the Hakomi Institute website: www.hakomiinstitute.com. Tell them Dr. Peg sent you.

Asian markets sell inexpensive ones adorned with the eight-sided ba-gua, the ancient symbolic arrangement representing feng shui's directional associations.

❑ *Hide it in a hole.* Some chi-blockers are "built-ins." What to do? Imagine you could slip the problem, at least symbolically, into a handy hole. Bamboo to the rescue! Decoratively hung bamboo flutes not only provide the magic hole but also bear a name, in Cantonese, that sounds just like the word for "disappear." Now *that's* handy.

❏ *Have a grand reopening party*. When your rearrangement is complete, throw open the doors in welcome.

Take the Waters

When we're in the water, we're not in this world.
— Gertrude Ederle (1905–2003)

We'll never know the worth of water till the well go dry.
— Eighteenth-century Scottish proverb

*T*wo hydrogen atoms, one oxygen atom. Put them together, and poof! Life is possible. Isn't that amazing? As astronomers probe for signs of life elsewhere in the universe, they keep a keen eye out for even the slightest hint of water, so linked is the H_2O molecule to the possibility of life. So far, all they've found is evidence of water erosion on Mars, but they're still looking.

Yet here we sit, on an earth so watery it's blue, inhabiting bodies that are themselves two-thirds water. Need a reason to feel happy today? Well . . . got water? There you go!

From Baptism to Boating

Okay, so our very survival depends on the stuff. Yet even that doesn't tell the whole wet, wild, wonderful story of water in our lives.

"Nowadays, if I have a church, it's my bathtub," emailed Alexa. "I *live* in it during the cold months." She's onto something — as any worshipper in the water knows. We're talking about one of the four sacred elements here. (The Orient has five, but the West has four: earth, air, fire, and . . . you guessed it!). No wonder we install hot tubs and fountains and backyard lily ponds. We yearn to commune with water.

Whether you're drinking it, swimming in it, cooking food in it, or washing stuff clean with it, water is the best friend your body ever had. And let's face it, to age is to shrivel, so . . . *hydrate, hydrate, hydrate*! Crown yourself the Monarch of Moisturizer and bask in Your Royal Hydrance. (It's not a real word, I know, but it should be. Because, obviously, I do not mean *hydrants*!)

SCRIBBLES & DOODLES
A River Runs through You

Write an ode (or, better, an *eau d'*) to your own personal Body of Water. Bless your blood, salute your sweat, tout your tears, even marvel at your mucus! Imbue your every H_2O molecule with the power to shine like a crystal. (Ever read anything by Masaru Emoto? Google him!) Or simply get out your *water* colors and render your flowing inner landscape.

I Can't Get Enough of Your Love!

Staying juicy may be something you crave for vanity's sake alone, but the importance of adequate hydration goes far beyond skin-deep. *Every* bodily function is aided by proper hydration: digestion, metabolism (weight loss!), cleansing of toxins, elimination, temperature regulation, even the ability to think. And it doesn't take much *de*hydration for a body to suffer the effects — just 1 or 2 percent to impair physical and cognitive performance, according to the *International Journal of Sport Nutrition*. When water loss approaches 7 percent, you may flat-out collapse. Yikes!

So, drink up. Alcohol and caffeine don't count — at least, not toward hydration. As diuretics, they have the opposite net effect. For thirst, water is almost always the best choice.

DOC IN THE BOX: *Stay Moist Inside and Out (Hydration)*

Water. The stuff of life. Both our bodies and the earth are about two-thirds water. While you can live without food for months, you'll die in less than two weeks if you don't have water. How much is enough? Most people need eight to ten cups of water a day to maintain good hydration. If you exercise or sweat heavily, you'll need more. Two good rules of thumb: Drink *before* you get thirsty and drink till the water runs clear. If you're dehydrated, your kidneys hang on to as much water as they can, resulting in concentrated, dark urine. If you're taking in plenty of water, the extra will come through clear (and probably loud, too!).

Your skin is another indicator of hydration, although less sensitive than your kidneys, of course. Chapped lips? Flaky skin? Could be dehydration! Most skin hydration happens from the inside out, but a good moisturizer can help. Make sure it has at least 15 SPF, and apply it even on cloudy days. Use plenty of sunscreen to protect all exposed skin (don't forget your hands!), and make sure to reapply every two hours, even if the stuff calls itself "sweat-proof."

I had a professor in college who never drank water. "Do you know what fish *do* in that stuff?" he used to joke. Personally, I think it was just his excuse to drink more beer. But if you're like him and find eight cups of water a day to be too much of a good thing, you do have some options, as you know from cruising your local grocery store or sports outfitter. You can spend your retirement egg on fancy bottled sports drinks. Or you can opt for fruit or vegetable juices, or even make your own rehydration remedy: Dissolve one level teaspoon of salt and eight level teaspoons of sugar in ¼ cup hot water. Then add one quart of water or juice or mixture of same.

By the way, it is possible to get too much of a good thing when it comes to water. Overhydrating can actually kill you, by upsetting your delicate chemical balance, so keep it under two gallons on a regular day. Drink, drink, drink, but don't drown!

 COOL MOVES

Wash Between Your Ears!

Sinuses giving you trouble? Give them a good rinse! Surfers and other ocean dunkers reap this benefit more or less automatically. For the rest of us, there's the neti pot, a small, squat pitcher shaped like a genie's lamp, designed to pour salt water in one nostril and out the other. If you're troubled by allergies, make "netting" a daily practice. Or reduce the misery of a cold or sore throat by rinsing your sinuses several times a day, beginning with the first sneeze or tickle.

✓〜 THINGS TO TRY AT LEAST ONCE

❑ *Jump in*. Water aerobics is ideal exercise for those who have been sedentary for a long time or have joint problems. It is ultra-low impact, but the resistance of the water provides a good workout. Try it.

❑ *Get wet*. Have a pool party. Institute a daily swim. Make it your goal to swim the English Channel. Plumb the depths of your water love!

❑ *Marinate and baste*. Fill a big bubbly tub with beneficial salts or aromatherapy oils, and place burning candles all around. Pour yourself a tiny little cordial, and sip it leisurely while you soak in the baahth. Or, if you're feeling flush, find a day spa and go all out.

❑ *Drink up*. Make water your only liquid libation for a whole day (or a whole week). Next time there's a toast-worthy occasion, fill the goblets with sparkling mineral water. Let everyone be a designated driver!

Spurn Your Bra

You like pain? Try wearing a corset!

— Elizabeth Swann (Keira Knightley) in the film
    Pirates of the Caribbean: The Curse of the Black Pearl

*R*estrictive clothing cuts your chi." I don't remember where I heard this, but it rang true for me immediately. Or maybe I simply welcomed any good excuse for flinging my bras into the trash. Apparently, the bra hasn't been built yet that can fit the likes of me. I'm always chasing errant shoulder straps or tugging the whole contraption back into place. I saw a candid photo of myself once, elbow aloft, hand fishing down through the neckline of my blouse. After that, I went strapless. I call it my breastplate now, and as soon as I walk in my front door, pwoink! It's outta there, and I'm hangin' with my homies.

In the Clearing Stand Your Boxers

Gentlemen, I wouldn't dream of leaving you out of this discussion. You've got a couple of homies of your own, after all. The "bra" of this Way's title is really just a metaphor for discomfort. *Removable* discomfort. Discomfort you can do something about. Besides, guys, snug bindings cut *your* chi, too.

So spurn them, I say! Cast aside all tighties, be they whitey or otherwise.

And about that necktie, *any* necktie. I mean, the very idea of tying on a little noose each morning is a little nuts. What fashion wizard came up with that one? Sorry, Fernando Lamas (née Billy Crystal in a previous incarnation): it is *not* better to look good than to feel good! Nor should anyone ever have to choose between the two. (You look mahvelous, by the way!)

"What's *Sarong* with That?"

Bras, tighty whiteys, neckties, pantyhose (*oy, pantyhose!*), belts, fake fabrics, stays, itchy tags — come to think of it, let's round up *all* the fashion wizards, sit 'em down, and have a serious word. At least, let's round up all the "cut-cloth" fashion wizards.

On his first visit to Japan, my friend Michael, a Shibori silk artist and avid kimonophile, observed that, in general, the East is (at least traditionally) a "whole-cloth" culture, while here in the West, cut-cloth (i.e., tailoring) has always been the norm.

Comfortable Clothing Unlimited

While literally going braless is not likely to fly — not in business class, anyway — the mix of world cultures, together with the shopping ease of the Internet, has vastly expanded the rack, so to speak, of comfortable clothing options. We could call it the Global Village Shopping

Mall. And there's no need to fly, after all, since a click or two can get you there.

COOL MOVES

Shoulder Strap Tap

Energy blockages in the body are sort of like ketchup in a bottle. How to get them out? Well, if bonking the bottle works for ketchup... "Body tapping" can move the chi, anywhere sensations of tightness or tenderness indicate blockage. Since bra-spurning is the Way of the moment, let's focus on the chest. (Again, despite the lingerie lingo, these taps work for any gender.)

Shape your right palm into a cup (any cup size will do!), and tap the top of your left shoulder. Don't be shy. You deserve a robust pat on the back — even if it is your shoulder. After, oh, let's say thirty-six to forty-two of those, move your cupped palm down from the top of your shoulder to the front of it, just above your left breast. Tap out another count of thirty-six to forty-two. Finish by sweeping your hand from your shoulder down your left arm and the left side of your chest several times. Make it a "cross your heart" treatment by doing the same thing on the other side of your body.

SCRIBBLES & DOODLES
"Banter with the Boobs" or "Say It to the Scrotum"

"Listen to your body," speaks the gentle healer, but how can we expect to hear anything when our parts are bound and gagged? Time to unfetter and let it all hang out. In your journal, engage in a good, long chat with your body or any specific body part(s). Write some dialogue, as in a script. Work quickly, and don't edit. Ask your (fill in the blank) what's on its mind, and let it answer with *the very first words* that come to mind. Allow the conversation to be lively, organic, even argumentative, but do coax it toward resolution. After all, you and your parts are stuck with each other. Can't you all just get along?

DOC IN THE BOX: *Do Not Spurn Your Mammographer! (Breast Cancer)*

By the time you're fifty, I'd wager a confident bet that you have known (or been) someone with breast cancer. I can think of seven such women I've known well, not counting patients. One died from her cancer, one died from something else, three are survivors, and two are still in treatment. Each is someone's dear mother, beloved wife, cherished daughter, and/or prized sister. It's a sobering, all-too-common reality.

Thankfully, things are looking up. Detection is improving, and deaths are decreasing. Money is flowing toward research and treatment, thanks to the pioneering efforts of the Susan G. Komen for the Cure Foundation and the like. By now, pink bows to raise breast cancer awareness are everywhere, even on specially marked boxes of this and that. Still, this cancer remains a looming threat to every woman.

So what's my advice? Get regular mammograms!

You'll hear different recommendations about how often you should do this. I squeeze it into my schedule (pun intended) every year and advise my patients over forty to do the same. It's worth it to catch a cancer when it's still tiny.

If you're like me, one mammogram is one too many. But sometimes we have to suffer for the greater good, right? You can minimize your suffering, however, if you:

1. *Schedule your mammo for a midcycle time.* If you're still menstruating, with roughly predictable cycles, don't plan to get your breasts squashed like pancakes when they're at their most swollen and tender. In other words, not when you're premenstrual. I've goofed on that one myself. Ouch!

2. *Keep quiet.* I'm one of those patients who tend to be chatty and friendly with medical staff. But this is one procedure during which I just shut my yappy trap. The mammographer has a job to do, and the less you distract her, the quicker she'll get it done. And you do want it done quickly, right? Listen to her instructions, follow them exactly, and keep your mouth shut. And just when you think you can't stand the pressure one more nanosecond, it's over.

3. *Practice.* Lie down in the driveway and have your "love interest" run over your — I'm kidding! Once a year is bad enough.

Last word(s): Hands on! Many women find their own breast cancer before the X-rays do. Get to know your breasts with a monthly

self-check. Nothing fancy, just feel 'em up thoroughly (and here's where your "love interest" *can* help) in the shower or in bed. Remember to avoid those tender times of the month.

∿➔ THINGS TO TRY AT LEAST ONCE

❑ *Go in for custom tailoring*. Sure, it's pricey. But this is your Big Five-oh, dahling, and you deserve to both look good and feel good!

❑ *Erin, go braless*. If you're not exactly the "full-figured" gal made famous by Jane Russell, forego all those expensive, heavily constructed bras in favor of a light, brief bralet. Or try a camisole or clingy tank top beneath your blouse instead.

❑ *Don your bedsheets*. It's an Animal House party. "Toga! Toga!"

❑ *Go beyond clothing*. Ready to invest some big dollars in Big Comfort? Need a gift idea for the new fifty-year-old? Three words: La-Z-Boy!

W A Y 14 — Keep on Rockin' Me, Baby

Did you ever do it to Ravel's Bolero?

— Jenny (Bo Derek) to George (Dudley Moore), in the film *10*

*H*ave we come to the end of the Body section so soon? Well, we'd better get busy talking about sex, then. Who'd like to begin?

Oh, all right, I will — but only if I can dish on an old friend. I'll call her June.

June was fifty and I barely thirty when, in casual conversation, she gave me my first consciousness-raising glimpse into midlife sex. How we got on the subject, I can't begin to recall, but she described how she'd caught a reflection of herself, quite unexpectedly, while "in the act" and on top.

"Oh, my God!" she exclaimed, while scrunching the flesh of her face between her hands. "All *this* was hanging forward! It was *not* a pretty sight. Since then, I've always tried to be, you know, *below* — or at least more or less upright." By now she was blushing. "Good heavens! You get to be my age and, seriously, you've got to use all the help you can get!"

Oh, I'm sorry. Was that too much information? Okay, let's turn it around and talk about the menfolk for a moment.

Sex and Drugs and Rock and Roll

I ran into my old pal Chris at our twenty-year high-school reunion — can it really have been nine years ago already? As we took to opposite sides of the buffet table, I learned Chris had become a doctor, just like his dad. Correction: not *just* like his dad. Ol' Dr. Adducci is a gynecologist. Young (okay, middle-aged) Dr. Adducci is a urologist. The serving line was moving at a snail's pace, and I'd already asked about his wife and kids. So I brought up the only urology-related story I could think of, "torn from the day's headlines," as they say, since the first of the erectile dysfunction drugs had just hit the market.

"How 'bout that Viagra?" I said, perhaps a tad too loudly, as I think I perceived a tiny little shock-wave in my midst. But before I could even chastise myself for forgetting I was back in my hometown, among the good, honest, decent people I grew up with, Chris — Dr. Chris, the urologist *and* my long-time fellow smarty-pants and covaledictorian — was there, in a heartbeat, to save me from myself.

"How *'bout* that Viagra!" he practically shouted. Now everyone laughed and finally exhaled.

"Writing a lot of prescriptions for it these days, are you?" I asked.

SCRIBBLES & DOODLES
Euphemistically Speaking

"Rock and roll," the label bestowed on the wildly danceable music we all grew up with, was always a double entendre hinting at sex. How many more euphemisms can you think of for "doing it"? This can be a fun game at parties, all the more so if inebriants are served. Challenge your guests to come up with at least fifty, the more creative and outrageous, the better. For more laughs, Google it — there are online lists like you wouldn't believe!

"Am I ever!" he said. "My partners and I got so tired of writing scrips for Viagra that we actually had prewritten prescription pads printed up. Now all we have to do is sign."

Chris and I were soon at the desserts, and that's where the conversation ended. But I have always wondered (despite the fact that it's none of my bleepin' business): Did Dr. Adducci (the Younger), uh, sign any "autographs" that night? I'd like to think so — just for happy endings' sake.

 DOC IN THE BOX: *You Still Got It, Babe! (Sex in Midlife)*

Remember when we were eighteen and tried to imagine people over forty having sex? We couldn't, right? No way those old farts could still get it on! And even if they could, *ee-yew*, who'd want 'em? Now we *are* those old farts. And we're still "doing it." Or are we? Does sex change in midlife? Does it get better or worse? Does it even happen? Or is laundry day the only time we shake the sheets?

It turns out there is no simple answer. Midlifers are all over the sexual map. More sex, less sex, higher drive, lower drive, new partner, old partner, no partner . . . it's all there. The only thing that is constant across the board is change. Our priorities are changing, our relationships are changing, and none of us experiences sex and sexuality the same way we did when we were twenty-something.

For one thing, we don't have the bods we used to have, and that takes some getting used to. Youth defines sexuality, or so the ad execs would have you believe, and one thing we ain't is young. The mortal flesh is settling; we're not the Gumbies of yore. But you and I know that, beneath the wrinkles and the graying hair, we are just as sexy as we used to be. Probably sexier, given a half-life of experience under our belts (so to speak).

This is not to deny the very real physical and hormonal effects of aging. Drying tissues and waning libidos are common. Don't let those things spoil your fun. Talk with your partner. Pick up your favorite personal moisturizer, and allow yourselves to enjoy nonsexual touch if you're not in the mood. Cuddling rocks!

Treasure your sexual self. Be open to change, but celebrate too, because babe, you still got it!

Sex and the Celibate Girl

The last word in *sex* is *ex*. If you're not gettin' any, maybe it's because you don't really care for any, *thanks*. And if you don't, you are not alone. According to AARP's latest study on the subject, 14 percent of survey respondents (age forty-five and up) reported having had no sex in the past six months, and 12 percent said they'd "be very happy never having sex again."

People give all kinds of reasons for choosing celibacy, from anatomical to spiritual, with long stretches of "not in the mood" and "got nobody to love" in between. Well, as with Dr. Anybody and his or her prescription pad, "it ain't nobody's business if you do" — *or don't*. But if you find yourself in that "not in the mood" group — not particularly interested in developing your sexual self — now is as good a time as any to explore why.

COOL MOVES
Rock & Roll, the Exercise!

Also called tumble hugs or rolling-back exercise, this one loosens up a stiff spine. Sit on an exercise mat or carpeted floor, and hug your knees close to your chest. Round your back, and tuck your chin slightly. Inhale deeply and, as you exhale, roll backward onto your back and shoulders, then, with your inhalation, rock forward again to a seated position. For extra challenge, get enough momentum going that, when you rock forward, you can lift your bottom off the floor and balance on your feet for a moment before rolling backward again. Repeat ten times.

∿ THINGS TO TRY AT LEAST ONCE

☐ *Do the wild thing!* Orgasms move big chi, so . . . do a lot of wild things. Explore Tantra yoga. Read the *Kama Sutra* (or just look at the pictures). Shop for naughty lingerie and sex toys. Rent erotic movies. Read aloud from your volumes of torrid love poetry, yes! And bodice-ripping prose. Yes! Yes! YES!

☐ *Whisper sweet somethings.* Speak up during sex, if only at a whisper. Guessing games can be fun in bed, but not every time. Give your lover a hint. If need be, give your lover a whole how-to demo!

☐ *Rock around the clock.* Or rock any way you want! Rock on with your garage band. Rock preemies at the hospital. Create a rock garden. Refinish an old rocking chair. Or pick up a lowly "gratitude rock" for your pocket, to remind you to notice how great the world is.

PART TWO

MIND

Please Make a Note of It

Inscribe it in the remembering tablets of your mind.

— Aeschylus, *Prometheus Bound*, 1.789

*H*ave you heard the one about Emma and Ivy, two old friends getting on in years? One day out of the blue Emma says, "Ivy? We should think more about the hereafter."

"Why?" asked Ivy. "I think about it all the time as it is."

"You do?" Emma said, her eyes growing wide. "I had no idea."

"Sure!" Ivy responded lightly. "Seems every time I walk into a room, I think, 'Now . . . *what* am I here after?'"

It Helps to Have a Jot Spot

I hardly have to ask whether you can relate. Welcome to the realm of Mind, of remembering and forgetting, yes, and of learning and imagining and of so much more. But let us begin with memory loss, since the Swiss-cheese brain is so famously associated with midlife. Guess you could call it Baby Swiss at this point.

Solution: pen and paper, don't leave home without them! Pencil,

SCRIBBLES & DOODLES
Brain Dump

A regular writing habit goes a long way in shoring up the forgetful mind. Try it for a week. Writing first thing in the morning works for a lot of people, or at least during the first quiet moment of the morning. Just do it! Open a notebook, and write — anything and everything — until you fill several pages. This ain't English comp, so go on, mix metaphors. Punctuate creatively. Spell with reckless abandon. Let participles dangle. Just dump your thoughts onto paper; get them out where you can see them. In the process, you're bound to snag (i.e., remember) myriad details that might otherwise have slipped through a crack. Dr. Peg recommends a daily writing practice to her more anxious patients, encouraging them to dump out their worries — like taking out the trash! — so that they can go on with their day.

crayon, fine. Just always have writing gear handy. As memory aids go, nothing beats words on paper. Okay, words on *screen* can serve the purpose, too, but let me sing the praises of plain old pen and paper a moment longer. I know the marketplace beeps and hums these days with electronic note-taking/scheduling/texting devices of every description, but I still prefer the lowly little notebook. For one thing, there's no better doodling to be had than the kind you do with a ballpoint pen. For another, you don't need batteries.

Brain on a Chain

My friend Mary keeps her writing gear around her neck; calls the cute little spiral-bound notebook her "brain on a chain." She wore it everywhere during a recent vacation. When a shopkeeper, an older fellow, commented on it, Mary said, almost apologetically, "Yeah, now that I'm getting older, I can't remember a damn thing anymore."

"Okay," he said, pointing at the door. "I'm gonna ask you to go back out there, then come in and reframe that answer." He and Mary were both laughing, but the shopkeeper insisted. Well, Mary is nothing if not good-natured, so she did as the man asked. With relish. Upon reentering his shop, she marched right up to him, big fat grin on her face, brandished her little necklace notebook, and announced, "Hi! Do you like my 'brain on a chain'? I get so many *great* ideas, I just have to write them all down."

The older fellow beamed and nodded.

Are You of Two Minds?

But let us speak of larger notebooks, whether spiral-bound or fancier volumes. For there is something more to writing by hand, something more than remembering, something almost magical. When you go beyond mere note-taking (or doodling) to explore your thoughts in writing — and especially when you let your pen be fast and free, allowing words to come of their own volition — you may find a wisdom emerging that you didn't even know you possessed.

This is precisely why so many of this book's journaling prompts (the "Scribbles & Doodles") instruct you to use the freewriting approach: if you can write faster than the English teacher in your head can lecture, you may actually allow your quieter, intuitive self to be heard. Think of it as tapping the subconscious. This deeper part of you doesn't give a rip, frankly, about the rules of composition — or logic, for that matter. But it is wise in ways great and small, and you can trust what it tells you, I guarantee it. Those "slips" of the pen that turn the word *eight* into *light*, for example, or *saw* into *say* — look closely! Turn them over in your mind. Are they really slips? Or is your subconscious mind sending up clues for your conscious mind to consider?

Your Handwriting Will Die with You

A headline in my newspaper this very day reads, "Writing may be on the wall for penmanship." Cursive writing, the story goes, may be a dying art form. What with all the keyboards in classrooms these days,

DOC IN THE BOX: *What Were We Talking About? (Memory in Midlife)*

This is a test. Read the following words out loud and remember them: *lizard, book, grape*. Good. Now on to the topic at hand.

There are two basic kinds of memory: implicit and explicit. Implicit memory is what we use to learn skills. These memories tend to stick. Like when you get back on a bicycle after years of not riding, and presto, you're rollin'!

Explicit memories are the kind that you can recall consciously and describe verbally: people, places, facts, objects. Explicit memories are short-term, recent, or long-term. An example of short-term memory is knowing the color of the socks you put on five minutes ago. Long-term memories go back as far as your childhood and stick with you the longest. Recent memories, like what you ate for breakfast or where you parked your car at the mall, are the ones most commonly affected by normal aging. These memories are stored in a part of the brain fittingly called the hippocampus. (Can't you just imagine a ponderous hippocampus slogging through the swamp of your brain, searching for that elusive fact?)

I should note here that in addition to normal aging, memory can be affected by depression, menopause, medication, substance abuse, head injuries, and strokes. If you see yourself in that list, get help.

Here are some ways to help sharpen your memory, regardless:

- Get regular aerobic exercise.

- Learn new things and engage in intellectually stimulating activities, such as crossword puzzles or Sudoku.

- Do what you can to retain your sense of control in life, because those who do have been shown, on average, to stay sharper longer.

When you find yourself in a panic of forgetting, slow down, try to relax, and focus. Visualize an image of the desired person or object. Or run through the alphabet, saying the letters aloud to trigger a memory of the word you seek. (Be open but skeptical regarding touted miracle cures such as ginkgo biloba or apple juice. The jury is still out.)

Keep lists, make a detailed calendar, and organize yourself as much as you can. For example, have a designated "key spot" inside the front door, and always put your keys there. Follow routines, repeat names back when you meet a new person, or repeat other new things you learn. Pay attention and concentrate when learning new things. Create associations. In learning someone's name, for example, ask yourself, "What does this name remind me of?" and really think of that association as you repeat the person's name aloud. All these tricks will help improve later recall.

Speaking of which — no peeking! — what were those three words from the beginning of this discussion? Relax, focus, recall. See? You're not as bad off as you thought.

even if kids learn to write fluidly, connecting the letters, an increasing number of them are losing the know-how from lack of use.

Not to be Debbie Downer or anything, but cursive writing is not the only dying art form; *you* happen to be one, too! Since this Way is about both writing and remembering, why not *write* a little something for people to *remember* you by? By hand, *por favor*, in your unique penmanship, even if your writing does look more like printing. Compose long letters or silly poems to everyone you love. Keep a special journal for a special someone (a grandchild, perhaps), to present as a gift someday. Write your life story! Or maybe just fill a card file with your favorite recipes, written out in longhand. Your descendants (by blood or by bond) will treasure it, all the more so for the way you loop your *g*'s and cross your *t*'s.

COOL MOVES

Carpal Tunnel Ahead: Prepare to "Ex" It

Repetitive-motion injuries, such as carpal tunnel syndrome, are a bear to cure. Better to prevent them in the first place. Make absolutely sure your computer workstation is ergonomically correct. (Revisit "Things to Try" in Way 3.) And, should you experience pain or tingling in the hands or arms, don't ignore it! Seek treatment (and deeper schooling on the issue) promptly. Whatever your situation, *take frequent stretch breaks*. Here are a couple of my faves:

- *Swing time:* Stand with plenty of space all around, and swing your arms in unison, forward and back, as far as they'll go. Do ten to twenty swings. If you're at a keyboard all day, enjoy a bit of swing time every hour on the hour.

- *Push me, pull you:* Place hands palm to palm and raise elbows until your wrists form right angles (or thereabouts). Push your fingers back one way, then the other. Work up to holding each push for thirty seconds.

⌐∿➔ THINGS TO TRY AT LEAST ONCE

❑ *Take gingko biloba.* Even though Dr. Peg is cautious and correct in saying that the jury's still out, I happen to know she takes this stuff every day — and she gave me permission to report as much.

❑ *Try aromatherapy.* The scents of lavender and peppermint have been shown to improve memory, while citrus and floral scents may help a person learn things faster.

❑ *Keep it sharp.* People who continually challenge their minds, even in small ways, stay smarter longer. So! Play Scrabble. Do math in your head. Work out crossword puzzles. Juggle. Square-dance. Paint by number! Watch the reverse-sequenced movie *Memento* (you may actually want to take notes, I kid you not). Read, read, read. Use your brain every which way you can — early and often.

❑ *Make your own journal.* Shop for a book-art kit or class, and stock up on handmade papers, ribbons, book cloth, whatever you need to make this treasure uniquely yours and uniquely "now." Then buy the perfect pen. Let money be no object.

❑ *Take your journal on a date.* Attend a journal circle or memoir-writing workshop.

Fuhgeddaboudit!

You worry, you spend energy, you get nothing.
— Sun Lee, Dahn master

*I*t wasn't but two seconds ago that I was writing about the importance of remembering. Well, *fuhgeddaboudit!* Sometimes remembering is overrated. Ever get a song stuck in your head? Need I say more? *My kingdom for an erase button!*

I Meant to Do That

Seriously, though, some memories are not worth keeping. They're just a drag on the system. If, for instance, your Inner Accountant has dutifully filed a mental note about every hurtful experience you've ever had — gosh! Think what a load off it would be to dump those files! While you're at it, ask yourself if you really, *really* need to hang on to those assumptions about what "always" happens, those regrets over a long-ago decision, and those worries about dying homeless and penniless with a garbage bag for a raincoat.

Fuhgeddaboudit! What are you, nuts?

"Where Mind Goes, Energy Follows"

A funny thing happened on the way to writing this book. I had just discovered Dahn yoga and the writings of its founder, Ilchi Lee (including the above-stated mind/energy principle and its converse, "Where energy goes, mind follows"), when suddenly it seemed as if every author I read was telling me the same thing. Caroline Myss, Eckhart Tolle, Deepak Chopra, David R. Hawkins, Thich Nhat Hanh, Roger Mills and Elsie Spittle, Wayne Dyer, Pema Chödrön, and many others underscored the same essential truth: *thoughts have power.* Indeed, thoughts *are* power. What we do with our mental energy determines, to a huge degree, what happens in our lives. And, most important, though it may seem as if our thoughts are running us, it's really the other way around.

Like it or not — like *them* or not — *you* are the author of your thoughts.

SCRIBBLES & DOODLES
Rewrite the Ending

Okay, so things didn't go as well as you'd hoped. Take to your journal, and write about "what went down" up to the point when, in your opinion, things went wrong. Fictionalize from there. Sometimes just playing out, or writing down, the things you *wish* had happened (or the snappy rejoinders you *wish* you'd said right then and there) can be your one-way ticket to Forget-It-Ville.

Kvetch Me Not

Give a thing mental energy, and it grows. Don't want it to grow? Then *fuhgeddaboudit!* Give it no oxygen. Pay it no mind. Why? Well, to blatantly misquote that advice-giving gent in *The Graduate*, I've got one word for you: *plasticity.* The human brain is plastic, changeable. Its architecture is never set in stone, although (surprise, surprise) an adult's brain is not nearly as plastic as a child's. Still, think of it! You can literally change your brain's architecture by thinking in new ways. Even *moving* in new ways alters the array of neural connections in your brain.

So, back to forgetting. It's the old "use it or lose it" thing, turned on its head. *Don't* use it. *Do* lose it. Get off the mental treadmill of worry, regret, self-pity, and the like; let those unhelpful thought patterns atrophy and die. How? For starters, practice "thought stopping," the "Cool Move" in Way 32. And keep reading! Not to call anyone an old dog or anything, but Dr. Peg and I have plenty of new tricks we'd like to teach.

COOL MOVES

A Thingamajig by Any Other Name

Ready to blow your mind — or at least rewire it a bit? Try forgetting the names of things! This Renaming Exercise, adapted from Ilchi Lee's *Brain Respiration*, is designed to improve your mind's agility by teaching it to slip the "insidious cage" (preconceptions) created by names. "We experience resistance when we try renaming," Lee writes, "because the name associated with an object is . . . hardwired in our brain as a pattern of neural connections. Renaming is an attempt to change the pattern intentionally."

Here's how to do it: (1) Make or buy a set of picture cards showing common, easily recognizable objects. (2) With the deck facedown, flip one card over and, as fast as you can, call out a name *completely unrelated* to the pictured object (e.g., if it's a banana, don't say orange; if it's

DOC IN THE BOX: *Prescription for Brain Play (Crossword Puzzle)*

What? You were expecting maybe some high-falutin' medical treatise here? Well, *fuhgeddaboudit!* Doctor's orders this time are to kick back and have a little fun, for goodness' sake. You can start with this easy crossword puzzle. Even as you relish how swiftly your vast intellect makes history of this puzzle, your memory centers will be getting a subtle tune-up. Won't hurt a bit! (Solution to the crossword puzzle on page 88.)

ACROSS

2 put on your _____ _____
4 instinctive understanding
6 noodle
8 find the answer to a problem
12 like brains over brawn (3 words)
15 didn't remember
16 "He's crazy! Lost his _____!"
17 remember
20 noggin
21 colorful name for brain (2 words)

DOWN

1 source of brilliant ideas
3 Einstein was one
5 "Just the _____ of you . . ."
7 brain cell
9 out cold
10 wisecracker (2 words)
11 something to be solved
13 nerdy bright guy
14 whatcha got if you're brainy
18 mental picture from the past
19 awake to your surroundings

a hat, don't say feather). (3) See how long it takes you to go through the whole deck. Try to improve on your speed every time you play, even as you call out new replacement names each time. (Party game alternative: play this in a group, either as a competition between teams or as a cooperative round-robin.)

⚡ THINGS TO TRY AT LEAST ONCE

❑ *Adopt some amnesia.* A little "purposeful forgetting" will improve your mood and your relationships. Accept that nobody's perfect and that grumpiness happens. Let the little hurts and slights slide off your back like water off a duck.

❑ *Raise the bar sinister.* Word is out: that red circle-slash thingie — the international symbol for "don't" — has a name: "bar sinister." Next time your thoughts are straying in a direction you'd rather they didn't, mentally "circle-slash" them in *achtung!* red.

❑ *Ignore the news.* Take a break from the daily blow-by-blow of politics, war, celebrity gossip, and the tragedies of just plain folks. It'll all be there, should you ever decide to go back to it.

❑ *Let begonias be begonias.* Release a grudge. Forgive someone, even yourself. Plant some begonias to celebrate that you're over it.

❑ *Play Scarlet O'Hara for a day.* Even if you do have a lot to remember, you don't have to remember it all *right now*, this minute. After all, tomorrow *is* another day!

Solution to crossword puzzle:

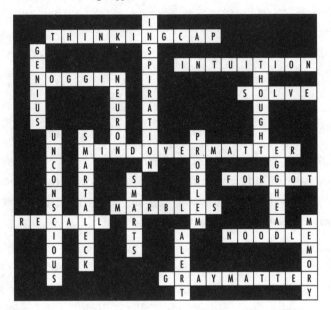

17 Go with the Flow

But one creature said at last, "I am tired of clinging. Though I cannot see it with my eyes, I trust that the current knows where it is going. I shall let go and let it take me where it will. Clinging, I shall die of boredom."

— Richard Bach, *Illusions: The Adventures of a Reluctant Messiah*

*S*ometimes you must yield to forces bigger than you. Any good sailor will tell you that, even in the fairest weather, it pays to align your "vessel" with the winds and tides. That's the gist of this Way, in a tiny little walnut shell of a boat, drifting along on a steady stream.

Ahoy! Where Are You Bound?

Thoughts have power. Thoughts are power. What you do with your thoughts — *how you direct their flow* — largely determines the course of your life.

So... where are you bound? Are your thoughts, like sails, properly set to take you there? Or are you tacking back and forth, only angling at your goal? Heaven forbid you're in the doldrums, with not a breath of air to move you! If the last be true, take heart in this, at least: the doldrums are a common midlife predicament.

SCRIBBLES & DOODLES
"O Captain, My Captain"

In his book *Flow: The Psychology of Optimal Experience,* Mihaly Csikszentmihalyi describes "flow experiences" as those in which everything just clicks. You feel buoyed along, time stands still, and nothing matters but the task at hand. Create such an experience for yourself, in writing. Do this in advance of that big important and fast-approaching *voyage* (event, sales presentation, whatever) for which you're the skipper. Script the details exactly as you want them to flow. Then, anchors aweigh! When the big moment arrives, you may be surprised by your own smooth sailing.

Become the Prevailing Wind

Oh, but remember the power you hold in your head! Imagine how that sailboat of yours would speed ahead if you but set your mind on it like a prevailing wind, blowing in exactly the right direction.

You *can* power your own sails. Especially if you take to heart our advice in the previous chapter: "forget" to waste energy on treadmill thoughts such as worry, regret, and self-pity. Save your mental juice for riding the wave!

Dare We Call It the "Wu-Wave"?

Some hear "go with the flow" as a call to give up or give in. To be passive, even lazy. To set yourself adrift. Others hear a call to assimilate, the old "go along to get along" routine. I don't mean "go with the flow" in any of those ways; I mean it in the "wu-wei." (Pardon my puns, but silly wordplay really can help fix a new concept in the mind.)

All silliness aside, *wu-wei*, the Taoist principle of "doing by not doing," is one of those ideals I categorize as Simple but Not Always Easy. It describes a beautiful way of being in which individuals feel connected to one another and to their own environments, indeed, to all creation. Through this deep sense of connectedness, "right action" occurs spontaneously, effortlessly, and at the appropriate time and place. Stress is low, productivity is high. Everything just... *flows*! You know?

COOL MOVES
Bladder Channel Opener

Can you touch fingers to toes with your legs straight? As stretches go, this is the gold standard. If you're "too short by half," chances are you're one of untold bazillions of people with tight (which is to say, short) hamstrings and back muscles. This Dahn yoga exercise stretches the whole back side of your body, with the Eastern-medicine bonus that it opens up the major chi meridians associated with the bladder, enabling the release of tons of stagnation. *Got restless legs syndrome? Do this stretch before bed.*

Lying on your back, lift your legs toward the sky. Keep your knees straight, and cock your feet slightly, enough to feel the stretch in your calves. Depending on your level of flexibility, take hold of your toes, ankles, calves, knees, or thighs, and use your hands to gently pull your legs toward your head to deepen the stretch. Don't overdo it! Most important is that you keep your knees straight and your feet flexed. Relax all muscles not engaged in the task. Breathe with your mouth open. *If your legs start to shake, let them!* Indeed, if the shaking stops, deepen your stretch and see if you can bring on more involuntary shaking, since it is a sure sign of release. Hold, and repeatedly deepen, the stretch for five minutes or more, taking it (if you're able) all the way to Hatha yoga's Plow Position, with toes touching the floor beyond your head.

Then slowly lower your feet to the floor close to your bottom, "windshield wiper" your knees back and forth a few times, then straighten them, and rest a while in Corpse Pose (see Way 38) before getting up.

 DOC IN THE BOX: *Keep the Flow Going (Urinary Health)*

At this time of life, there are other, more practical kinds of flow that might concern you. Gals may have "gone with the flow" even without meaning to (cough, sneeze, oops!). Guys may have felt the need to flow but just couldn't go. Not to mention the big C-word whose risk lurks in every system now that we're aging.

We tend to take our elimination systems for granted, until they develop problems. But even if your flow is still a go, it's never too late for preventive maintenance. Most important, to head off bladder (and other types of) cancer, stop smoking! Beyond that, here are some ways to maintain healthy plumbing:

- *Flush it.* From the inside out. Running fluid through the pipes regularly can wash out carcinogens. Eating lots of cruciferous (cabbage family) vegetables helps prevent bladder cancer, too, so learn to love broccoli. Flushing can also decrease the risk of urinary tract infections, which also in turn lowers your cancer risk. Drink lots of water and other noncaffeinated beverages.

- *Tune it up.* The muscles that support the bladder and urethra are weakened in women by pregnancy, childbirth, and being overweight. Weak muscles cause embarrassing leakage. Getting these muscles in shape can plug the leak and make it less likely that you'll need a pessary (a ring device in the vagina) or a surgical procedure to correct urine leakage. Tighten your pelvic muscles before sneezing, lifting, or jumping. Best of all, firm up your pelvic floor with the infamous Kegel exercise. It's easy:

- *Kegel! Kegel! Kegel!* To learn how, sit on the pot and start to pee, then stop yourself. That's the sensation you're after. From now on, squeeze those deepest muscles (*hard!*) and hold 'em (*long!*) whenever you think of it: at a red light, while doing dishes, in the movie theater, anywhere! Hundreds of Kegels a day would not be too many. Fringe benefit: increased sexual pleasure for all parties involved!

⌇ THINGS TO TRY AT LEAST ONCE

❑ *Learn to sail* — or just go sailing!

❑ *Go ahead and cry*. It's healthy to flush the pipes now and then.

❑ *If it's yellow, let it mellow*. Water will be a defining issue of the twenty-first century. Please don't waste any.

❑ *Contemplate flow*. Sit by a babbling brook or a rushing river and just be. Listen, watch, enjoy. Or visit an active volcano — from a safe distance — to watch the lava flow.

❑ *Open your channels*. Get your chi flowing with a professional massage or other chi-moving modality. Remember to drink lots of water afterward.

Book 'Em, Danno

> Wholly unprepared, we embark upon the second half of life.... But we cannot live the afternoon of life according to the program of life's morning — for what was great in the morning will be little at evening, and what in the morning was true will at evening have become a lie.
>
> — Carl Jung (1875–1961)

*I*f you watched TV as a kid, you'll know whom we mean when we say, "Book 'em, Danno." *Dut-dut-dut-duhh-daah-dahhhh:* can't you just hear the theme song's opening horns?

So maybe you're thinking this Way is about leaving your forties in state number fifty. *Absolutely!* If an authentic *Hawaii Five-O* birthday is what you'd like, then go for it! Because this Way is about getting everything you want out of life.

Tick-Tock, Y'all

Mention "biological clock," and most folks think of waning fertility, usually of the female persuasion. But there's another biological clock ticking for each of us, men included. More commonly called your "life-time," it dings, and you're dead. What're you gonna do?

Seriously! The life expectancy of today's average fifty-year-old American is 84.2 years, an expanse of time not at all guaranteed. It could all stop short tomorrow! But just in case it doesn't, what are you going to do?

This Way says, "Plan!" Give serious thought to what time you (ahem) *may* have left and decide what you want to accomplish before D-day. Then book it! Even if now's not the time to schedule it firmly, at least write the would-be accomplishment down. Get it on your to-do list.

It's All in Your Head

In Way 15 we discussed what a good idea it is to write stuff down. It's memory enhancing and brain relieving, both of which are good, but this is even better: a special magic comes from committing your life's big dreams to paper. (Okay, it's not really magic; it's evolutionary biology.) Henriette Klauser explains, in her book *Write It Down, Make It Happen*:

> At the base of the brain stem, about the size of a little finger, is a group of cells whose job it is to sort and evaluate incoming data. This control center is known as the reticular activating system (RAS). The RAS sends the urgent stuff to the active part of your brain, and sends the non-urgent to the subconscious

SCRIBBLES & DOODLES
Write Your RAS a Memo

Send a shout out to your reticular activating system. Maybe even draw it a picture (*several* pictures) in the form of a "storyboard." List all the things you want to do before your biological clock goes "ding." Think big. Be bold. Think small, too. And outside the box. Do you still wish you'd had braces as a kid? Well, it's never too late to get your teeth straightened! Write down every one of your want-to's and wish-I-coulds, no matter how much the very thought of them makes you giggle with dreamer's delight. Then draw a storyboard (or a comic book!) starring heroic you. Depict yourself accomplishing everything on your list. Can you think of fifty dreams-come-true to draw? Post your storyboard (or written to-do list) prominently — or put it away! Either way, the sentries of your RAS division will have been briefed. They'll be on the lookout, 24/7, for anything that might help you get what you want.

DOC IN THE BOX: *Book 'Em Daily (Vitamin and Mineral Daily Minimums)*

"I only eat junk food, but I take a multivitamin so I know I'm getting everything I need." I have heard this from too many of my patients. As if all your nutrition could fit in a tiny pill. Not so, Horatio! Our poor overstressed bodies need far more than that. In fact, I was taught that vitamin supplements weren't even necessary, that a good healthy diet contained all the vitamins we need.

Well, *that* was wrong. Like many medical pronouncements, it had to be modified. It's looking now like vitamin supplements are in fact important tools for our bodies. Let me explain.

A vitamin is a nutrient you have to get from food because your body can't make it from scratch. Vitamins have also been called *micro*nutrients, since the amount we need is tiny. The body can use them as is, without breaking them down any further.

Vitamin deficiencies, though quite rare in modern society, can cause serious health problems. For example, rickets (thin, fragile bones) from lack of vitamin D, or scurvy (bleeding sores and gums) from lack of vitamin C. (British sailors got the nickname "limey" from the limes they ate to prevent scurvy.)

It is possible to overdose on vitamins, a risk increased by the current popularity of mega-dosing. While it is more difficult to overdose on the water-soluble vitamins (B's, C) since the excess gets eliminated in our urine, the fat-soluble ones (A, D, E, and K) can accumulate in our fat tissue and build up toxicity. Clearly, more is not always better.

However, new research is verifying that vitamins play very important roles in our bodies, and that some vitamin supplementation is good for us after all, no matter how balanced or "healthy" our diet. The table on the next page summarizes current knowledge and recommendations.

The take-home message is this: Take a good multivitamin supplement every day. *Mineral* supplements are a whole different issue, but I will say that a calcium supplement is a good idea for most women.

One good resource for vitamin information is Dr. Andrew Weil's website, drweil.com, on which he has an individualized "vitamin advisor" questionnaire to help you decide which vitamins and supplements to take.

Vitamin	What It's Good For	Optimal Daily Intake
A (retinol)	• helps us see in the dark • makes white blood cells • remodels bones • keeps body linings healthy • regulates cell growth	• women: 4,000 IU • men: 5,000 IU *IU = International Units Take it as beta-carotene to avoid getting too much.
B6 (pyridoxine)	• might help fight heart disease • might help fight cancer • might help stress	Unknown (at least 1.7 milligrams)
B9 (folic acid/folate)	• prevents spina bifida birth defect • might help fight heart disease • might help fight cancer	Unknown (at least 400 micrograms)
B12 (cobalamin)	• might help fight heart disease • might help fight cancer	Unknown (at least 6 micrograms)
C (ascorbic acid)	• helps control infections • antioxidant • makes collagen	300 milligrams
D (calciferol)	• builds bones • keeps cancer cells from dividing	15 minutes of sunshine or 1,000 IU
E (tocopherol)	• might help fight heart disease • might help healing	400 IU
K (phylloquinone)	• clots the blood • builds bones	• women: 65 micrograms • men: 80 micrograms

.... Once you write down a goal, your brain will be working overtime to see you get it, and will alert you to the signs and signals that ... were there all along.

Don't believe that writing it down can make it happen for *you*? Guess there's only one way to find out.

COOL MOVES

For Eyes That Love Books

As with every one of this book's fifty Ways, there is more than one way to "book 'em." Here, for example, is a bit of vision reeducation advice for the avid bookworm, to reduce eyestrain while reading:

- Blink softly and quickly on *every* punctuation mark.

- Move your nose in unison with a pointer (such as a toothpick or finger) gliding steadily beneath the text you're reading, until it's a habit to move your nose (then let go of the toothpick).

- At the end of each paragraph, close your eyes briefly, and inhale. While exhaling, open your eyes with your focus on the far distance. This is like a leg stretch for your eyes.

THINGS TO TRY AT LEAST ONCE

❑ *Be here, aloha!* Bring the luau to your house. Greet guests with leis, crank up the Don Ho tunes, and serve Hawaiian punch, mai tais, shish kebab, and desserts of pineapple and coconut. Grass skirts, anyone? Let's hula!

❏ *Pencil yourself in.* Schedule time to read for pleasure, go see a movie, reconnect with a loved one, or just do whatever you feel like doing when the time comes. Forget penciling, on second thought, and *ink* this deal.

❏ *Reread 'em, Danno.* Just for fun, dig out your old journals and "book" back through your earlier days.

❏ *Look to your books* (as in finances). Age fifty is an ideal time to reevaluate (or, ah, *begin*) your retirement planning. Procrastinators, don't despair! Instead, make a catch-up retirement plan the best birthday gift you ever gave yourself! Operation Hope can help (www.operationhope.org).

Lay a Feast for the Muses

The day of days, the great day of the feast of life, is that in which the inward eye opens to the Unity in things.

— Ralph Waldo Emerson, "Fate," *The Conduct of Life*

*A*ny birthday is a time to celebrate, of course, but the half-century mark? *This* calls for a feast! And not just any old feast, either, but one fit for the gods!

Now, to put the very finest point on this, let me say, "Not just any old feast fit for the gods, either." For we are not talking literal feasts here — at least, not *only* the literal kind. Recall that this Way is in the Mind section, the realm of imagination, dreams, and symbolism. This feast is metaphorical, and the guest of honor is You!

Guess Who's Coming to Dinner?

Those nine Greek lovelies, the Muses, are credited as the bringers of inspiration — exactly the kind of guests you want at your table, especially in times of doldrums. Feeling stuck or bored in midlife is no surprise when careers grow long in the tooth and relationships feel as comfortable as bedroom slippers (and about as sexy). Even if you happen to love both your marriage and your career, these days may find you sleepwalking through your routines, and — like I need to tell *you*! — that's no way to live.

Hence this feast for the Muses, darling, in celebration of Your Most Essential Self — the proverbial "true you" — that you may bloom, fully actualized, in this lifetime!

Be the Food of the Gods

Hosting a feast calls on us to be our best. We bring out the fine linens and china. We plan an exquisite menu and scour the market for special ingredients. We scour our homes until they shine! As the earth turns toward the day of our feast, we're up before the sun, preparing the food and setting the table. We break open our finest wine to honor our guests most richly, even as they honor us by their presence at our table.

So it must be in our lives, when the guest of honor is Self. You know that old Woody Allen quote, "80 percent of success is just showing up"? *Hear, hear!* You've got to *show up for yourself*, if you're to bloom fully.

Will you go the extra mile to make this the very best feast, knowing that it's for *you*? Will you forego the drive-through, fast-food, protein-drink

SCRIBBLES & DOODLES
Menu of the Gods

Don your thinking cap — or no, a fresh white chef's toque would be more appropriate for this — and design a menu fit for a Muse. What do Muses eat, you ask? Why, *you*, naturally! Course upon course of your willingness, readiness, and ability to turn divine inspiration into something wonderful. Think of this menu as your cosmic résumé, and tell your royal guests what's good here. Perhaps the appetizers are your inborn talents and traits; the soups and salads, your accumulated wisdom; and the entrees, your values and outlook. What's to drink? And for dessert? Have fun presenting your many delicious and nutritious qualities in fun or fancy menu language. Extend this exercise into an arts-and-crafts project, to produce a beautifully finished menu. Get it laminated. *Bon appétit!*

lunch on the go, and actually sit down to *dine?* Not just this once, for your birthday — but regularly? Can you treat yourself as a Royal Guest at your own table?

The Four Basic Food Groups

Eating is how we draw the earth's energy into our bodies, and every mother's child knows that a balanced diet is very important. Once again, let us feast metaphorically. The ancients saw creation as having four essential elements — earth, air, fire, and water — and all four came together in the cooking pot. Food from the earth, water from the well or stream, fire to cook it, and — (deep breath) — *smell that?* Dinner!

The four elements correlate with the divisions of this book. You've got your earthy Body, the airy thoughts of Mind, the forging fire of Soul, and the watery emotions of Heart. To become the very best food for the gods, your True You should "get enough" of all realms of life. Leave no aspect of Self to starve.

Answer your creative urges. They are the Muses knocking at your door.

COOL MOVES

The Dancing Waiter

Be like a waiter drawing figure eights with his tray. Why would a waiter do that? This Brain Respiration exercise is a profound chi mover!

Stand with feet together, and take a double step forward with your right foot. Extend your right arm forward, with elbow soft and palm

DOC IN THE BOX: *Lay a Feast, Raise a Toast (Health Pros and Cons of Alcohol)*

Your fiftieth birthday feast. The table is groaning with roast meats, loaves of fresh-baked bread, steaming vegetable dishes, fruit-stuffed cornucopia, fancy baked pastries. And of course, goblets! What would a birthday feast be without the nectar of the gods? Pass your glass and enjoy. It turns out a drop of "the grape" is good for you!

Notice I said a "drop." You won't find a doctor anywhere advocating a case a day. Alcohol is one of those double-edged swords, where a little is good, but a lot is *not*!

Let's start with the bad news. At the extreme negative end of the distilled and fermented spectrum are the day-long drinkers. These people are at high risk for cirrhosis of the liver, heart muscle damage, brain atrophy, pancreatitis, and sudden death and are more likely than their neighbors to drink themselves into a cancer ward. (Cancers of the pancreas, mouth, pharynx, larynx, esophagus, liver, and breast all correlate with heavy drinking.) Not to mention the well-known and tragic consequences of drinking and driving, and of mixing alcohol with anger or depression.

It's enough to make you want to become a teetotaler. Thankfully, with alcohol, as with much in life, it's a matter of degree.

Here's the good news. A little bit goes a long way when it comes to alcohol. If you include one or two drinks (12 oz. beer, 6 oz. wine, or a level shot of liquor) on your daily menu, you are actually less likely than the teetotaler to develop vascular disease, less likely to die of a heart attack, even less likely to get gallstones. Research is also suggesting that you might have a lower risk of strokes and diabetes, and you might even have stronger bones. Tip: of all the drink choices, red wine seems to convey the most health benefits.

If you're currently a nondrinker, I'm not suggesting you take up the habit against your personal or religious principles. And if you overindulge, please get some help and cut down. But if you enjoy a glass of wine with your dinner, or a bottle for your birthday feast, here's a guilt-free "bottoms up" to you!

upward, as if holding a tray. Place your left wrist at the small of your back. Exhale as you bend forward slightly, and move your "tray" counterclockwise (toward your body and loosely under your right armpit). Continue this counterclockwise movement as you straighten up and shift your weight to the back (left) foot. Inhale deeply as your tray draws a second large circle, this one over your head: looking upward, move your tray in a clockwise circle. Keep your palm upward (don't drop the dishes!) as you complete your first figure eight and begin again by bending forward with your exhalation. Move fluidly with your breath as you continue alternating the two sets of moves — (1) exhaling/forward/looking down/counterclockwise arm movement/in front of body and (2) inhaling/backward/looking up/clockwise arm movement/overhead — until you've completed ten figure eights. Repeat on the left side.

〰️ THINGS TO TRY AT LEAST ONCE

☐ *Name the nine.* Pop quiz! List all the Muses, and, for extra credit, name the art or science each inspires. (Answers appear just below.)

☐ *Invent a tenth.* Make up a new Muse to fit any needful moment: "Hail Asphalta, full of grace, help me find a parking place" (an impromptu prayer by rising-star comedienne Amy Boyd).

☐ *Have an amusing affair.* Invite your guests to dress up as their favorite Muse, and ask them to prepare a little something for recital — be it poem, song, scientific theory, or dance. Serve spanakopita and dolmades. Don't forget the ambrosia!

☐ *Consult an oracle.* Rune stones, Tarot cards, and the *I Ching* are three well-known means through which the Muses may point the way. Or just let a favorite book fall open, plunk your pointing finger down on any page, and start reading. Many people consult the Bible in such a manner.

❑ *Be a gallivanting gourmet.* Make it a point to sample some fancy foods such as caviar, real truffles, steak tartare, crème fraîche, escargot, or vichyssoise. Finish with a chocolate-covered grasshopper.

❑ *Indulge in a Visual Feast.* Enjoy a food-movie marathon. *Eat, Drink, Man, Woman*; *Like Water for Chocolate*; *The Big Night*; *Chocolat*; and *Tampopo* are just a few of the great movies starring food.

Answers to the pop quiz:
The Greek Muses are Clio (history), Calliope (epic poetry), Erato (love poetry and mimicry), Euterpe (music), Melpomene (tragedy), Polyhymnia (sacred poetry), Terpsichore (dance), Thalia (comedy and playful poetry), and Urania (astronomy).

WAY 20 — Say It Loud, Sing It Proud

O that my tongue were in the thunder's mouth!
Then with passion would I shake the world.

— William Shakespeare, *The Life and Death of King John*, act 3,
scene 4

"I remember when I was in my thirties," Tuko emailed, "I hated telling people I was over thirty.... Now I proudly tell them I'm fifty. What's up with that?"

No kidding! Fifty years on the planet is no mean feat. You've earned bragging rights! As recently as 1901, life expectancy for a person born in the United States was just forty-nine years. Nowadays most of us hit fifty *hard* and keep right on going. We *should* shout it from the rooftops. We should break into song! We should put our hands together and make a joyful noise. Then — *you* heard the bard — with *passion* would we shake the world!

Rhyming and Stealing

Shakespeare said a lot of stuff best, but it was the Beastie Boys who gave us the phrase "rhyming and stealing." I, for one, am much obliged,

106

since I happen to do a little rhyming and stealing myself from time to time, pairing silly faux lyrics with (often tired) pop melodies, to comic effect — at least in the eyes of my young children.

Now that my kids approach teendom, however, clearly my career as a comedic singer-songwriter is near an end. No matter. I'll just pick up my soap-on-a-rope microphone and hit the shower.

Rhyming and Remembering

Seriously, here's a thing worth singing about: musical memory is stored in the brain differently than other types of data. As such, it can aid learning. For instance, can you speak the language you studied in high school? Unless you've been using it regularly since then, probably not, at least not fluently. But what about the *songs* you learned in that language class? You can sing them straightaway, right?

Try this the next time you have something important to remember (say, a new, healthier habit). Just hitch it to a fitting melody. (Affirmations, anyone?) It'll stick in your head!

When You Can't Find the Words, Hum!

Vocal vibration is comforting, and not just to babies. Remember audible sighing from Way 1, how it helps relax the body from head to tail? One day, while driving in dangerous weather, I spontaneously

SCRIBBLES & DOODLES
*"Splish, Splash,
I Was Havin' a Flash"*

Weird Al Yankovic is known for his hilarious skewering of pop tunes (though, in case it's not obvious, "Splish, Splash" is not one of his). Whether by "rhyming and stealing" or by penning an original composition, write a song or poem in honor of leaving your forties. Need inspiration? Give Weird Al a whirl! And don't stop until you give voice to your creation in at least one "public" performance. (Family members crowding 'round with ears to bathroom door? That counts, I guess — but only if they really, *really* enjoy the show!)

began voicing *every* exhalation, to calm my nerves and center my mind. It worked! I thought I'd made quite a discovery — until I remembered that yogis and monks have been chanting mantras since time out of mind.

Russill Paul writes as much, in *The Yoga of Sound*: "Mantra has always been central to healing in India, where sonic formulas have been used to promote well-being for thousands of years. . . . Research shows that chanting produces natural painkillers, lowers the heart rate, and reduces blood pressure." Through our voice, Paul explains, we can sync up sonically (musically) with the universe.

And here I thought I was just sighing out loud.

COOL MOVES

"I'm an Ape Man, I'm an Ape-Ape Man!"

If this one makes you cough, keep doing it! Coughing is a great, percussive releaser. Seated or standing, tap on your chest (hard!) with cupped palms in unison, one high on the sternum, the other directly beneath. Follow three rhythmic taps with one vocal blast on the fourth tap, a loud, clipped "AH!" (tap, tap, tap, "AH!"). Do three cycles. Next, follow your three unvoiced taps with *three* voiced ones (tap, tap, tap, "AH! AH! AH!" = six taps). Repeat, repeat. Finish by switching from taps in unison to alternating beats, and don't be shy about regaling your housemates with your best (loud) chest-thumping imitation of King Kong. Or Tarzan, if you prefer. Just make it the longest and most spirited "AHHHHHHHHHHHHHHHH" possible. And remember, coughing is good!

DOC IN THE BOX: *Sound Effects (Healing Uses of Sound)*

For me it's running water, soft wind chimes, or Brazilian crooning. For you it might be drums, violins, or Elvis. The sounds that soothe, energize, or lift the spirit. Sound is powerful stuff. Shamans since forever have used chanting and drumming in healing rituals. In the Navajo tradition medicine men use chanting, drumming, and dancing as crucial elements in their healing ceremony; they even call this ceremony a "sing." Healers among the Yanyuwa Aborigines of Northern Australia sing a healing song directly "into" the top of the head of the sick person. Chanting the Indian Vedas, proclaimed to be the voice of the Lord that was heard by the seers of yore, is a sacred act for millions. These are, of course, just a few examples.

Sound is used in modern healing as well. Practitioners of sound therapy approach humans as vibratory beings, whose every cell and organ possesses unique vibratory properties. Sound therapists, with the help of tuning forks, chimes, music, or electric sound generators, use specific frequencies to resonate with certain organs and support healing. Some of the applications include relaxation, pain control, birthing assistance, death transition, and chakra balancing.

Do you doubt that sound has energy? Consider the fact that sound waves are used to break up kidney stones, or think back to the last time you heard a sonic boom or clapped your hands over your ears when something was too loud. Invisible yet powerful.

If sound therapy sounds too weird to you, just go with what you like. Make a listening library of different music or sounds for different moods or desired effects. Pick your favorites, and treat yourself. And don't forget that silence is one of the richest sounds of all.

THINGS TO TRY AT LEAST ONCE

❑ *Sing!* In the shower, in church, along with the car radio, around the campfire, at karaoke night. Every chance you get, *sing*.

❑ *Chant!* Think you can't sing? Phooey! Choose your most comfortable vocal pitch and a simple word or phrase to repeat like a mantra. (Jack Nicholson's "shrink" character in the movie *Anger Management* uses "Gooooz-frah-bah," a big fave at my house. Your mantra can be real words, if you want, or any sounds that you find soothing.) Relax, breathe, and let your voice do the rest. Keep it up for several long minutes.

❏ *Speak!* Join Toastmasters to develop your public-speaking skills or just for fun.

❏ *Don't speak!* One way to better appreciate the power of your voice is to practice silence. Start small — an hour, a whole morning — and work up to a days-long silent retreat.

Know Your Yin from Your Yang

There's nothing constant in the world,
All ebb and flow, and every shape that's born
Bears in its womb the seeds of change.

— Ovid *Metamorphoses* 15.177–78

*W*ho was it that said, "Fifty is the old age of youth and the youth of old age"? A writer for Hallmark, perhaps? Whoever it was, we stand now at that nexus. Gone are our days of pleading "young and stupid"; the world expects "older and wiser" from us now. You know what the old-timers say: get to be our age, and we really ought to know our [bleep] from shinola (whatever the [bleep] shinola is).

But since we live in a global village, let me put it this way, no bleeps about it: in this day and at our age, what we really should know is our yin from our yang.

A Speck of Spice in the Cosmic Soup

The Chinese creation myth begins with a great cosmic egg in which was floating a shapeless *won-ton* ("no thing"), until the day the egg hatched to reveal the giant Phan-Ku. As Phan-Ku grew at a rate of ten thousand feet a day, he lifted the upper half of the eggshell skyward,

SCRIBBLES & DOODLES
Trading Places

Write of a recent experience or exchange you had with someone of the opposite sex, but do your best to tell it from the other person's point of view, using his or her voice as first person. (Tempted though you may be, refrain from an attitude of "Okay, you be me, and *I'll* be the [bleeeep]!")

which then became the heavenly principle yang. And he ground the lower half beneath his feet, which became the earthly principle yin. Thus was born the duality of all things.

Before the story ends, Phan-Ku dies and gives his bones to be the mountains, his blood to be the rivers, his hair to be the forests, and — are you ready for this? — his *fleas* to be the people. Now, don't jump to any conclusions! Such lowly beginnings are not meant to suggest that humans are like vermin — only that we are but a teeny-tiny part of creation. Chinese brush painters reflect this notion in their towering monochromatic landscapes. See that tiny figure? Barely more than a dot? It's like Where's Waldo, without the crowds.

Things Change

The yin-yang symbol expresses creation's never-ending cycles of change in simple, stark black and white. The bright-as-day yang side and dark-as-night yin side are ever in flux, as symbolized by the S-curved boundary between them. And each side contains the seed of its opposite: a white spot on the black half, and vice versa.

Honestly, I could never remember which was which until I struck on this simple mnemonic device: yin contains the word *in*, and it's the *inward*, receptive, feminine principle, the one that's dark, cool, and reflective, like the moon. Yang, then, is the outward, active, masculine principle — bright, hot, and radiant like the sun. This is not to say, of course, that a man can't be cool and reflective, or that a woman can't be active and outgoing. No one is all yin or all yang; recall those spots of the opposite color on each half of the yin-yang symbol.

Here's another mnemonic: **yin** is *yi*elding (*yi-yi*), ya**ng** is stro**ng** (*ng-ng*). (Or, as Dr. Peg likes to say, "Yang is like boing.") Because right-handedness is vastly more common than left-handedness, yang correlates with the (strong) right side of the body, and yin with the (yielding) left. Again, let me hasten to add that I know plenty of strong left-handers and plenty of yielding right-handers, and I bet you do too. We are, every one of us, a mixed bag.

It All Hangs in the Balance

Indeed, each of us embodies an ever-changing mix of the dual energies, as does our environment. The opposing principles hold each other in check, never conquering. In the event that either energy grows too strong, there always comes a tipping point, a revolution. To better understand the beauty and poetry of this concept, study translations of China's ancient *I Ching*, also known as *The Book of Changes*.

Revolutions can be harsh! If change is truly an inescapable fact of nature (and it is), then we do better to manage it as gradually as possible, rather than waiting for things to blow. For example, if one of your relationships is out of balance, communicate your needs with gentle persistence — and be open to hearing and addressing the other person's needs — before it's too late!

DOC IN THE BOX: *Unblocking the Yin-Yang River (Acupuncture)*

As a medical student, I had the great good fortune to spend a winter in Beijing, China, at an urban children's hospital that used traditional Chinese medicine as well as modern Western methods. Eager to learn all I could, I asked one of the doctors to give me an acupuncture treatment. She readily agreed, asking what was wrong with me. Well, since my arrival, I had been severely congested with thick yellow mucus, probably because of the heavy coal-dust atmosphere. Hearing this, the Chinese doctor proceeded to stick several tiny needles into my face and neck. She twirled and adjusted each needle, saying, "Tell me when I hit the spot." My confusion about this cleared when, with each needle, I felt a sudden sense of pressure and warmth that passed in a flash; the needle had obviously hit the "spot." After she finished, I sat there like some kind of fleshy porcupine until she returned (ten minutes later) to remove the needles. The following morning, I awoke snot-free and with a mind as open as my sinuses.

Acupuncture is almost as old as Phan-Ku himself and has been used for centuries by the Chinese to control pain and treat illness. The purpose of acupuncture is to balance the flow of chi through the meridians. (Remember Sheila's bus-route description from Way 4.) If chi flow is blocked in one place, or if it is too heavy in another, illness results. Stimulating certain prescribed points on the body meridians restores balance.

In recent decades, acupuncture has become increasingly accepted outside China. The needles have been shown to stimulate certain hormones and biochemical mediators, like endorphins (natural painkillers), but beyond that, the exact mechanism remains unexplained in Western terms. Regardless, the record of millions of successful treatments carries a certain weight that many health insurance companies will now take to the bank, covering acupuncture treatments alongside prescription medications and surgery. Check www.nccaom.org to find a certified acupuncturist.

 COOL MOVES

Yin-to-Yang Shower Scrub

In the body's energy system, the meridians are designated yin or yang, depending on the direction of their chi flow. In general, the yin channels run along the front and inner planes of the body, and the yang ones run along the back and outer planes.

This washcloth scrub helps stimulate proper chi flow, from yin to yang, in the upper body. It can also be performed (*sans* washcloth) as a lotion rub, after showering. For greater chi-moving benefit, replace the rubbing or scrubbing with Dahnhak-style rhythmic body tapping (with cupped palm; see Way 4), in the same sequence.

In the shower, soap up a washcloth and spread it over your right hand. Hold your left arm in front of you, at shoulder height, with palm upward. Run the soapy washcloth down your arm, in one smooth swipe, from shoulder to palm. Scrub palms together several times, then turn the left arm palm downward and run the washcloth upward in a single swipe, from the back of the hand to the shoulder. Now, with your left arm still at shoulder height, point your thumb upward and swipe the washcloth down the arm, from shoulder to thumb. Finally, as you lift that left arm, slide the washcloth up the underside of your arm, from pinkie to armpit. Scrub the armpit and down the ribcage several times. Repeat the series a time or two on the same side, then several times on the other side.

⌇ THINGS TO TRY AT LEAST ONCE

☐ *Order up some wonton soup* and contemplate the shapeless "no thing" that existed before creation. Or, if your taste runs more to sweet-and-sour, order the fried wontons and dip 'em in that "dualistic" sauce, as you contemplate yin and yang, the pervasive duality of nature.

☐ *Eat your yin-ables!* Menopause is said to be a time of relative yin deficiency — too hot! need cooling energy! — so, ladies, eat your "yin foods," including almonds, apples, asparagus, bamboo shoots, bananas, barley, bean curd, bean sprouts, beer, broccoli, cabbage, celery, clams, corn, corn flour, crab, cucumbers, duck, eels, fish, grapes, honey, ice cream, lemons, mushrooms, mussels, oranges, oysters, peppermint tea, pineapple, salt, shrimp, spinach, strawberries, soy beans, white sugar, and tomatoes. Water also provides a boost of cooling yin, so drink up!

❏ ... *And your yang-ables*. In case you're feeling too yin (cold, reclusive, overly passive), eat more "yang foods," including beef, black pepper, brown sugar, butter, cheese, chicken liver and fat, chilies, chocolate, coffee, eggs, smoked fish, garlic, green peppers, goose, ham, kidney beans, lamb, leeks, onions, peanut butter, roasted peanuts, potato, rabbit, turkey, walnuts, and whisky. Oh, and drink wine.

Seize the Night

Night, the beloved. Night, when words fade and things come alive. When the destructive analysis of day is done, and all that is truly important becomes whole and sound again. When man reassembles his fragmentary self and grows with the calm of a tree.

— Antoine de Saint-Exupéry, *Flight to Arras*

*N*ight owls! Call me bird of a feather. All hours of the night, I hoot with thee, my wide eyes gleaming and engaged, despite the silent darkness all around. Oh, but I must be sleeping, because a moment ago I was a bird, and now suddenly I'm a knight dressed in black, whose white stallion rears up beneath a full moon, at the very moment a coyote howls — and that kind of thing usually only happens when I'm dreaming.

Of *Course*, the "Night" Was Dressed in Black!

And the horse can fly, did I mention? Isn't dreaming just the trippiest? How better to begin a Way titled "Seize the Night"? Whether or not you do it for serious self-analysis, dream interpretation is some of the best fun you can have with your brain. Take that howling coyote, for instance. I don't know what the dream dictionaries would say, but my guess is she cries for every nocturnal Joe or Jane who ever had to hold down a day job.

SCRIBBLES & DOODLES
Dash It Down before It Dashes Away

Keep a dream journal for at least a week. Details vanish through the crack between the worlds almost as soon as you wake up, so keep a pen and pad next to your pillow. Don't worry about writing style, but do try to get down as many details as you can remember. Rereading your notes later, ask yourself (in writing) what the different images mean. Trust your own intuition before someone else's. If you are thoroughly stumped, consult a book or website on dream interpretation. Or talk the dream though with your mate or a trusted friend or therapist. Sometimes we figure it all out in the process of narrating.

If you've been known to howl (however silently) at the moon, then maybe, metaphorically speaking, you're a wolf in human's clothing! I'm only half-joking. You may want to read up on the fascinating shamanistic lore concerning animal totems. Who knows? Could be, according to your animal nature, you were born not to be wild, exactly, but at least to work the swing shift.

Great Mysteries Unfold in the Dark

Pity the poor Dark Side, demonized since time out of mind. But in a dualistic universe, we truly *must* have both the light and the dark, and not just so the Good Guy will have a Bad Guy to vanquish. Consider the true dark side of nature: the night, the winter, the rot, the countless hidden mysteries that occur in the dark — beneath the soil's surface, for instance, or inside a pregnant belly or cocoon, or way out in the deepest, star-birthing reaches of space.

Even in the pitch blackness, anyone ought to be able to see that the so-called dark side is neither evil nor empty. On the contrary, it is replete with rich potential. And, to a lazybones like me, here's the very best part: you can tap into the richness of this vast potential *while you sleep*.

Don't believe it? Try a little fairy-tale magic! (Insomniacs, take note: Dr. Peg tells me that the following activity is not a good one for people who get wound up by dwelling on problems at bedtime. If that's you, please skip this and proceed directly to her "Doc in the Box" instead.)

The Elves and the Shoemaker

You know the fairy tale, right? A poor shoemaker cuts out his last bit of remaining leather and then goes to bed. In the morning, he discovers that the leather has been perfectly stitched into a fine pair of shoes. A customer comes to the store and buys the shoes for twice the usual price, the shoemaker buys more leather to make two pairs of shoes, and the story continues like this till the shoemaker and his wife are famous for their fine shoes, and wealthy to boot (pun intended).

Before bed, metaphorically cut out the shoe leather of whatever problem is vexing you, by reviewing your notes on the matter, journaling about it, praying — whatever works for you. Just give it a good going-over in your mind. Then lay it aside. Utterly. Leave it on your "workbench" and go sleep the sleep of an exhausted shoemaker.

Come morning, don't be surprised if the solution pops into your head almost as soon as you open your eyes, or as soon as you open that vexing project file. The "elves" of your subconscious mind have a wonderful way of cobbling together the pieces while you sleep and leaving the solution, whole and ready for your discovery, like a gift on your pillow. It may not happen over one night, but keep practicing.

DOC IN THE BOX: *You Are Getting Sle-e-e-py! (Clinical Hypnosis)*

It was after lunch, and I had a conference headache. That's the one that comes from too much sitting, too many cups of free coffee, and too much rich dessert. Lucky for me, the topic of the day was hypnosis, and the instructor asked for a volunteer. I settled into the chair, eager to think my headache away.

"I'll put you in trance," the instructor explained, "then you'll go (in your mind) to a control room, the one that manages all your body functions and sensations. You'll find the pain dial and slowly turn it down." In keeping with the philosophy of clinical hypnosis, there would be no surprises. Knowing what was coming, I'd be able to relax more fully. This would allow my parasympathetic system to take over, opening access to my unconscious mind and thereby to my body.

Hypnosis is simply the process of attaining a state of deep relaxation and heightened suggestibility. Contrary to popular belief, hypnosis does not turn you into a powerless zombie, at the mercy of the hypnotist. As I discovered, even in trance you remain aware of your surroundings and in control of your behavior. Anyone can be hypnotized if she wants to be, and nobody in trance can be forced to do something she is not willing to do. People use hypnosis to ease symptoms of a variety of illnesses, to calm anxiety, and to help them change behaviors. It has a very good track record with helping people to stop smoking and overeating.

Back to the chair. The instructor's smooth, deep voice helped me into relaxation using guided imagery. From there I "went" to the control room in my mind, found the dial, and turned down the pain, bit by bit, until the headache was gone. Pain-free, I signaled my success to the hypnotist, who brought me out of trance with a countdown and a smile.

Sounds simple, doesn't it? Well, it is. You can even do it to yourself, to an extent. Books on self-hypnosis abound. If you'd rather start with a professional, look on www.medicalsupporthypnotherapy.com, or call the Hypnotherapy Academy of America at 877-983-1515, toll-free.

This Too Shall Pass

At our age, I don't recommend pulling an all-nighter, except *maybe* on the winter solstice. A common Longest Night observance of old was to gather the neighbors to await the "return of the light" (that is, the seasonal tip back toward lengthening days). These must have been the original "slumber" parties, since the whole point was not to slumber at all, but rather to sing, and eat, and party on through the long, dark hours, all the more earnestly (and exhaustedly) to appreciate the glorious sunrise. To me this ritual is emblematic of the mystical or shamanic "dark night of the soul," during which an individual endures long adversity, persevering through many tests of spirit (and bodily exhaustion), to emerge transformed as the new day dawns.

No one can be "all sweetness and light" *all* the time. Embrace your shadow self. It has so much to teach you! Listen for its whispers. Observe the waxing and waning of your energies, and retreat, *hibernate*, as necessary. And even if you should stub your toe painfully in the discovery, be glad for whatever wisdom you stumble on in the dark. As always, the shadow and the light are in cahoots.

COOL MOVES

Sleeping Tiger

Don't be fooled by the name. Even in repose, the tiger can be fierce! This Dahnhak "accumulation" pose feeds the *dahn-jon*, recharging the body's major "battery" in the lower abdomen, by drawing chi through the palms and soles.

Position yourself like a big cat on its back, all four limbs aloft, with 90-degree angles at the shoulders, wrists (palms up), hips, knees, and ankles. Keep your legs parallel, with knees and ankles about a fist-width apart. Curl your tailbone upward, and press your lower back against the floor. Do your best to maintain proper form as you hold the pose for five minutes. Focus on your *dahn-jon*, and keep affirming, "I can do this; I am strong." Discomfort indicates areas of blockage; keep breathing and *will* them to open. Visualize them opening. Increase hold time by a minute a day; work up to a half hour. If it helps, lift your head off the floor for some of the time. Finish by lowering your hands to your belly, then your feet to the floor near your rump. Move your knees from side to side, like windshield wipers, to relieve your lower back. Rest a few minutes in Corpse Pose (see Way 38) before getting up.

∿ THINGS TO TRY AT LEAST ONCE

☐ *Celebrate thirteen moons.* Honor a whole year's worth of moon cycles. Meet with friends when the moon is full. Write in your Dark of the Moon journal when the moon is new. Or come up with your own moon-honoring activities.

☐ *Practice lucid dreaming.* For starters, watch *Waking Life*, Richard Linklater's 2001 live-animated masterpiece, or read Carlos Castaneda's *The Art of Dreaming*. Or try this: the next time you realize you're dreaming, see if you can make yourself look at your hands, in your dream. Once you've mastered that, who knows? You could be flying like Superman in no time!

☐ *Get up dark and early.* Whatever your dream — better fitness, a grant for your art project — *find the time* to make it happen, even if it means getting up at 4:00 a.m.!

☐ *Moon someone.* If you dare!

23 Shake It Up Baby, Now

They always say time changes things, but you actually have to change them yourself.

— Andy Warhol (1928–1987)

*N*ever let it be said of our generation that we are old and set in our ways. Quick! *Everybody out of the box!* After five decades of letting your habits settle, how refreshing to give them a good shake.

Hey, wanna dance? The abrupt shift into body movement is intentional. Shake it *up*, baby! (Lest you "twist and shout," however, please warm up first.) Does your brain sometimes feel like a gerbil on a wheel? Let dance throw open the cage door. Let your gerbil run wild, into rooms you may have forgotten even existed. There's much to be said for using *all* parts of your body. Keeps you young!

The Road Less Traveled

Try this: Interlace your fingers and clasp your hands together. Notice which thumb is on top. Now switch it, interlacing fingers so the other thumb is on top. Feels weird, huh? The first way was your habitual clasp. The second feels strange because you're using a slightly different set of neural pathways. These roads of the central nervous system carry the brain's electrochemical impulses to all parts of the body, and — news flash! — you either use 'em or lose 'em. This is the brain plasticity I mentioned in Way 16, in the context of undoing deeply entrenched habits.

Naturally, plasticity works in a positive way, too. It's the reason practice makes perfect. Well-rehearsed neural pathways ("habituated" ones, in neuro-speak) are like the freeways of the body's neural infrastructure. But what of your side roads and surface streets? Are *they* getting any practice, practice, practice? If not, the brain's "paving crew" is under strict orders to ignore them, leaving them to grow over like dirt roads reclaimed by the earth.

SCRIBBLES & DOODLES
Two Hands, Two Shapes

Get your brain hemispheres buzzing with this coordination challenge. Put a pen or pencil in each hand. Simultaneously draw a triangle with one hand and a circle with the other. Keep trying! Do your best. Switch directions. Try swapping shapes, hand to hand. See if you have better luck with a square and a triangle. Your struggle for mastery sends the call to your brain's paving crew. Keep practicing, and you and your crew will have traffic on those neural pathways up to full speed ASAP.

And Now for Something Completely Different

To keep all your neural pathways in serviceable condition, get off the beaten path as often as possible. Shake up the same-old same-old with a healthy dose of chaos. It's disorderly, sure, but also rich with possibility. The original Chaos, the Greek goddess of emptiness and confusion, gave birth to no less than the universe! Not too shabby.

So shake it up, baby! Rearrange the furniture. Knit. Practice doing things with the "wrong" hand. Contemplate a vexing Buddhist koan.

Take up a new language. Go *out of your way* to gain a different perspective — anything to wire new connections in your brain.

DOC IN THE BOX: *May the Force Be with You (Consciousness)*

If you are reading this, you are conscious. Awake and alert, as we say in the business. That is a very basic definition of consciousness. It seems fairly straightforward, until you get out the scalpel and attempt a dissection of this slippery concept. In recent decades, physicists have joined philosophers and mystics in an upsurge of interest in this, the very essence of our existence. The questions are unending, and the answers may surprise us all.

At Princeton, scientists in the Global Consciousness Project (http://noosphere.princeton.edu/) are exploring the nature of consciousness, with very interesting results. They have found evidence of what they call a "growing global consciousness." To study this, they placed machines called random event generators all over the world. These machines produce random numbers, usually with a certain average pattern, but the researchers discovered something fascinating: when something momentous and unexpected happened, something that caused a similar emotional reaction in a large number of people, the random event generators showed what might best be described as a "disturbance in the force." Deviating significantly from the average, the "random" behavior was no longer random. The terrorist attack on the United States on September 11, 2001, was one of these events. The Russian school hostage crisis in September 2004 was another. Consternation and grief swept the globe, and the Princeton machines went haywire. Could group consciousness be an actual physical force? Or a shared energy, through which shock waves can travel?

What exactly is consciousness? And *where* is it? Even apparently unconscious people show brain activity in response to speech, blurring the line between consciousness and unconsciousness, a line that is itself the subject of much exploration and debate. Scientists can also tell a lot about what someone is thinking just by examining the blood-flow patterns of the brain, and can even cause hallucinations by stimulating certain areas of the brain. Is consciousness nothing more than electrical and chemical events inside the head?

Philosophers, naturally, are asking more esoteric questions, such as, Why do we even have subjective, first-person experiences? Why do we need unconscious thoughts?

This is heady stuff. The plot will undoubtedly thicken. Stay tuned.

COOL MOVES

Two "Great Shakes"

- *Spaghetti limbs.* This one is best done after exercising or stretching. Lie on your back, with "all fours" straight up in the air. Let your limbs be as loose as cooked spaghetti, and shake them for all they're worth! Increase speed and intensity while slowly (s-l-o-w-l-y) counting to ten. Now drop the spaghetti, fast. Let arms and legs lie where they fall. Savor the sensation of spent energy releasing through your hands and feet.

- *Lasagna loca!* Stand with your feet parallel (even slightly pigeon-toed) shoulder-width apart. Soften your body — be a lasagna noodle this time — and move it rhythmically. Consciously breathe through the tight or painful places, exhaling through an open mouth. Don't think. Just bounce and wiggle, wobble and bobble, for ten minutes or more. Add body tapping (see Way 13) for a more prodigious release of blockage. This exercise is nice to do in the morning, while waiting for the tea kettle to whistle, or any time you can catch a private moment to shake off stiffness.

THINGS TO TRY AT LEAST ONCE

- ❑ *Get hip to belly dancing.* Talk about giving things a good shake! Work up a sweat while strengthening those all-important core muscles. Search online for a local instructor.

❏ *Shake up city hall* — or the government entity of your choice. Attend a city council meeting or a political demonstration. Canvass for a cause. Write a letter to the editor or your congressional representative.

❏ *Get a fresh perspective.* Lie at the base of a tree, looking up into its canopy. Or climb up on the roof. Literally look at the world in a new way.

❏ *Take a spirited leap.* Career change? Early retirement? Relocation to a whole different culture? Shake it up, baby!

24 Imagine All the People

There is only one admirable form of the imagination: the imagination that is so intense that it creates a new reality, that it makes things happen.

— Seán Ó Faoláin (1900–1991)

I never had the pleasure of meeting Mr. Ó Faoláin. If I had, I most certainly would have agreed with him about the splendor of an imagination so intense it effects change. Then, depending on the Irish writer's amiability at the moment, I might also have added, "But that can't be the *only* admirable form of imagination, can it? I mean, consider the Beatles during their *Yellow Submarine* period . . ."

Spend Some Time Moodling

"Imagination needs moodling," Barbara Ueland wrote, "long, inefficient, happy idling, dawdling and puttering." Sounds plenty admirable to me!

It can look an awful lot like airheadedness, moodling can. But please don't make the curmudgeonly mistake of equating imagination with idle fantasy. Of course you're free to enjoy imagination as an end in itself. Even curmudgeons are entitled to idle fantasies! But, as long as you're dreaming it all up anyway, you might as well make it a *good* dream, a happy dream for "all the people."

Visualize World Peace

During the summer of 1993, larger and larger crowds gathered on the Mall in Washington, D.C., to meditate for peace. This was not an antiwar protest, but rather a carefully designed research project of the Institute of Science, Technology, and Public Policy, at Maharishi University of Management, in Fairfield, Iowa. Its aim was to measure the effects of mass meditation on the U.S. capitol's violent-crime rate. As the assembly grew over the eight-week period, from several hundred participants to nearly four thousand, city police documented a staggering 23 percent drop in incidents of homicide, rape, and assault. You can read all about this remarkable study and others like it at www.istpp.org.

Meanwhile, I feel duty-bound to ask the obvious question: How come we, as a people, are not gathering to meditate for peace in every violent city in the world?

Mind Becomes Matter, Thoughts Become Things

Our thoughts have power, remember? Put them together with those of many like-minded others and . . . *that's a lot of power!* How could they *not* have an effect?

In his book *Power vs. Force*, David R. Hawkins, MD, explains collective consciousness in computer terms: "The individual human mind is like a computer terminal connected to a giant database. The database

SCRIBBLES & DOODLES
"You May Say I'm a Dreamer"

Imagine all the people — in your family, in your workplace, in your city of residence — pick a "people" and imagine all of them, for twenty-four happy, harmonious hours, living life in peace. "Live" through the day with these people, in present tense — not "we would be," but "we *are*"! And don't limit yourself to what seems reasonable or possible. Change the world with your vision!

is human consciousness itself." Not only do we draw from the database — it is the repository of all human works, after all — but our every thought, word, and deed feeds *into* the database, too, as do the thoughts, words, and deeds of *every human who has ever lived.* Guess that's why they call it the "collective" consciousness, eh?

"The proofs can be complex," Hawkins writes — and indeed, he fills a whole book making the case — but he doesn't have to convince me. For better or worse, our individual thoughts affect the world. Collectively, our thoughts shape society. Voting in an honest election is important, absolutely, but it is by no means the only power you have in changing the world's leadership. Nor is out-and-out political activism, though that helps too, obviously. Gandhi famously told us to "be the change you want to see in the world," and in order to be that, you first have to . . . *imagine* that!

"Think Good Thoughts!"

For me, the most compelling takeaway message in *Power vs. Force* is this: a person's *individual* energy will always aspire to the level of the collective energies in his or her immediate surroundings. If you've ever witnessed mob behavior, you know the dangerous extremes of this. At the other end of the spectrum are groups of people supporting each other to better themselves. "Just bring your body to a meeting" is

DOC IN THE BOX: *"I Can Just See It Now!"* *(Visualization in Healing)*

We all daydream. Remembering yesterday, planning tomorrow, wishing we were somewhere else . . . and when we do, we usually see pictures in our heads. That's visualization, of a sort.

Jack Nicklaus, arguably the greatest pro golfer of all time, visualizes every swing before he takes it. Many big-league sports teams retain visualization coaches. These modern experts help players imagine in detail the successful swing, or shot, or throw before game time. The athletes do more than just daydream; they mentally experience the physical movements, the feel of the ball, even the emotional surge of success. Why? Because it works. The brain, having rehearsed the firing sequence ahead of time, guides them smoothly through the actual event. The players perform better.

The second habit of Stephen R. Covey's renowned *Seven Habits of Highly Successful People* is "Begin with the end in mind." Experts in visualization recommend that you imagine a complete and perfect picture of what you want. The idea is not that making a visual picture will magically make your dreams come true, but that it will imbue your life with a sense of hope and purpose, and that it will harness your creativity, even at a subconscious level, to actualize your success. You can use this technique for anything. Visualize your remodeled home, your slim bod, your ideal job.

Visualization is also a good way to solve a myriad of physical and emotional problems: headaches, hypertension, anorexia, addiction, insomnia, arthritis, cancer, and many more. The success stories pile up.

The basic technique, according to Gerald Epstein, MD, in his book *Healing Visualizations,* is to sit quietly and comfortably, state your intention (aloud or silently), close your eyes, take a few deep, relaxing breaths, then focus on the desired image in your mind. You can find a prescribed image or make up your own. Do it for as many minutes as you like. You will find more detailed instructions, as well as imagery exercises for numerous specific ailments, in Epstein's book.

Go ahead. Think big. Conjure it up. Make it happen!

something people in 12-step programs often say to their downtrodden companions.

Imagine! It's the same for working stiffs who drag their sorry butts to the gym after work — even if they proceed directly to the sauna or whirlpool. *How invigorating,* even at a standstill (or a lie-down), to dwell among bodies bent on getting in better shape! Imagine it happening to you! Imagine *all the people* giving you the "lookin' good" nod as you pass by. It'll happen. See it. Do it. Be it.

COOL MOVES
Fifty Laps Around the Sun

Here's a simple birthday ritual to do alone or with friends. Rituals (like altars and shrines) are symbolic; they rely on imagination. When you imbue an object, action, or sensory stimulus (color, scent, taste, texture) with meaning, you speak in symbols to those parts of yourself that don't "do" words. And, since these preliterate parts date all the way back to your stay in the womb, learning at this level can be profound.

Place a lit yellow candle in the center of the room or outdoor space. *Behold the (symbolic) sun!* Carry a globe, or wear Planet Earth colors of blue and green, as you walk counterclockwise around the candle fifty times. Contemplate the years of your life as you complete each circle. Happy birthday!

∿ THINGS TO TRY AT LEAST ONCE

❏ *Picture yourself.* Have a new portrait done for your fiftieth, alone and/or with others.

❏ *Show, don't tell.* Participate in a group ritual, or create an altar or meditation space around the theme "Imagine All the People." *Use your imagination!* Really *feel* it!

❏ *Use healing visualization.* Read anything by Shakti Gawain or Louise Hay to learn how to transform the facts of your life through the power of your imagination.

❏ *Share the vision of Juan Mann.* Watch the short video at www.freehugscampaign.org. Like the vision? Aid the "hundredth monkey" effect by sending the link to everyone you know.

Believe It, or Don't

Alice laughed. "There's no use trying," she said, "one can't believe impossible things."

"I daresay you haven't had much practice," said the Queen. "When I was your age, I always did it for half-an-hour a day. Why sometimes I believed as many as six impossible things before breakfast!"

— Lewis Carroll, *Alice's Adventures in Wonderland*

I cannot *believe* I'm turning fifty!" Who can relate? Raise your hand! It is an astonishing age, is it not? Ever think about it as a kid, what it would be like to be so ancient? Well, golly, look at us now! Not so very ancient after all!

In any case, this Way leaves you an out.

Deny, Deny, Deny

"Dana" swore me to secrecy before admitting, in whispers, that she belonged in this book's "target demographic." She said she had taken her mom's advice to start fudging her age downward at around age thirty, so naturally, whenever her birthday rolls around now, none of her friends knows what to believe. I only met Dana once, so I'll never know, but I'm guessing that the only fiftieth birthday mail she got was her invitation to join AARP. Poor Dana!

The point is, you're free to believe whatever you want, even if it doesn't always jibe with reality. What *is* reality, anyway? And does fifty years amount to a hill of beans in this crazy world? Heck if I know; you tell me!

Albert Einstein summed it up nicely: "Not everything that can be counted counts, and not everything that counts can be counted."

One Person's Fairy Tale, Another Person's Truth

Beliefs can be a double-edged sword. Belief in yourself, your cause, your God(s) — these can see you through when the going gets tough. On the other hand, beliefs that cut corners on critical thinking (preconceived notions, in other words) can prevent you from seeing the truth, or from even *considering* different possibilities.

Eastern medicine (indeed, holism in general) is a perfect example. Although these ancient ways have begun to permeate Western society, plenty of folks still flat-out "don't believe in that nonsense." They *might* accept that there's a connection between stress and disease, especially now that Western doctors are saying so, too. But though their bodies are stiff and sore and their chronic health problems grow serious with age, these disbelievers scoff at the notion that their energy is blocked up. Or maybe they'll buy that much, but not the part about the blockage being caused by "stagnant energy," the physiological residue of a lifetime's

SCRIBBLES & DOODLES
This I Believe

Quick! As fast as you can, list your Top Ten Beliefs. Write complete sentences, beginning with "I believe..." You can ponder and clarify *later*! Right now, just dash off the first ten complete "I believe" sentences to flow out of your pen. Ready? Go!

Not as easy as it sounds, is it? Or *is* it? If, on reflection, you find that all or most of the beliefs on your list paraphrase church dogma, I invite you to dig deeper on your next go-round. In any case, after your "flash list" is complete, take all the time you need to clarify ten of your most dearly held beliefs, religious or otherwise.

worth of stuffed emotions. Besides, they're not about to try acupuncture, herbal medicine, or any of the other chi-moving modalities that could open them up and get their meridians flowing. Too "woo-woo." Oh, well. Different strokes, right?

The good news is that *any* type of physical workout helps release stagnant energy. It's one of the reasons exercise feels so darned great, both during and after.

 DOC IN THE BOX: *The Power of Prayer*

"I'm praying for you." "You are in my thoughts." Sound familiar? Many of us pray for others, in our own way. And we may be convinced that it works, particularly if we adhere to a religious faith. Churches have prayer circles for ill members. Hospitals have chaplains. Clearly there's some kind of common belief at work here. But can it be proved scientifically? It turns out the answer is yes.

Larry Dossey, MD, in his remarkable book *Healing Words*, reviews evidence, provided by hundreds of researchers, that thoughts actually can have influence outside our bodies. And not just on other humans, but on plants, blood cells, mice, chicks — the list boggles the mind. Thoughts even affect the growth rates of bacteria. (Maybe you want to take a moment to bless your food?) From heart disease to cell growth, directed thoughts can cause change outside the thinker. In short, prayer works.

Another name for this process is Distant Intentionality. That means focusing your intention on another person (or mouse, or...) from a distance. Holding them in your mind. Wishing them well. Hundreds of experiments have provided evidence that we can generate some kind of force with our minds, and that this force has power.

"With great power comes great responsibility," as even Spider-Man is aware. Given what he knows now, Dr. Dossey believes that *not* to pray for a patient is tantamount to medical malpractice. While I can't imagine such a lawsuit anytime soon, I urge you to imagine the implications of this information, take it to heart, and use your prayers — whatever that means to you — to improve the lives of those around you.

See the World as It Is, Not as You Are

"Argue for your limitations," writes Richard Bach, "and sure enough, they're yours." In our minds, opinion can harden into perceived fact in the wink of an eye. Such thoughts are like bricks, write Roger Mills and Elsie Spittle in *The Wisdom Within*. Once we build our bricks into elaborate houses, we convince ourselves that these thought patterns are immutably real. But, no, they're still just hardened thoughts, stacked up the same old way.

Inevitably, if you undertake to rearrange brick walls, heavy lifting will be involved. But take heart! Your thoughts may be as brick, but your mind is marvelously *plastic*, remember? Preconceptions are nothing more than well-worn neural pathways in the brain, and you don't "hafta" go that way.

You can blaze new trails. Believe it!

COOL MOVES

"Tell It to the Hands" (The Yes/No of Kinesiological Muscle Response)

I introduced Hawkins's book, *Power vs. Force*, in the previous Way. His conclusions about what he calls the "hidden determinants of human behavior" are based on the science of kinesiological muscle testing, which many people frankly have to feel to believe. Well, here's your chance.

Find a partner. Stand with your dominant arm at shoulder height, out to the side, palm downward. Have your partner stand behind your arm and place both hands on it. On the count of three, resist with all your might while your partner briskly pushes your arm down hard. Repeat the test three times, to really get the feel of your arm strength. Now, spend a few moments talking to your body, or even just your heart. Tell it how much you appreciate all it does for you, that you know it's working night and day for you, that you'd be a goner without it. Thank it. Express your sincere love for it. All the better if you do this aloud. Now repeat the muscle test three more times. Notice any difference? Dr. Hawkins and others have found that, by vast margins, most test subjects are noticeably strengthened by such self-nurturing.

∿ THINGS TO TRY AT LEAST ONCE

❑ *Make believe.* Play Dungeons & Dragons or other role-playing games. When in the kitchen, *dress* the part of the world-class chef you want to be. Or just hang out with a kid for a while.

❑ *Question your beliefs.* Strike up a conversation with someone whose beliefs are significantly different from your own, and consciously work to open yourself, to "try on" that person's beliefs. Or attend an unfamiliar religious service. Keep an open mind.

❑ *Vote with your feet.* Giving money to a cause you believe in is great. Putting your belief into action is even greater.

❑ *Never say never.* Period.

Dance on the Head of a Pin

How goodness heightens beauty!
— Milan Kundera

*T*his Way is about balance. It also speaks of grace, integrity, and what Abe Lincoln once called the "better angels of our nature." Remember your yin and yang from Way 21? In the Eastern view, the dualistic energies of heaven and earth meet within the human body. Many Western traditions say as much: we are soul made flesh.

I picture the divine in each of us as a ballerina *en pointe*. Exquisitely balanced, gorgeously graceful, she (or he) hovers between heaven and earth, barely alighting. She goes by the name Best Self, and as good as she is, even she slips sometimes. Too much earth, not enough heaven — or vice versa — and things go off-balance. We're only human, after all. Forgive yourself, as any angel would. Regain equilibrium, and strive upward once more, as if on angel's wings.

Pondering the Imponderables

Puzzling over how many angels can dance on the head of a pin is a job for the so-called higher brain, seated in the frontal lobes of our cerebral cortex. Seated, you might say, as if on a throne, for this most highly evolved region of the brain is our skull's resident scholar, the one who can do what the very best brains of other animals cannot: crunch numbers, use reason and logic, collect arcane trivia in hopes of winning on *Jeopardy!* someday... that sort of thing.

Well, were I to risk it all to speak truth to power, I would put this question to that royal-highness of a brain: "So tell us, Your Majesty! With all those super, human smarts of yours — not to mention your savvy for programming machines to think like you — how come you haven't designed a robot yet that can even walk with the grace of a human, let alone dance like one? Eh, Yer Highness? How high is your 'higher brain' functioning now?"

Enough, enough. Lest I forget, I'm making a case for the better angels of our nature, here.

Jack Be Limbic, Jack Be Quick

I got snotty there for a minute to make this point: the higher brain may be clever enough to do math and use logic and even win on brainy game shows, but it doesn't know — nor does it care — one bit about hurt feelings (or sex or food, for that matter). What's worse, it couldn't run you out of a burning building to save your soul.

Higher brain, my foot. If dancing with angels is what you want, come

SCRIBBLES & DOODLES
Everything's Better in Balance

Put your life on the scales. Size up the various parts of it. You can think in terms of yin (inner life) and yang (outer life), if you'd like, and see how the two sides compare. Or go at this exercise pie-chart style, carving slices for "family," "career," "fitness," "reading for pleasure," "sleep" — whatever. Now step back. Don't *feel* the slices are fair? (That's a limbic judgment.) Make a new pie. Keep tinkering with the recipe until you get the pieces divided just the way you want them.

on down to the limbic level, what Peg and I like to call the Limbic Lounge, 'round the bend from the frontal lobe, in the temporal lobes on the sides of the head. The limbic system may not rank as high as the higher brain, but it's the more feeling brain, the brain who cares! It knows where your edges are and senses beyond them. Gut feelings plug into the limbic brain, and its fight-or-flight sentinels stand ready to save you. Thanks to the limbic system, rock-a-bye motion soothes the crying babe, and deepening *emotion* transforms strangers into friends and mere sex into soul union. . . .

Yeah, life would be mighty dull without a limbic brain in our heads. Except for the even sadder possibility that we'd all be extinct by now.

Be an Angel, Will You, Love?

The compassionate limbic brain evolved to aid survival. Before it emerged, about 100 million years ago, the most sophisticated animal brains were "reptilian" — and you know how snakes can be. If they happened by as their own eggs were hatching, they'd be like, "Hey! Lunch!" But not us mammals. Our limbic systems ooze with emotion, and we *fall in love* with our babies, just as we fell for their daddies or mommies before them (not to mention countless grannies and aunties, cousins, and buddies). Forget saving ourselves: we'd run *into* burning buildings for these guys!

My sister Theresa gave our brother Sean two-thirds of her liver. The risks were enormous, her children were still at home, but she never wavered in her decision to try to save Sean's life. And she did. The way I see it, Theresa now dances among the angels — in a beautifully scarred body *still living* right here on earth!

DOC IN THE BOX: *Walk the Line (Proprioception and Balance)*

People with great gifts are easy to find, but symmetrical and balanced ones never.
— Ralph Waldo Emerson (1803–1882)

Quick, which way is up? Where is your left hand? No-brainers, right? That's because you have proprioception. This word comes from *proprio*, from the Latin *proprius*, meaning "one's own," and *reception*, meaning "to receive." Proprioception is a fifty-dollar word for the body's ability to know where it is in space, without peeking.

Proprioception is also what helps us to walk without looking at our feet or falling on our faces. Thanks to proprioceptors (position sensors), our brain knows when our feet are landing or pushing off. We adjust our leg muscles to compensate for uneven terrain without even thinking about it. Proprioception is essential for balance.

Alas for our aging selves, this particular body function goes the way of eyesight and hearing. If, that is, we let it. Rusty proprioception is a major cause of falls as people get older. Dull proprioceptors and slowed reflexes mean that by the time our bodies have figured out that we're off-kilter, we're already on the way down, headed for a bruise or a hip fracture. But just like so many things, if you use it, you won't lose it.

Keep your proprioceptors in shape by doing things that require balance. This can be as simple as taking frequent walks and varying the underfoot terrain. Even better are deliberate balancing exercises, like standing on one foot (as in this chapter's "Cool Move"), or walking heel-to-toe in a line. Strength training, for the whole body, is also essential.

Ralph Waldo Emerson was a wise man in many ways. But in this one instance, let's all prove him wrong, shall we?

 COOL MOVES

Balance Challenge!

Practice hatha yoga's Tree Pose (*Vrksasana*) every chance you get. Stand tall with your feet together. Place the right foot against the (inner) left leg at the level of ankle, knee, or thigh (mid-thigh or higher up), as you're able. Higher placement = bigger challenge. Fix your gaze on a low spot about ten feet in front of you. Inhale and raise your arms overhead, with palms facing each other or touching. Straighten the elbows, arms to ears, chin slightly tucked. Breathe mindfully. Grow upward! Hold for twenty to thirty seconds. Repeat on the other side.

⟋⟍→ THINGS TO TRY AT LEAST ONCE

❑ *Dance.* With a partner, alone in your room, fast, slow, cha-cha-cha! Take dance lessons — ballroom, ballet, *belly* — whatever moves you. Just get up and booooogieeeee!

❑ *Pick an angel, any angel!* Consult a deck of Angel Cards and let them lift you with their single-word encouragements.

❑ *Take on balance challenges.* Ride a bike, play hopscotch, climb rock walls, spin a ball on your fingertips, play tennis or soccer, balance a yardstick vertically at arm's length, or pretend the curb is a balance beam and that you're going for Olympic gold!

❑ *Host a Dancing Angels film festival.* Invite your friends (or not) for a marathon of movies about angels and dance. Might I suggest Wim Wenders's *Wings of Desire*, the American remake of it, called *City of Angels*, and anything by Busby Berkeley?

PART THREE

SOUL

27 Get Your Hands Dirty

Hard work spotlights the character of people: some turn up their sleeves,
some turn up their noses, and some don't turn up at all.

— Sam Ewing III (1921–2001)

*M*anual labor — what a pain, eh? Oh, but how gratifying when
it's finished! The tidy garage, the newly planted garden, a
dozen sparkling jars of homemade jam: the mess got worse before it
got better, right? And now the ol' muscles are buggin' a little. But look
at the results. Behold what your hands have wrought!

Mundane Tasks Are the Hiding Places of Joy

With this Way we move into the realm of the Soul. If the Body is solid
like Earth, and the Mind plucks ideas out of thin Air, and the emotional
Heart ebbs and flows like Water, then Soul is life's productive Fire.
Cook the food! Forge your tools! What matters here is not what you
think, feel, or say, but what you *do*! The soul is about action and agency.
Why are you here? What is your purpose in the grand scheme of things?

These are not necessarily career questions, by the way. Or, to put
it another way, the answers don't always come in the form of paying

gigs. Still, somehow, the work is yours to do, and you would do well to tend to it mindfully, for mundane tasks hide not only joy but also meaning. Somewhere within them lies the very reason you were born!

If You Build It, They Will Come

What if Ray, the Kevin Costner character in *Field of Dreams*, had heard the whispering in the corn and said, "No, thanks"? (We're talking about the 1989 movie based on W. P. Kinsella's *Shoeless Joe*, in which an Iowa farmer becomes convinced by a mysterious voice that he is supposed to construct a baseball diamond in his cornfield.) What would have happened had Ray given in to — take your pick — financial pressure, family pressure, public ridicule, *his self-doubt*? Or what if, all pressures aside, he'd simply been the kind of guy who just *hated* to get his hands dirty?

Nothing, that's what. All the magic in that cornfield would have whispered away on the wind and come to naught. The field's *potential* as something much more special than a struggling farm required an agent — someone taking action — in order to be brought into *form*, namely, the baseball field that ends up attracting ticket-buyers from miles around, people of all ages yearning for the happiness to be found there. So Ray steps in, does the work, and everyone lives happily ever after.

Call It *Cosmogenesis*

Kinsella's story is a fairy tale, of course, but also a potent allegory symbolizing both the transformative power and the spiritual engagement of hard work. You build it, they come. It's a nice arrangement; it works for everybody.

Theologian Matthew Fox, in his book *Original Blessing*, posits that Creation is still unfolding, and that you and I — all of us — are "cocreators" of it. He then asks, What are *you* cocreating, and is it constructive or destructive? The old guns-or-butter question. I'll leave that more heavenly debate to the theologians, and instead bring Fox's concept of *cosmogenesis* to this more mundane concern: Do you like your job?

If you don't like your job, chances are you're not exactly thrilling to the daily "transformative power" and "spiritual engagement" of hard work. Chances are the daily grind is just that: a grind, grinding away at your quality of life, week in, week out, while your years on earth slide by, never to return. *Don't let it!* Build something new, something that engages your passion. It doesn't have to be a whole new job; maybe there's a way to change the job you're in. Even if not, and even if you decide to stick it out until retirement, you still have your off hours in which to build a passion-engaging something to feed your soul — and possibly (probably!) the souls of others.

Do What You Love, the Money Will Follow

Marsha Sinetar wrote a book by that title a few decades back, and it was the very thing that

SCRIBBLES & DOODLES
Compost Journaling

Choose a blank book to serve as your metaphorical compost bin, and toss into it all the "rot" of your life, the things that, in your opinion, went wrong. Pile onto this never-ending list all the regrets you're ready to scrap but whose rich organic matter should not go to waste: the stinky cheese of painful relationships, the banana peels of countless slipups, the moldering crusts of bad habits, the dried leaves of forgotten dreams. List them by name, and feel free to repeat them, layer upon layer. Moisture is crucial to composting, so go ahead and cry. Finally, "turn the pile" now and then: reread your list and glean from it all the rich black soil you can — lessons learned, perspectives gained — to support your blossoming in life's second half.

emboldened me to make the leap to self-employment. Many, many people in midlife dream of going into business for themselves. If you're one of them, let me encourage you with all the thumbs-up enthusiasm I can muster: *Go for it!* It may take until your Big *Six*-oh to finish "building it." All the more reason to roll up your sleeves and get started now!

Sometimes the only way to get to the life you'd rather be living is straight through the muck. But what's the big deal? You're stronger than dirt, right?

COOL MOVES

"My Hands Are Healing Hands!" (Palming the Eyes)

Speaking of hands, dirty and otherwise.... Recall from Way 4 the seven *dahn-jons* of the body's energy system. Two of these energy pools are centered in the palms. Dahnhak, the Korean tradition I study, teaches that we can all learn to sense and control our chi flow. Healing tools come standard on the human body; we've only misplaced the operating manual.

Next time your eyes feel tired, "palm" them with your healing hands! Clap your hands briskly ten to twenty times, then rub them together to create heat. Cup them firmly over your eyes so that no light is visible. Keep your eyes lightly closed to receive the energy emanating from your palms. If you're aware of any floating splotches of color, mentally paint them velvety black. Move your eyes in every direction: up, down, left, right, in circles. Bring up pleasant, happy memories as you imagine your eyes growing brighter. Come out of palming slowly, first opening the "window blinds" of the fingers, as you gently blink your eyelids, waggle your brows, and breathe mindfully.

 DOC IN THE BOX: *Drawing from the Depths (Art Therapy)*

According to the American Art Therapy Association, "art therapy is an established mental health profession that uses the creative process of art making to improve and enhance the physical, mental and emotional well-being of individuals of all ages." Sounds to me like something for everyone!

In art therapy, the client produces some kind of artwork that he or she then interprets, with the help of a therapist. The medium is usually visual, for example painting or drawing, although some art therapists work with music, dance, or even film.

The purpose of this kind of therapy is multifold. First, when you are creating a piece of art you are absorbed, focused, "in the zone." This can be very useful for taking your mind off your pain or chronic illness. Second, art can unearth memories that have been buried, probably because it provides another pathway to the memory when the usual one has been blocked off by trauma or neurological disease. Third, it can be used to express feelings by people who are unwilling or unable to use words to do so. Fourth, art can be used for communication if someone's language is either undeveloped (kids) or impaired (those affected by dementia or a stroke).

Try it yourself. Get out your favorite art tool and just draw something. Or grab a hunk of clay and sculpt! Some suggest warming up with your nondominant hand. Work quickly and intuitively without making a formal plan. When you're done, examine your work and see what thoughts and feelings come up. If you are interested in pursuing art therapy further, contact the American Art Therapy Association at www.arttherapy.org.

∿ THINGS TO TRY AT LEAST ONCE

❑ *Plant a tree.* Better yet, make it a lifetime goal to plant fifty trees. Your Big Five-oh will live on, and you'll leave your planet breathing easier.

❑ *Henna your hands.* How about a little *artful* dirtiness? Find a beauty parlor that plies this Indian art form, and have your hands decoratively stained.

❑ *Get a tetanus shot.* Don't wait for a rusty nail to find you. Tetanus boosters are good for ten years. Get one now, and you'll be due again on every big-oh birthday.

❑ *Get your hands clean.* It's a germy world out there. Make it a good-health habit to wash your hands every time you come into the house. With soap.

Go Win One for the Team

I had never expected that the China initiative would come to fruition in the form of a ping-pong team.

— Richard Nixon, on the first friendly overture by the People's Republic of China, March 1972

T was twelve when Nixon said that, and was just beginning to pay attention to world news, which took me every night to the war-torn jungles of Vietnam. "But what are they fighting *about*?" I asked my mom. She gave a deep sigh and said, "It's complicated." That's all. I suppose China-U.S. relations were complicated, too.

But not ping-pong. Ping-pong is, was, and always will be a perfectly simple concept. I dare say, Forrest Gump could set up a table in any culture, begin pinging and ponging, and the locals would catch right on. With language barriers smashed, everyone would be grinning in no time.

Can't Win if You Don't Play

Forrest Gump, the title character of the 1994 movie (based on the novel by Winston Groom), won one for a lot of teams in his day. Not just for his obvious teams — football, army, ping-pong — but also for the families of every man he carried out of battle, especially those of Bubba and Lieutenant Dan. He won a big one for humanity, by loving Jenny so truly and by providing a stable home and family for little Forrest to grow up in.

"Stupid is as stupid does," his mama taught him. By that measure, Forrest was brilliant. Who needs superior intellect when you already possess the heart of a champion?

Our Diversity Is Our Strength

Maybe you saw the title of this Way and thought, "But I'm not really much of a team player." Me neither, frankly. So it's a darned good thing for Team Human that "lone wolf" is not the only available personality type. Teams succeed where individuals fail, not just because "many hands make light work." Many hands also possess a wider variety of skills. As any sweaty one-man band could tell you (between gasps), "concerted efforts" are a whole lot easier with the entire orchestra!

Teams hold out the possibility of success even when you yourself are off your game or on the injured list. While my brother Sean lay in a big-city hospital after his liver transplant, his posse back home was racing to finish the renovation on his home. They raised money, got materials donated, and gave up months' worth of evenings and weekends — all to play makeover on Sean's extreme fixer-upper. What the Mayo Clinic's medical team

SCRIBBLES & DOODLES
"Who's on First?"

Quickly list the "teams" in your life, and pick one. Today you're team captain. Size up the organization and your position in it. What are your strengths (individually and as a group)? Your weaknesses? Your signature plays? In a pinch, are your players equipped to sub in for each other? What should be the drills at tonight's practice?

did for my brother was amazing, absolutely, but no more amazing than the winning efforts of the *home* team, who did it all for love.

Running with the Pack

My friend Lynne, the leukemia survivor I introduced in Way 6, was a lone wolf–type runner before she got sick. Walking back to health after five months of chemotherapy, she decided to join the Leukemia & Lymphoma Society's Team in Training (TNT) program and do her first marathon. The event drew some sixteen thousand participants, nearly a quarter of them TNT people.

"I *really* felt like a part of something," Lynne recalled. "TNT raised $12 million that day, and our purple jerseys were *everywhere!*" But that wasn't the biggest joy. "The patients on the sideline, cheering us on — oh, my God!" Lynne exclaimed. "Some were in wheelchairs, some were bald from chemo.... They'd spot us in our purple jerseys and shout and wave: 'Team-in-Training! *Thank you! We love you!*' It was — I can't think of words special enough. They kept me going, they helped me finish. I really, truly did not run that race by myself."

We All "Made" the Team

In case you missed it, *win* is not the operative word of this Way. *Team* is, and we all "made the team," so let's cheer. "We're the Earth Humans, mighty Earth Humans!" There really ought to be no losers in the human race. If we can all just work together and get our poop in a group.... But wait! That's the next chapter.

DOC IN THE BOX: *Donate One to Team Human (Organ Donation)*

This is a test. True or false?

1. There are plenty of available organs for those who need them.
2. If I'm injured or sick, they won't try as hard to save me if they know that I'm an organ donor.
3. My family will get hit with a big bill for harvesting my organs.
4. My religion forbids it.
5. I have to be dead to donate my body parts.
6. I won't be able to have an open-casket funeral if I donate.
7. I'm too _____ (young, old, sick, etc.) to donate my organs.

Answers:

1. False. Every day nineteen people in the United States die for lack of a donated organ that could have saved their lives. And every day, more than five thousand people die of other causes. If only a fraction of them had checked the yes box. . . .
2. *Totally* false! What do you take us for, a bunch of unscrupulous mercenaries? Well, whether or not you do, it's still false.
3. False. There is no cost to the donor or the family for being a donor. There is also no financial gain, so don't get any ideas about Grandpa!
4. Probably false. Most major religions support this life-saving practice.
5. False, believe it or not. There are living donor programs for liver (it grows back), kidneys (you've got two), and, of course, blood, marrow, and plasma.
6. Also false. Your organs are inside you, remember? They can be surgically removed from the inside, and you will still look peaceful and whole on the outside. Yes, even if you donate your corneas (they put in a filler to preserve the shape of the eye).
7. By now you're on to the pattern here: false. There are no age limits on organ donors, and while some of your organs may not be usable, others might. Possible organs for transplant include cornea, kidney, heart, liver, lung, pancreas, intestine, blood vessels, bone, and skin. Surely at least one of those is in decent shape. Don't let your age or health status stop you from checking the yes box.

Perish the thought, but someday it could be you or one of your loved ones on the waiting list. Please, please become a lifesaving donor for Team Human. See www.organdonor.gov for more information, or contact your local Red Cross.

COOL MOVES
Spider's Web

You'll need a team for this one, natch. If you're the competitive type, get two teams together, and make it a race.

Find a pair of strong posts or mature trees spaced six to ten feet apart (one pair for each team). Using string or twine, fashion a spiderweb between the trees, with at least as many holes as you have team members. Purposely create a variety of hole sizes, shapes, and heights. The object of the game is to get your team through the web, one player at a time, with each available hole to be used only once. Players may receive help from teammates, but once someone is on the other side, he or she can only help from there, so consider your players' diverse strengths and limitations, and strategize carefully. Gooooo, team! Note: it's always a good idea to analyze a new thing after trying it, but never more so than when a team is involved. So talk! What worked? What didn't? What did you learn? Make sure everyone gets a chance to be heard.

THINGS TO TRY AT LEAST ONCE

❑ *Be the designated runner.* Do a charity walk or run to raise money and awareness for a cause. Dedicate your run to the one who most personifies the cause for you. During the race, wear a custom-made T-shirt bearing that person's photo.

❑ *"Have some of mine!"* Donate leave time for a co-worker who's seriously ill.

❑ *Join something*. Or start it, then join it: a reading group, a volunteer effort, a healthy trend!

❑ *Get your game on*. Go win one for an actual sports team: the city league, a pickup game, the fifty-plus division of your favorite sport, *whatever* — just get in the game.

❑ *Encourage cooperative play*. "Face-up" Scrabble and Jenga are two examples. Think of more games in which all players work toward a common goal. Everyone loves to win, and this way everyone does!

29 Sh@t or Get Off the Pot

Get busy livin', or get busy dyin'.
— Stephen King, *Rita Hayworth and the Shawshank Redemption*

*F*orgive the vulgarity of this Way's title. Believe me, I seriously considered changing it to "Poop or Get Off the Potty" — in a book about turning fifty, no less! Couldn't replace it with "Fish or Cut Bait" because, well, Dr. Peg and I have some serious stuff to tell you in this chapter, about digestion, constipation, hemorrhoids, and such. Besides, uh, sh@tting is a normal bodily function, right? (At least, we *hope* that from day to day it's functioning normally!)

So even at the risk of offending delicate sensibilities, we decided the title had to *stay put*, as ironic as that may seem. For good measure, we *softened* it with a fashionable @, a fitting symbol for getting "at" the biggest, boldest thing on your life's to-do list.

It Is *In* You Somewhere!

That thing you're always talking about doing "someday"? It's in you. Otherwise you wouldn't keep feeling it. The only reason you're still "on the pot" with it is *you've got too much other stuff in the way*. Could be anything — a job you hate, an unfair share of the workload at home, or those troublesome preconceptions we discussed in Way 25. Whatever it is, as long as all that stuff just sits there, in the way, what hope do you have of ever getting your much-desired "gonna do" *done*?

Preparation Helps

And I don't mean the kind labeled *H*. But go ahead and groan if you want, or laugh right out loud, because on the literal pot at least, low-pitched, deep-bellied vocal vibration can truly help *move things along*. Women sometimes learn this in childbirth: "As above, so below." If you want to open up *down there*, then open wide *up here*, at throat level. No squeaky, closed-throat noises, please. Moo! Bellow! Sing long, slow dirges. Whatever it takes!

So Does Moaning and Groaning, but Only up to a Point

But back to your big dream and getting that job done. As with childbirth, it makes no sense whatsoever to start pushing too soon. Give your dream the proper care and feeding it requires. Put in the metaphorical fiber, the water, the time. Work at it with (double-groaner alert!) regularity and, you know what they say, everything's sure to come out all right!

SCRIBBLES & DOODLES
*"Like Sands through
the Hourglass..."*

As above, so below. For me, it's wind across the rolling wheat fields of my native North Dakota. For you, it's... *what*? Maybe you already have a visualization to hasten your success in the bathroom each day. If not, create, in writing, a kinetic image whose gentle, rhythmic motion (in your mind, "above") may whisper *peristaltic* encouragements to your bowel, "below." For added impact, engage in this visualization while also doing the "toe gazer" stretch, described in Way 5. The two together make a terrific toilet topper!

DOC IN THE BOX: *To Cleanse or Not to Cleanse? (Colon Care)*

"Death begins in the colon." This was the mantra and founding principle behind "autointoxication," a theory popular early last century. Adherents asserted that all illnesses were caused by self-poisoning. The poisons supposedly came from our own colons, products of unabsorbed crud that got stuck on the walls like so much moss. Enemas and cleanses were all the rage, as efforts were made to purge our gunky guts of decades' worth of slime.

Medical science debunked that myth once, but history repeats itself, and autointoxication is making a comeback. Drinkable colon-cleansing products can be purchased for a (phe)nominal fee, and there are even websites where enthusiasts share photos of their "results," believe it or not. (The knotty ropes they pass are caused by the cleansing product itself — a cast formed as the colon does its job of removing water from waste.) Or, if you'd rather take the low road, you can see a colon hydrotherapist, who will slosh the barnacles loose from below with gallons and gallons of enema water.

Now, I'm willing to consider lots of ideas outside the traditional Western medical box. But it just plain irks me when charlatans cheat good people out of their money.

This is how your digestion works. First your teeth chop up your food. Then your stomach breaks it down with acid. Your small intestine absorbs the good stuff. Your colon collects the bad stuff and pushes it out of the body. All of it. Your gut is a beautifully designed and highly efficient machine. It doesn't need an outside cleaning job, unless you're getting prepped for a colonoscopy or the like. Not only that; some of the products out there can actually harm you.

Sure, you can get constipated. Many people do, and that is uncomfortable. Not to mention the fact that it can cause hemorrhoids to rear [*sic*] their ugly heads. If you aren't making a well-formed stool regularly — and *how soft* is more important than *how oft* — you probably need to increase one (or all) of the following: water intake, fiber intake, or exercise.

It really is as simple as that.

COOL MOVES

"You Put Your Belly In, You Put Your Belly Out . . ."

Actually, to do this exercise, what you put out first is your breath. Hatha yoga's Uddiyana Bandha massages the internal organs to help relieve constipation or bring on a stubborn menstrual period. (Do not do this exercise if you think you may be pregnant.)

Bend over at the hips, place your hands on your knees, and exhale as hard, fast, and completely as possible. Lock out the breath and pull your tummy muscles in as deeply as possible. For as long as you can comfortably hold your breath, deeply manipulate the abdominal muscles, rolling them in and out and from side to side, like a bent-over belly dancer. Move your hips in every direction. Release the breath, and breathe easily for a few moments. Repeat two or three times. (Bonus! Speaking of "belly in, belly out," see Way 9's "Cool Move," too. Dahn-style Intestinal Exercise is another constipation buster.)

〰️ THINGS TO TRY AT LEAST ONCE

❑ *Get a colonoscopy.* It's time.

❑ *Say "good riddance" to 'roids.* See a proctologist to have hemorrhoids "banded." It's quick and practically painless.

❑ *Ramp up the roughage.* One tip is to fill *half* your plate with fresh or steamed veggies at every lunch and dinner. Another is to get in the habit of reading nutrition labels on packaged foods and buying those with the highest number of dietary fiber grams. Snack on fruit instead of junk. Eat your oatmeal. And wash it all down with plenty of water.

❑ *Happy bathroom to you!* Re-do one of yours. Switch to low-flow fixtures, and consider installing a gray-water reclamation system, the water-wise way to keep your landscaping lush and green. Finish with a throne-side bookshelf to house *this* little tome, bookmarked at Way 29!

30 Hit the Road, Jack

Roam abroad in the world, and take thy fill of its enjoyments before the day shall come when thou must quit it for good.

— Saadi (1184–1291)

*E*ver been to Sturgis? I'm not even a biker chick, but for some reason, as I close in on fifty, I'm thinking, "World's biggest Harley-Davidson rally — *why not?* I'm the adventurous sort, have plenty of friends and family up that way. And the rally campground is called Hog Heaven, for heaven's sake! How can it *be* that I've never *been?*"

Okay, it's true I don't actually own a "hog," nor would I know how to ride it if I did. But if I have learned even two things from this book you're holding, it's that we — you, me, everyone our age — are *nowhere near too old* to learn a few new tricks. That's one. And two: our brains *love* cruising new vistas. All that newness makes our noggins light up inside and ding and whir like happy-go-lucky pinball machines.

Drive, She Said

If you want to get out of town, of course, you don't need to pull the whole *Easy Rider* rebel-on-the-highway thing. Cars and trucks are a lot safer anyway. But please, for the sake of this Way, do cruise the vistas! Ride the surface of this beautiful planet. Don't go anywhere near an airport. Train station *maybe*, but listen.

Only by going your own speed can you explore off the beaten track. Whether you work out a detailed itinerary to pay visits to all your old college chums or the older folks in your family, or just pick a general direction and go, let me share three of my favorite ideas for making any trip more interesting, with or without passengers along:

- *"Baby, you can drive my car."* If you don't have a particular route or destination in mind, let someone else's need to have their car driven from point A to point B decide for you. Search the Web for a drive-away gig.

- *Find a road with your name on it.* Whether in the city you call home or a new one you'd like to explore, do a map search for a street that shares your first or family name. Then go find it.

- *Go letterboxing.* This one, which combines treasure hunting and rubberstamping, is especially useful for spicing up those oft-driven trips, such as long hauls cross-country back home to see the folks. Craft your own stamp (any rubberstamp supplier can turn the least little scribble into a stamp). Next, search online for directions to letterboxes people have hidden along your intended route (www.letterboxing.org). If you're clever enough to uncover a letterbox, by all means, stamp the book inside it with your unique mark and carefully re-hide the box before going along your merry way. Could be you'll want to hide a few letterboxes of your own here and there, too, and visit them once in a while, to see how your "stamp collection" is growing.

COOL MOVES

Ease on Down the Road (Visual Habits)

Circulation is health. Dawn Rose of the Vision Re-Education Center in San Diego was the first healer to tell me that, and it was in the context of why it's important to keep the eyes *moving*. "See one point best and all others second best," Dawn teaches, "and keep that one best point *moving*, from point to point to point." In other words: hard stare, dead stare, squinting — no good, not a one! Drawing on Dawn's gentle teachings, permit me to (re)teach your eyes how to drive, in five easy steps:

1. While driving, waggle the eyebrows up and down at a comfortable pace.

2. Lift and straighten (I like to say "shift and lift") your posture. Relax. Breathe.

3. Blink regularly. Keep waggling. (No one's looking at you; don't worry.)

4. Move your focus from point to point to point, alternating near and far. Look from car to car in traffic. Trace the horizon lightly with your eyes. Check your odometer and both rearviews. Outline a billboard. Look at the dashboard. Visually caress any beautiful architecture as you pass by. See always "one point best and all others second best." Keep waggling, breathing, blinking, lifting, relaxing.

SCRIBBLES & DOODLES
There and Back Again

Keep a travel log (a combination journal and scrapbook) during your next road trip. Choose a sturdy, compact volume, something up to the rigors of what you've got planned, and preferably a book with unlined pages, the better for sketching. Pack along invisible tape, an acid-free gluestick, and a small pair of scissors, and you're good to go. Some nice extras: sticky stars of various colors, highlighter or glitter pen (mark the map!), and, if you're the kind to *really pack it in*, a couple of sturdy rubber bands or a tie-around sash for storing your travel journal, safely closed.

5. Smile a big, bright, "I'm going somewhere *fun!*" smile. Enjoy the ride.

 DOC IN THE BOX: *Moving On (EMDR)*

This chapter's "Cool Move" reminds me of EMDR: Eye Movement Desensitization and Reprocessing. When I first heard about this method for healing traumatic memories by moving your eyes back and forth, my own eyes did an upward roll. "You mean to tell me that a woman who was raped and is now experiencing nightmares, insomnia, sweats, and anxiety will be cured by looking from side to side?" It isn't quite that simple, as I found out, but yes, in fact, such a woman could, through EMDR, come to feel vastly better. This repetitive-stimulus technique is a highly successful and efficient post-traumatic stress reliever.

EMDR has been used with war veterans, victims of sexual assault and other crimes, survivors of trauma and natural disasters, and many others. It doesn't erase their memories, but it does ease the pain and allow these folks to return to normal functioning. Often it only takes a few sessions.

The idea behind this kind of therapy is that some traumatic events don't get properly processed in our brains, and as a result they remain very painful. It's as if the memory gets stuck in the feelings, like tires in the mud. For some unknown reason, the act of moving your eyes back and forth or attending to a rhythmic tapping sound, while holding certain images or phrases in your mind, helps to unstick the memories from the emotional mud — sort of like rocking the car back and forth until it pops free. The memory remains, but the awful emotion around it has dissipated. The incident is then available for normal processing and can be motored sedately into the background like your other memories. Well, never *just* like them, but at least it is out of the foreground. And you are free of that paralyzing fear, or anger, or grief.

If you want to learn more, go to www.emdr.com.

THINGS TO TRY AT LEAST ONCE

☐ *Mosey*. Be not a slave to the clock. Find the scenic byways and visit roadside attractions.

- ❏ *Accessorize your ride.* Add some fuzzy dice and a nodding dog, maybe a big hood ornament. Or hang a "spirit caller" from the rearview mirror: hand-strung beads, baubles, and bells collected during your travels.

- ❏ *Pedal.* Leave the gas-guzzler in the garage for a change and "bike it" for a week.

- ❏ *Shrink your carbon footprint.* Next car purchase, buy a hybrid or the eco-friendliest model your budget can handle. Visit www.carbonfootprint.com to calculate your personal impact on global warming and how to reduce it. Then reduce it.

- ❏ *Read Kerouac.* His signature work, *On the Road*, recently turned fifty itself. And it's still the road story to... *beat*!

WAY 31 — Get Lost

> Buddha wandered. Jesus wandered. Muhammad wandered. Abraham wandered. They all did! They didn't just sit back and say, "I want to know why I'm here, who I am, and what I'm supposed to do. Come on, let's go!" It doesn't work like that. . . . You're under contract to wander. Get used to it.
>
> — Caroline Myss, *Sacred Contracts: Awakening Your Divine Potential*

*M*y friend Judie, now a globe-trotting documentary filmmaker and travel writer, was for many years a scriptwriter in Hollywood (the "lie about your age" capital of the world). Come birthday time, she'd typically skip town.

"So when I turned fifty, it just seemed like such a heavy age, and I did *not* go away," she said. "Instead, I went with my husband and just lay under a tree and looked up. . . . I just calmed down my nervous system and looked up at the stars."

Ahh, to lose oneself for a while — what a pleasure! Reverie is a beautiful place; we should all go there as often as possible. And this Way invites you to go beyond reveries, to go get literally lost — *out there*, in the great big world!

Dancing Lessons from God

Judie seconds that emotion. "When you get lost in travel, that's when adventure happens," she says emphatically. "I tell people, 'Put down

168

the guidebook, the map, the whatever, and go wander. Get *lost*!' The mind, the spirit, they need new
information in order to grow. Getting lost is new
information. Getting lost is a great, great teacher."

Which is not the same as saying, "Getting lost
is great, great *fun*," of course, because — while it
often is fun, and we certainly always set out hoping
it will be — sometimes it is anything but. Here's
the old yin and yang again, the shadow and the
light. Being lost can feel exhilarating, adventurous.
It can make you feel wildly alive! Or it can feel frus-
trating, scary, even desperate. By fifty, many of us
are so trained to the beaten track — it's easier, we
tell ourselves, and safer — that we could walk it in
our sleep.

SCRIBBLES & DOODLES
Find the North Star

For the nearly 90 percent of humans who call the Northern Hemisphere home, Polaris points the way north, and with that, navigation is possible. Write about your life's metaphorical North Star. What orients you when the world seems topsy-turvy?

Feeling Your Wei in the Dark

Remember *wu-wei* from Way 17? "We do without doing, and everything gets done" is how many folks understand this Taoist principle,
but it has also been defined as "purposeless wandering." The point —
and the hardest part for many to accept, frankly — is that right action
will flow through us spontaneously, effortlessly, and at the proper time
only if we remain unattached to outcomes.

Shocking as that may be to the goal-oriented among us, the fact remains that nary a soul — not even the likes of Jesus and the Buddha —
gets to know ahead of time the whole "what, where, when, why, and
how" of his or her life. And yet, *count on it*, each of us will be exactly
where we're supposed to be when the time comes.

It's like that old Lewis Carroll line that George Harrison made into a song: "If you don't know where you are going, any road will take you there."

 DOC IN THE BOX: *Navigate Your Way Out of Pain (Magnet Therapy)*

Magnets: useful for finding your way in the wilderness, for sticking pictures of the kids on the fridge, and now, perhaps, for treating your achy-breaky back.

Magnets as tools of healing went through a phase of popularity once before, in the 1700s. During that time, a Viennese physician named Mesmer (of the later-coined word *mesmerized*) claimed widespread success with magnet treatments and posited the existence of "animal magnetism" in people, particularly in himself. This not-so-humble gentleman claimed to be able to heal people by increasing the flow of magnetic "universal fluid" between himself and them. His technique became so popular in Paris that King Louis XVI established a commission (which included our very own Ben Franklin) to check it out. Alas for Dr. Mesmer, the illustrious group debunked his work as pure power of suggestion, and magnets got stuck in the history books for a time.

But everything old is new again, and magnets, like bell-bottoms and the Beatles, are making a comeback. From bracelets and back wraps to shoe inserts and mattresses, magnetized objects are attracting a lot of cash, and a number of supporters, including some prominent professional athletes. Health claims are mostly for relief of joint pain. Although precisely how magnet treatments work remains unclear, there is some scientific evidence that the claims are valid.

A respected study from the Baylor College of Medicine showed a distinct drop in knee pain in postpolio patients who used magnets compared to those who used a placebo. Another small study from Harvard suggested they might work in the short term for back pain. And an English research group found evidence for the positive effect of magnets on arthritis of the hip and knee.

Like many of the edgier therapies, magnets have garnered their share of bad press and negative studies, not to mention their share of gold diggers and opportunists. The jury is still out. But while they deliberate, if you feel *pulled* to it, and as long as you keep a bearing on your coffers, you might just try altering course toward this new kind of pain relief.

COOL MOVES

Lost Inside Yourself

When I read on my friend Diane's blog that one of her favorite pastimes is "whirling," I simply had to find out more. Here's the scoop, straight from the Whirling Woman herself.

Sufi whirling is an ancient type of dance meditation. If you want dance to become meditation, free your mind of everything but the music, and get lost in it, and in the whirling. (If you are particularly prone to dizziness, balance problems, or nausea, choose a more comfortable type of dance movement: figure eights with your arms, for example, or seated leg movements.)

Whirl as you did when you were a child, with eyes open and arms outstretched, with one palm up, the other down. Move knowing that your True Self is the center, and your body but the wheel that revolves around the center. Start slowly and gently. Whirl faster and faster as you are able. Move in the direction that feels right. If you feel dizzy, it helps to look at your "leading hand." When the music stops or you've had enough, fall gently to the floor and roll over onto your stomach. Keep your eyes closed, and feel your body merge with the earth. Work up to forty-five minutes of whirling and fifteen of belly-lying.

THINGS TO TRY AT LEAST ONCE

❏ *Take an orienteering class.* Wield your compass and maps like a pro.

❑   *Go a-wandering.* Travel to an unfamiliar neighborhood and just wander. Or cruise a mall. Or a childhood haunt. "Waste" an afternoon, just riding the city bus. Or get safely lost out in nature, with Outward Bound, REI, or another adventure company.

❑   *Carry on, my wayward son (or daughter).* When on a familiar road trip, pass up the usual pit stops. Press on for a few miles and find a new road stop.

❑   *Lose yourself in a good book.* Venture into an unexplored genre of the literary forest. Be sure to leave crumbs so you can find your way back!

WAY 32   Stop, Look & Listen

To neglect our ears is to neglect our soul.
— Russill Paul, *The Yoga of Sound*

"I see," said the blind man.
— Anonymous

Four minutes, thirty-three seconds. That's all he was asking. Just a quick "take five" to sit in relative silence, hearing only the ambient sounds of the environment. Such a lovely gift for every soul who was there, it seems to me. Yet John Cage's seminal work for silent piano met with considerable scorn when it premiered, in 1952. Reading about the event fifty years later, I was enthralled to learn that the venue (Maverick Concert Hall, in Woodstock, New York) opens at one end onto the woods, and that during those fateful four and a half minutes, "there were sounds of a breeze, then the first drops of a light rain on the roof and finally, the composer said many years later, 'the voices of disturbed listeners, some of whom may be said to still be walking out.'"

Awww! So close and yet so far! But can't you just hear them, those departing audience members, huffing about their precious time getting wasted (all 273 seconds of it)? *What* breeze? *What* rain? I bet they didn't even notice.

Where Mind Goes, Energy Follows

Noticing is the heart and soul of this Way. And did you *notice* that the title mentions stopping, looking, and listening, and that it doesn't mention judging, talking, or getting up and leaving? Rather like the enduring kindergarten lesson it's named for, "Stop, Look & Listen" simply asks that you be still for a while and pay close attention.

The disgruntlement that Cage's *4'33"* provoked is a good example of the Dahnhak principle "Where mind goes, energy follows, and where energy goes, mind follows," first mentioned in Way 16. Had audience members chosen to focus on what they could hear *because* the piano was silent, they might all have had an enjoyable, possibly even a poignant, experience. Instead, some chose to focus on the seated pianist and his persistent silence and *What did it mean?* and *Was this some kind of joke?* and *How long are we expected to put up with this?* and *How very pretentious of that composer!* and on and on until they'd worked up quite a head of steam, not just in their own heads, but also in several heads nearby. Meanwhile, nature's symphony played on and nobody heard, for all the grumbling.

You Stand at a Crossroads — Always

Everything you do expends energy, *everything*, even such seemingly passive activities as looking and listening. Except for the autonomic processes — the beating of your heart and all — decisions about how to spend your energy are entirely up to you. What to look at, dwell on, read about, listen to, talk about . . . *you* call the shots, babe, like a movie director framing scenes between fingers and thumbs. Please be choosy.

Because whether or not you buy the notion that life serves up more of whatever you dwell on, the fact is that whatever you dwell on becomes the content of your life, just as surely as the director's choices become the content of the film.

 DOC IN THE BOX: *Listen to Your Body (Body Awareness)*

When I say, "Listen to your body," I don't mean hearken to the creaks and snaps of aging joints, or blush at the rumble of your no-longer-iron guts. I'm talking body scans. Not the high-dollar kind with the big magnetic tube, but the kind you do with your own senses. Costs you nothing. Try it right now. Like McCoy on *Star Trek*, run your mental tricorder from head to toe, making note of any and all sensations. Is your jaw tense? What's the pace of your breathing? How does your back feel? Is that chair turning you into a numb-butt? Are you cold? Warm? Hungry? Tired? Just *observe*, with nonjudgmental curiosity.

Practicing awareness of your bodily sensations is extremely useful, for a number of reasons. The most important is simply that *the body never lies*. Ask a mortified teenage boy who catches sight of his sister's Victoria's Secret catalog, or a concert violinist with stage fright. The body will give you away every time.

This is a good thing. I know, the two in the previous paragraph may not agree, but hear me out. Too many folks still live by the die-hard social code called Stiff Upper Lip. You know what I'm talking about. Pull yourself up by your bootstraps. Chin up. Big boys don't cry, and nice girls don't yell. Stuffing our feelings is an American habit as old as chewing tobacco, and about as healthy. Unexpressed feelings cause stress, and stress causes illness.

Thankfully, our bodies are wiser than our brains, and if we just pay attention, we can learn to discover and express our emotions. Tensed muscles? Might be anger. Butterfly belly? Might be excitement. The details may be different for everyone, but the wisdom of the system is universal.

Equally vital is the fact that skilled body awareness can alert you to illness. If you recognize sensations early, you can sometimes nip sickness in the bud. We medical types really appreciate a good symptom description; it helps us help you. And, going one level deeper, this skill will aid you in *healing* both physical and emotional wounds. We go through life with our whole selves, after all, body and brain, and what injures one will damage the other.

Convinced? Good. Now fire up that tricorder, and scan your bod again!

Filter out the junk. Focus on the good stuff. Especially in conversation, look deeply and listen hard. Give full attention to what's being said, both verbally and nonverbally. Oh, and speaking of good stuff, please don't take leave of your *other* senses: taste, smell, touch. Take them out on regular dates, really woo them, and savor, savor, savor.

Keep a Sharp Eye

Middle-agers often bemoan their failing vision, but my friend Gina has a different take: "I did the videotape course *Yoga for Your Eyes* with Meir Schneider, and by gum, my vision came roaring back!" she emailed. "What I've found is that my vision parallels my 'vision.' In other words, when I am confused on the direction my life is taking, when I'm not seeing *that* clearly, my actual vision blurs a bit, too."

Yup. As Dawn Rose (my former vision therapist) would say, "There's a lot more to vision than eyesight."

In 1989, when I corrected my vision (without surgery) at the Vision Re-Education Center, in San Diego, many eye doctors scoffed at the very idea. "Impossible," they said. But here's an important clue: on determining that I no longer needed contact lenses, my miffed optometrist swore he'd never refer another patient to vision re-ed. He said it right out loud! Couldn't have more and more of his patients saying "no, thanks" to expensive corrective lenses, now, could he?

By now I hope that all healthcare providers understand and embrace the amazing plasticity of the human brain and that they'll encourage their patients to hone every bodily skill they can, vision definitely being one of them.

COOL MOVES
Derail That Thought!

Don't like where a habitual train of thought is taking you? Stop it! As soon as you spot an unwanted thought on the horizon, pound your fist into your open palm (or snap a rubber band you wear around your wrist) and call out, "Stop!" Practiced regularly, this derailment technique will soon have those habituated old "train tracks" (neural pathways) growing over from disuse.

COOL MOVES (BONUS ROUND)
Look! Up in the Sky! It's Bright!

Ditch your shades, at least some of the time. If you feel you can't survive outdoors without your sunglasses, it could be because your pupil-pulling muscles have atrophied from years and years of being kept in the dark. Brightness builds endurance. Being careful to look away from the sun, gaze into the sky with your naked eyes. Blink, breathe, waggle your eyebrows, and keep affirming the affirmative: "Brightness builds endurance." Wear a visor or a hat with a brim after twenty minutes in the sunshine.

THINGS TO TRY AT LEAST ONCE

☐ *Get your hearing tested.* I SAID, "GET YOUR HEARING TESTED!" Your vision, too, if it's been more than a year or two.

❑ *Replace your herbs and spices.* If you can't remember buying or drying them, then they probably taste like dust by now anyway. Bypass the grocery store's prepackaged selection (the typical bottles and tins), since the markup in price is astronomical. Seek out a bulk-foods store instead, and buy tiny quantities you can use up within a few weeks or months.

❑ *Stop thinking, look inward, and listen to the still, small voice.* The whispering soul can be hard to hear over the chattering brain, and its language is not always verbal. Stay quiet, and watch for signs.

Break on Through to the Other Side

Go as far as you can, then one step further.
— Ilchi Lee, *Wisdom of the Chun Bu Kyung*

There's something about turning fifty. Egads, it's a psychological barrier big enough to blot out the sun! But you know: the *only* alternative to waking up fifty one day is such a drag as to be no choice at all. So suck it up, man. You've got to go *do* this thing. And it's a piece o' cake, I promise you. Especially if you'll just put on a burst of speed and hit it with a bit of momentum. Ready?

Get Your Mojo Risin'

As any die-hard fan of the Doors knows, Jim Morrison copped his band's name from Aldous Huxley's *The Doors of Perception*, and Huxley, in turn, copped *his* title from a line from William Blake's *The Marriage of Heaven and Hell*: "If the doors of perception were cleansed, every thing would appear to man as it is, infinite. For man has closed himself up, till he sees all things thro' narrow chinks of his cavern."

Suddenly, it all becomes clear, doesn't it? What Morrison was yelling about in the song to which this Way pays homage? *Break on through those narrow chinks, by God!* Burst free of your self-imposed limitations.

"The Scales Fell from My Eyes!"

I've always been fascinated by stories of personal transformation, especially the sudden, profound, enduring kind. Take Bill W., for instance, the guy who started Alcoholics Anonymous. In the painful depths of his own addiction, Bill acted on a "breakthrough" intuition: that if he could team up with even one other alcoholic who desperately wanted to stop drinking, the two of them together could succeed in sobriety where, individually, they had failed. And so he did — and *they* did — and from that singular breakthrough was born the highly successful 12-step model for addiction recovery, and untold bazillions of lives were salvaged. *Way to go, Bill!*

Let me mention three others who sank to the depths of despair before rising like phoenixes, transformed: Eckhart Tolle (author of *The Power of Now*), Byron Katie (*Loving What Is*), and David R. Hawkins, MD (*Power vs. Force*). Want to change your life? You can start by reading these books.

Inching Toward the Tipping Point

Oh, to be transformed during one fitful night of the soul, like Spider-Man! But no. Most of us are on the slow road to enlightenment. Some of us are even on our hands and knees. The road is long, with many a winding turn. But no joke. I think of Frodo Baggins, at death's door on the side of Mt. Doom, in the finale of the Tolkien trilogy. The flutes wail with uncertainty and dread as our hero claws his way upward, inch by bloody inch. *Will he make it? Will his strength hold? Will good triumph over evil?*

Birth is painful. It makes sense that rebirth would be, too. The way I see it, hitting bottom is the Blessed Bonk that begins the hatching process. Your bonk may hurt, may knock the wind out of you, may even require medical attention. But Humpty Dumpty you are not; you, human, *can* put the pieces together again.

COOL MOVES

In One Nostril, Out the Other (Alternate-Nostril Breathing)

At any given moment, it's normal to breathe predominantly through one nostril. If it's the left nostril, your brain will be functioning predominantly on the right (spatial, intuitive, artistic, holistic) hemisphere. If your right nostril is more open, then you'll be more left-brained (analytical, verbal, linear) at the moment. A healthy person normally cycles from one nostril to the other every few hours, but the process can get sluggish in times of ill health or high stress. To shift nostrils (and thereby brain hemispheres) manually, so to speak, try this

SCRIBBLES & DOODLES
Riffin' on a Breakthrough

Peg and I call it riffing. You might call it brainstorming or free associating. By any name, it's a great way to help your own astonishing wisdom to break through. Write down the key word or phrase that best encapsulates the issue you have in mind, then quickly list *anything* that relates: similar words, opposites, old adages, pop lyrics, slang, book titles. If you're reminded of an experience, give it a name and move on. (Explore it later.) Work quickly. Write down *every* thought that pops into your head, even if you don't see how it relates. Did I say "pops"? Yes! As with popcorn, keep this process on the burner long enough for the straggling ideas to burst into consciousness. Any cool breakthroughs? Be patient. The magic has only just begun.

DOC IN THE BOX: *The* Other *Other Side* *(Near-Death Experiences)*

When severely injured or terribly ill people come very close to death, or actually die (by strict medical definitions) but then "come back," some remember a glimpse of what lies beyond. The near-death experiences (NDEs) described, by everyone from children to old people, from many different cultures, are far more alike than they are different.

Most NDEers describe a floating, out-of-body experience, during which they are able to perceive what's going on around them as if seeing it from above. This is followed by the sensation of a tunnel or dark passageway through which they travel. At the end of the tunnel is a light, or a being made of light. Brilliantly bright, this presence radiates total loving acceptance. Other friendly entities in various forms may be present. Communication in this realm is telepathic, and time and space don't behave the way they do in life. There is usually a rapid but in-depth review of the NDEer's life on earth, followed by some kind of border image — a fence or river, for example — beyond which there is no turning back. Nearly all report a sense of deep peace and contentment, and an overwhelming desire to stay right where they are. But eventually they decide to come back or are "told" that they must return, to complete unfinished tasks, or because it's "not their time" yet. By and large, the return to this life is made with some reluctance, and often with pain. Yet once they return, their lives are transformed. They may be reluctant to share their stories, fearing (and sometimes receiving) ridicule and disbelief. But typically they no longer fear death ("Death is not a life-threatening condition!" wrote one anonymous NDEer), and they find greater value in life, sometimes making radical changes to create enhanced meaning for themselves.

Of course such fantastic tales breed controversy and skepticism. Are they "real" experiences, or the hallucinations of an oxygen-starved brain? I figure I'll know for sure only when I get there, but meanwhile I am fascinated and moved by what I read.

You can learn more and read firsthand accounts online at the International Association for Near Death Studies at www.iands.org.

Pranayama exercise, known variously as *Anuloma Viloma*, or *Nadi Sodhana.*

Close the right nostril with your right thumb and inhale through the left nostril to a count of four. Close the left nostril with the right ring and pinkie fingers, while removing your thumb to open the right nostril. Exhale through the right nostril to a count of eight, keep your fingers where they are, and inhale through the right nostril to a count of four. Now close the right nostril with your thumb, as you did in the beginning, and exhale through the left nostril. (This completes one round.) Notice, once you get going, that when you first open a nostril, you exhale through it, then inhale through it, before switching to the other. Exhale, inhale, switch, exhale, inhale, switch. Do three rounds for starters; work up to seven or more.

〰➤ THINGS TO TRY AT LEAST ONCE

❑ *Push the envelope.* Pick one of your routine endeavors, and improve on your personal best, even in a small way.

❑ *Face your fears.* Do something that scares you. Public speaking, skydiving — or even just pool diving. Read *The Places That Scare You: A Guide to Fearlessness in Difficult Times* by Pema Chödrön. True phobics, get help! You need not give over the rest of your life to crippling fear.

❑ *Buy a piñata.* Talk about breakin' on through. Fill it with age-appropriate goodies — dental floss, say, and travel-sized bottles of SPF30 moisturizer. Okay, and maybe a *little* chocolate! They say a bit o' the dark stuff is actually good for you!

WAY 34 — Act Ageless

> Of all the self-fulfilling prophecies in our culture, the assumption that aging means decline and poor health is probably the deadliest.
>
> — Marilyn Ferguson, *The Aquarian Conspiracy*

*I*t took until my kids were almost teenagers, but sure enough, one day I opened my mouth and out it came: "Oh, act your age!" On the list of Stupid Things Parents Say All the Time, this one ranks way up there. I mean, it's so obvious! Any kid who provokes such an outburst from Mom or Dad is almost certainly doing an Oscar-worthy job of acting his age already.

And who, of any age, doesn't bristle at the very suggestion? Act my age, indeed! Unless, of course, the suggestion flows from the lips of Prince, the Artist Formerly Known as My Heartthrob — "Act your age, mama, not your shoe size" — in which case we could all just retire to the dance floor and (as the song goes) "maybe we could do the twirl."

Pop quiz! How old are we acting now?

(Is it a trick question? You bet it is! Age is so irrelevant.)

"This Is What Fifty Looks Like"

When Gloria Steinem uttered those famous words, I was half her age and didn't give them much thought. Now, of course (or terribly soon), I get to say them to my mirror each day.

But there are benefits to bringing up the rear of the baby-boom generation. *All* those aging bodies, *all* the money they spend on ... *everything*! Not to be too cynical — or to state the obvious — but the free-market system really caters to the boomers. Now is it any wonder, as boomers turn sixty at a rate of some 4 million a year in the United States alone, that Dove Soap would come out with a line of products called "Pro-Age"? Or that the youth-worshipping movie industry would dare to do nude scenes with not just the model-perfect ingénue but also the occasional middle-aged beauty? Have we come a long way baby, or *what?*

All sarcasm aside, it is a start. Genuine age reverence in our society may take a while, but every little bit helps — including the power of one: you, totally loving the fact that you're fifty. And getting older and better by the moment!

Don't Act Your Age — Act It Out

Putting the number fifty into action is a wonderful way to pass your semicentury mark. Peg's friend Sue, for instance, ran a marathon the day she turned fifty and now, a few years later, she is training for a fifty-miler. Another friend of a friend, during the summer of his fiftieth, drove U.S. Highway 50 from one end to the other and back, blogging

SCRIBBLES & DOODLES
"Dear Self, Happy Sixtieth!"

Think long and hard about your fifties, then write a letter to your sixty-year-old self. Stash it in a safe deposit box or a "tickler" file (maybe a time capsule; see below), or arrange to have a trusted (young! healthy!) friend actually mail it to you "next decade." Stamp it with one of those "Forever" stamps — or, for fun, guess how much it will cost to mail a letter when you're sixty, and affix that much postage.

all the way. And someone else I know organized the making of a friendship quilt for her best friend's fiftieth. The quilt incorporated fifty squares (five by five, times two sides) made by fifty different friends of the birthday girl. Wow!

But I'd have to say the official "Fifty Ways Award for Working in the Most Fifties" goes to summiting buff Thomas P. Martin. It's been a few years now, but this sports-medicine professor started his fiftieth birthday at 12:01 a.m. by doing several fifty-second stretches, fifty jumping jacks, fifty push-ups, and fifty sit-ups. He then proceeded to mountain bike and trek fifty miles from the shoreline (at sea level, natch) to the summit of Mauna Kea (13,796 ft.), the highest elevation in Hawaii, the fiftieth state of the United States, while pursuing his goal to reach the "high point" of all fifty states.

You get the idea. Even so, here's one more — a Big Five-oh gift that you can give: Put fifty-dollar bills into action. Peel off a Ulysses S. Grant or two for a good cause you've been meaning to support. If you're flush, give fifty of 'em, or even fifty grand! Now that would be one for the ages!

COOL MOVES
Child's Pose

Roughly "fetal position on your knees," this is a good pose for releasing lower-back strain. Begin on your hands and knees, with the top sides of your feet on the floor (soles up). Sit back on your heels, lower your upper body, and rest your head on the floor. You can keep your arms outstretched in front of you, folded in close to your sides, or laid alongside your legs, with palms facing upward next to your feet. Breathe normally, and relax deeply for a minute or two (or ten!). Let your mind be as untroubled as a sleeping babe's.

 DOC IN THE BOX: *"Fifty? But You Have the Body of a Thirty-Year-Old!"* *(Functional Age)*

"I've never had a problem!" lamented my friend Billy. "I exercise at least five times a week. I didn't think I had to worry!" He had just heard from his doctor that, in spite of his active lifestyle and normal weight, his cholesterol had crept up over the line.

At this time of life, many of us are confronted with solid evidence that the free ride of youth is over. We can't get away with what we used to. We are middle-aged. *The next thing you know*, we moan, *we'll get old and die!*

Much more likely in this day and age is that we will get old and live, according to Chris Crowley and Henry Lodge, in their book *Younger Next Year*. And this could be a daunting prospect. Nobody wants to live for years and years as a frail, drooling wisp of their former self. Getting old and living with the terrible restrictions of poor health might indeed be worse than the alternative.

However, assert these two vivacious and apparently ageless gentlemen, this does not have to be your story. To an extent, you can actually slow down the aging process, becoming functionally younger as the years go by. Read the books (there's *Younger Next Year for Women*, too) for the scientific details provided by Dr. Lodge, and the enthusiastic, in-your-face exhortations of Chris Crowley, a seventy-something whose body and lab results look more like those of a fifty-year-old. Why? Because he practices what they preach. Which is? *Exercise.* A lot. And start now. There is no fountain of youth, but through your own efforts you can slow down the clock a little.

THINGS TO TRY AT LEAST ONCE

- ❑ *"Break a leg!"* On second thought, do act your shoe size. If acting brings you joy, then do it however you can. Direct a school play. Lie about your age (older, younger: be bold)! Or just play charades.

❑ *Fake it till you make it.* Pretend you've been cast as the sort of person you truly want to be. Speak, move, dress, and behave as that person would, and *you may surprise yourself* by growing authentically into character.

❑ *Create a time capsule.* Here's another one "for the ages." Include items that capture the essence of now — today's newspaper, receipts for gas or groceries, photos of loved ones wearing today's fashions — and a contemplation about the future (a letter to your future self, say, or to future generations). Specify who should open it and when.

Mind Your Karma, Trim Your Dogma

You have your way. I have my way. As for the right way, the correct way, and the only way, it does not exist.

— Friedrich Wilhelm Nietzsche (1844–1900)

*L*et me start off by saying, to the stranger who helped my husband (then boyfriend) and me get back into the United States from our utterly budget-busting trip to Baja California, in 1983, *Thank you! We owe you one, man!*

It was only a buck or two — a few hundred pesos — but still, we didn't have it, and the uniformed Mexican official was showing no sign of letting us board the plane until we'd paid the full exit fee (times two). My heart was racing, my palms sweating. Mind you, we *had* carefully stuck away the *exact* amount we'd been told would come due on leaving Mexico, but it turns out we'd been told wrong. Luckily, a fellow *estadounidense*, overhearing our kerfuffle, dug into his wallet in the wink of an eye, and (karma bells!) my sweetie and I were free to board.

"We'll pay you back," I exclaimed to the guy, "just as soon as we get to Tucson."

Oh, but then! Back on home soil, where *was* he? Our ride was waiting; we didn't want to hold *him* up, so (karma buzz) we left without paying the guy back.

Do Unto Others...as Often as You Can

Who hasn't experienced such kindness from strangers? It's in our nature to help one another. Even before we meet, on some level we already care. And after we've been helped, we want to give something in return. It just seems right to go full circle. Alas, as happened to my husband and me and our cross-border benefactor, sometimes the only possible paying-it-back moment gets away. So, in the words of Catherine Ryan Hyde, whose novel was made into a movie, we "pay it forward." That's the simple karmic solution: here's some love — pass it on!

Wheel! Of! *Karma!*

Wouldn't it be great, though, if there really were gentle little bells and buzzers to help people get it about karma? Because doing the right thing is not always so cut-and-dried. Sure, maybe back when society *seemed* to be as homogenized as milk, the Golden Rule was all you'd ever need. But in this gloriously multicultural world of ours, there must be as many interpretations of "as you'd have them do unto you" as there are color combos of skin, eyes, and hair. A little karmic guidance wouldn't hurt.

Good news. When you listen to your heart, there actually are little bells and buzzers, though they're not the kind you hear so much as *feel*. Next time you're wondering how best to help someone, ask your heart. Listen for that still, small voice. Better yet, ask the person who needs help.

Your Help Is Only Helpful If People Want It

Let me say this with gentle-but-firm urgency, since it sums up "Mind Your Karma, Trim Your Dogma" in nine simple words: *Your help is only helpful if people want it.* It doesn't matter how pure your intentions are, how superior your religion is, or how great your ideas are for solving the problem at hand (or the *perceived* problem, if you get my meaning). Your help is only helpful if people want it.

Many of us find "helping" hard to resist. We can't...*help* ourselves. It's that doggone limbic brain of ours! That and our ego. Remember Mighty Mouse? *"Here I come to save the day!"* Craving security, recognition, and control, the mighty little ego likes nothing better than a chance to be the hero. After all, it has a crucial role to play in the all-important Survival of the Species, too. But in matters of spiritual growth, you'll have to pardon your eager ego. Kindly suggest that it step aside, so you can more truly consider the situation from the other person's perspective. The ego means well, but sometimes — lots of times — it only gets in the way.

SCRIBBLES & DOODLES
Downward Dogma

We haven't talked much about dogma yet, and here's why: in my humble opinion, the world has too much dogma in it already. I'm not calling it bad (*bad dogma!*), only excessive. Like the Golden Rule, the best dogma is short and sweet. What's *your* dogma, your code to live by? Would your credo fit on a bumper sticker? (Helpful hint: first do the "Scribbles & Doodles" exercise in Way 25.) For extra fun, make it into an actual bumper sticker and...stick it!

COOL MOVES

Downward Dog

Begin on your hands and knees, and make sure you're "square" (that is, that your hands are directly beneath your shoulders, and your knees directly beneath your hips). Lift your heels and curl the toes under, pointing forward. Straighten your legs and raise the hips until your body forms an inverted V. Relax your neck, and let your head hang. Press your heels to the floor and straighten your arms. Lift yourself through the wrists and shoulders. Flatten your back, press your shoulders toward the ground, and turn your tailbone to the sky, rather like a doggie wagging its tail. Hold the pose for twenty to thirty seconds, then bend the knees and rest a while in Child's Pose (see the previous Way). Repeat the exercise and rest again.

DOC IN THE BOX: *Health Karma's Gonna Get You...and Maybe Your Family, Too*

Remember John Lennon's song "Instant Karma"? Well, it may be more like "eventual karma" that gets you here, but by any chance does your list of future plans include "lose my independence" and/or "become a helpless burden on my family"? Of course not. So, as a doctor, I have to ask: Why are you still smoking? Or sitting on the couch stuffing yourself with junk food? Or avoiding your yearly checkups? Or _____? Fill in the blank; we all have something. Yes, even we docs, who *definitely* ought to know better.

I'm stepping into a very old-fashioned doctor role here (picture the mirror on the forehead and the house-call bag) to flat-out lecture you. Ready?

Do the right thing! Get healthy. Take care of yourself, if not for your sake, then for that of your loved ones. You don't want your kids to be stuck schlepping you around in a wheelchair because you lost your feet from diabetes, or your mind from a stroke. Right?

Right?!

Everything we do comes with consequences. Your bad habits and unhealthy behaviors *will* catch up with you (if they haven't already). But worse still, they can put a severe crimp in the lives (and bank accounts) of those who love you. Half of all personal bankruptcies filed in the United States are precipitated by unmanageable medical bills. So next time you're trying to overcome your own inertia, Do It for Them.

End of lecture. Thank you for listening!

↝ THINGS TO TRY AT LEAST ONCE

❑ *Be the (spare) change you want to see in the world.* Your help is *so* helpful when it's wanted! Create a magical moment of "yes" for both you and a stranger by giving a few coins — and a big, bright smile — to the next beggar you see. Please don't be dogmatic about what this poor soul may (or may not) do with the money. In my experience, the recipient of my fistful of coins never fails to look me right in the eye and say, "Bless you." And if that's not an even trade, well, then I'd have to say I'm getting the better end of the deal. The universe is abundant. Please share!

❑ *"Ever mind the Rule of Three."* Many people believe that the energies you "put out there" through your every thought, word, and deed do not merely come back to you; they come back *multiplied.* This is what Wiccans mean by the Rule of Three.

❑ *Catch a lecture at a Buddhist education center.* Now that the word *karma* is on the tongues of so many, you may think you know the fullness of its meaning. Then again, you may be surprised! Go find out: What is karma *really*?

❑ *Light a candle* for someone you know who is suffering.

WAY 36 (En)Lighten Up, Dude!

That you carry yourself forward and experience the myriad things is delusion. That the myriad things come forward and experience themselves is awakening.

— Dogen Zenji (1200–1253)

Don't worry. Be happy.

— Meher Baba (1894–1969)

"There really *is* something about leaving your forties," Kathy said, having been there, done that, a few years earlier. "Things change. Stuff you used to think was so important just isn't anymore. All that 'keeping up with the Joneses' crap. Oh, and that ten pounds I was *always* gonna lose!" She scoffed and waved her hand dismissively. "Who cares?"

Snatch the Pebble from My Hand

Such mundane matters — from "who's got what?" to the size of your jeans — are ego attachments, pure and simple, and I've heard enough stories like Kathy's by now to believe that they really do ease up in midlife. Maybe, with the nest emptying and the rat race in a groove, it's natural for people our age to look past the mundane, the earthly — as with a wide-eyed gaze into the starry night — and ask, "What am I missing? There's got to be more to life than just . . ." (lowering gaze) "this."

I agree. So does Peg. There is so much more to life than just what meets the eye. Thus we encourage you wholeheartedly to put Spiritual Quest on your to-do list. And if it's already there, then be bold and push it to the top!

Spiritual ≠ Religious

I'm no guru, but I think I can safely assert: enlightenment is not the sort of thing you can wedge in between appointments. Spiritual growth takes time and effort. *And* what my first-grade teacher Sister Corrine Marie called "stick-to-it-iveness." The very image of that mountaintop guru and his seeker's long, hard climb symbolizes as much.

Just to be clear, I am not necessarily equating the words *spiritual* and *religious*. While the two are practically the same thing in some people's minds, for others one is not even a subset of the other. Perhaps all your spirit longs for is more time to paint. Or to read. Or to practice tai chi out under the open sky.

Step Softly and Carry as Little as Possible

Whether you seek a deeper grounding in the religious tradition you've always known, or you yearn to explore other spiritual paths, the best advice I can give is "travel light!" I don't mean that just in the

SCRIBBLES & DOODLES
*From Half Empty to Half Full
(Reframing Exercise)*

That long wait in the grocery line: total waste of time, or a chance to chat with others and enjoy a few moments of standing still? The construction detour: pain in the behonkas, or an opportunity to see a new part of town? There are at least two ways to view everything. Pick something that happened recently, something negative. Now reframe it — give it the full (if metaphorical) gallery treatment, with dedicated lighting and proper placement in context, for ideal viewing. Write down what happened without changing any facts, but look at them from several different angles and see if you can lighten up on your interpretation and reaction. How does the situation look now?

obvious sense — you don't need material goods on a spiritual journey, so don't overpack — I also mean it in the more fanciful one: just *lighten up!*

Being your Very Best Self every moment of every day would be a steep climb indeed. Impossibly steep! Forgive yourself your stumbles, your backtracking, your need to stop and catch your breath. That you would embark on a Spiritual Quest at all is commendable. That you should persevere through adversity is more commendable still. Be patient enough to rest and recharge. Tend to your blisters lovingly. The morning will bring fresh light.

 ## COOL MOVES

Transcend the Mundane

For all intents and purposes, the chattering brain reflects the mundane world. Why else would so many spiritual traditions employ techniques for quieting (thus transcending) it? Choral music, chanting, meditation, prostration (repeated bowing), drumming, whirling, even self-flagellation — every one of them has the power to carry a soul to ecstatic heights. Now, if ecstatic heights are more than you're ready for just yet, try this much more down-to-earth technique from Dahn yoga. *Ji Gam*, Korean for "stop thought," focuses the mind on the physical sensation of energy in the body, beginning with the hands.

Sit comfortably, close your eyes, and raise your hands to about chest level, with palms facing each other about a foot apart. Notice if you can feel the energy in your palms or fingers — as a buzz or tingling, or as any sensation at all. Moving slowly, repeatedly bring your palms close together, not touching (feel the heat!), then apart again. Imagine that you have a shape-shifting ball of energy in your hands.

DOC IN THE BOX: *Be Here Now (Mindfulness)*

The only thing that is ultimately real about your journey is the step that you are taking at this moment. That's all there ever is.

— Eckhart Tolle, *The Power of Now*

Mindful. A word as common in this day and age as *natural* or *energy*, and just as often misused. I frequently hear it as an admonishment. "Be mindful of the traffic cones. Be mindful of your breathing. Be mindful of your to-do list." My blood pressure goes up just thinking about it. In truth, mindfulness is the opposite of stress. Real mindfulness brings peace, and that's the point.

Mindfulness, simply put, is paying maximum attention to this very moment and all that it contains, and nothing else. Experiencing the Now and accepting it fully. You may think you do this all the time, but do you really? How much time do you spend ruminating over the past or worrying about the future? If you're like most of us, the answer is, A lot!

What has happened cannot be changed. Stewing about it is nothing but wasted energy. The same goes for the future. It hasn't even gotten here yet, and when it does, presto, it's the present. And besides, that future you're fearing? It might not ever come to pass. Sure, it's important to look up at the horizon once in a while, to make plans, to think ahead. Life's practicalities have to be anticipated and seen to. But try not to dwell there. This moment, right now, is where *all* the action is.

If you have ever been totally wrapped up in something, like an art project or a very challenging physical activity, so involved that you forgot everything else and didn't notice the passage of time, you have experienced mindfulness. The peace that comes with that kind of focused concentration will leave you wanting more.

If you want to get a taste of mindfulness, so to speak, try the raisin meditation. Get a raisin. Look at it, feel it, smell it. Put it in your mouth. Hold it on your tongue and taste it. Focus all your attention on the raisin as you slowly chew and swallow it. Take your sweet time. Using your senses like this is an excellent way to be in the moment. You can do this in a myriad of small ways every day.

Or try formal meditation to still the mind. There are many techniques. One is simply to pay close attention to your breathing. Don't force it, just observe its inflow and outflow. Another meditation method is to envision, or actually look at, a burning candle, with the same kind of present-centered awareness.

When you are fully in the Now, there is no room for anything else. The past, lost and gone forever, and the future, as yet unknown, fade into the background. Your existence expands to fill this very moment — it's a beautiful place to hang out.

Raisin gazing may strike you as silly. But cultivate mindfulness as a way of life — bring your attention to the Now as often as you can — and you'll be amazed and delighted by how your life changes.

Notice all the sensations you can. If thoughts intrude, refocus on the feeling in your hands. Continue for several minutes. With practice, you may come to feel the movement of energy throughout your body, and the more you focus on *that*, the less the mundane world will intrude on your meditation.

〰️ THINGS TO TRY AT LEAST ONCE

☐ *Step lightly*. Literally! Bear yourself with elfin grace.

☐ *Forgive yourself ... endlessly!* Too much self-criticism stunts your growth.

☐ *Forgive everyone else, too*. Past, present, and future. Free your soul of those earthly bonds.

☐ *Life is funny — admit it*. Next time you do something stupid, take a breath, step back, and look for the humor in the situation. Failing that, label it an AFGO (Another Frikkin' Growth Opportunity) and laugh it off anyway.

W A Y 37 — Shine On You Crazy Diamond

> When I was young I was called a rugged individualist. When I was in my fifties I was considered eccentric. Here I am doing and saying the same things I did then and I'm labeled senile.
>
> — George Burns

*I*f you've never been a Pink Floyd fan (and what is up with that?), you may not know that Syd Barrett, cofounder (with Roger Waters, Richard Wright, and Nick Mason) of that seminal band, was the original Crazy Diamond; Waters wrote a beautiful, if melancholy, song titled "Shine On You Crazy Diamond" in homage to his lifelong friend.

A Real Face Melter

In Pink Floyd's early days, Syd once slathered his hair with goo before a live TV appearance of the band. Beneath the hot lights, the stuff turned to liquid, and during the broadcast Syd's face appeared to melt. Now, *that's* a bit of 1960s television I wish I'd seen. You've heard, perhaps, of the "face-melting" guitar solo? Leave it to madcap Syd to actually pull it off. Crazy *brilliant*!

Such white-hot creative genius can burn the one who bears it, of course, which is exactly what happened to Syd. Wasn't long before he

199

SCRIBBLES & DOODLES
Crazy Quilt (On Paper)

Break out your favorite art supplies and create a scatter page of your unique craziness. Turning your journal (or poster board) every which way, cover it with words, phrases, pictures, doodles . . . anything that conveys the particulars of your personal lunacy. Add shine, if you want, with metallic ink, glitter, and sequins, or display the finished masterpiece in a metal frame.

had a different kind of meltdown, and by the age of twenty-five, this rock god had retreated to the quietude of his mother's home, where he enjoyed tending garden, and where he lived out the last thirty-five years of his life.

It Takes All Kinds

Kind of a sad story, I know, but not as sad — nor as tragic — as some stories of the "crazy brilliant." Syd did not, for instance, stuff his pockets with rocks and go for a suicidal swim, like Virginia Woolf did. He opted for simple seclusion. Syd wisely traded in his rock stardom for healthier ways to channel his creative gifts. Hence the "shine on" of Waters's homage.

Just as that 1975 song honors Syd Barrett, this Way honors you! You and your particular craziness. Maybe you're a collector of Betty Boop memorabilia or an avid (some might say rabid) film buff. Maybe, despite being a peace activist, you enjoy a wicked-good paintball battle with your buddies now and again. Maybe you all but live at the flea market. Whatever your quirks, they are what make you you, and to that I say, "Shine on!"

Even in the Rough, Diamonds Rock

Brilliance need not be as white-hot as Syd's to be a hard thing to bear. If you have even a touch of it, you know. People often mistake true brilliance for common glare, shield their eyes, and ask that you tone it down. Envious others, recognizing your gift for how great it truly is, give you endless grief about it: *Hey Einstein! Drama queen! Brother from another planet!* Perhaps you decided long ago that it's just easier (safer, less lonely) to try to fit in — "I'm a plain, old, ordinary rock, honest!" — but the one-of-a-kind diamond of your soul goes right on craving the bright light of day. It's dying to shine! And I do mean *dying*. Tick-tock, remember?

Fetch your diamond-cutting tools and set to work, before it's too late. Knock away that dull facade you've been hiding behind. Dazzle the world with your signature brilliance!

Cosmic, Man!

There's actually a really important reason for you to do just that, at least according to Maria Montessori. Best known as a child educator, Dr. Montessori was first and foremost a scientist, with degrees in medicine and anthropology. She posited that every individual in the world — indeed, every thing in the universe — has a particular cosmic task to fulfill. There's a reason for everything, even the things that bug us. (Perhaps even the things — the quirks! — that bug us about ourselves!)

Talk about buggin'... let me use ants as an example. Crazy, frenetic ants. Their numbers are astronomical, and, hard workers that they are, they're forever racing around, hoisting objects way heavier than their own scrawny little bodies. And oh, what a bother they can be, biting and swarming! You'd be forgiven for wishing, as my five-year-old son, Sayre, once did, "that there wasn't even any such thing as ants."

Without *You*? Perish the Thought!

But can you imagine? All those bazillions of busy little bodies, gone? Just like that? Imagine how quickly *their* cosmic tasks would pile up. And what about the anteaters? Who'd feed them? Ecosystems can adapt, but they can also collapse. So, puny and annoying though they be, the ants must stay. Turns out they're of *cosmic* importance.

And so it is, my unique friend, with you! To put this matter in Tolkien-esque terms (paraphrasing elfin queen Galadriel), *your cosmic task has been appointed to you, and You Alone. If you do not accomplish it, no one will.*

Burn, Baby, Burn!

You may not grasp the full import of your works in this lifetime, any more than a carbon atom knows if it'll burn as coal at a backyard barbecue or sparkle as a diamond on the finger of a princess bride. Whatever your unique role in this lifetime, know that it's a worthy one, and shine on!

COOL MOVES

Sun Salutation (Surya Namascar) and Moon Salution (Chandra Namascar)

Careful Googling of these phrases will bring up easy-to-follow, animated demonstrations. These two series of hatha yoga asanas (poses) complement each other nicely: Sun Salutation moves from front to back, and Moon Salutation from side to side. Cycle through both a time or two, and you can call it a yoga workout!

DOC IN THE BOX: *The Quirk That Hurts (Mental Health)*

Yes, it's perfectly cool to be quirky. You are eccentric; you are unique. Celebrate that. But what if one of your "quirks" is hurting more than helping you? What if you have depression? Anxiety? A phobia? Maybe adult ADD or an addiction? Some quirks can really cramp your style, or even drive you underground. For example, the spontaneity of ADD might be outweighed by the chaos it wreaks, or the creative angst of depression might not be worth the pain. Or even if you're "just" a perfectionist, that can drive you (and those around you) a little nutty.

Our parents were offshoots of that "greatest generation" who kept their chins up and never complained. They worked hard and played their cards close to the vest. By and large, they didn't believe in mental healthcare unless someone was certifiable. It just wasn't cool to think or talk about emotional problems back then. So you may have been living with your sticky quirk since childhood.

Thankfully, the times they are a-changin'. Seeking help for depression or anxiety doesn't carry the stigma it once did. You don't have to be a raving lunatic or a wealthy heiress to get help. Advances in treatment have been made in the East and in the West, including refinements in pharmacology. You don't need to resign yourself to living with pain for the rest of your life.

So by all means, let your hair down and flaunt your *you*-ness to the max. But remember this: if the quirk hurts, don't settle. Get some help. You deserve to be the healthiest and happiest fifty-year-old you can be.

〰 THINGS TO TRY AT LEAST ONCE

❏ *Go fly a kite*. Really, do.

❏ *Visit Crazy Horse*. The likeness of this famous Lakota chief (and the horse he rode in on) is being carved into a mountainside in South Dakota's Black Hills, not far from Mt. Rushmore. Awesome!

❏ *Try out crystal healing*. Practitioners of this modality employ different types of crystals to treat different types of complaints. May sound crazy, but you never know.

❑   *Go to the source.* Syd lives! Actually, he died in July 2006. But the
    original "crazy diamond" shines on through his music. Check
    out Pink Floyd's first LP, *The Piper at the Gates of Dawn*, Bar-
    rett's masterpiece, or "Jug Band Blues," his only song on
    Floyd's second album.

38 # Look Death Right in the Eye

The fear of death follows from the fear of life. A man who lives fully is prepared to die at any time.

— Mark Twain

*T*hink Grim Reaper, and into your head lurches the ominous hooded guy with no face, right? He has no eyes to look into, yet, here's my bet: you know darned good and well when you've been eye-to-eye with Death, whether up close or from across a crowded room. It may have happened in a flash; it may have seemed like an eternity. *You* know. You were there.

Let me stop pussyfooting around this ghostly eminence in our midst. Fifty is big precisely because not everyone lives to see it. Bless their souls, some loved ones leave their forties the hard way. Their passing can't help but sound a deep knell within us and tinge our own remaining years (or will it be days?) bittersweet.

Jeez, Who Died?

If I may lighten the mood ... humorist Art Buchwald finally did. The widely syndicated columnist decided, at the ripe old age of eighty, that he'd had quite enough kidney dialysis for one lifetime, so he gave it up. When doctors told him, in February 2006, that he was likely to die within weeks, the Pulitzer Prize–winning author moved into a hospice to do just that. Friends from all over the world streamed to his bedside to say good-bye, and, when weeks stretched into months, many of them came to say good-bye again.

After five months of not dying at the hospice — indeed, of "holding court," as one write-up put it, and "having the time of [his] life," as another quoted the old joker — he decided to move back to his home on Martha's Vineyard and write what he called a "deathbed memoir" about the whole experience. Buchwald even lived to see the book published that fall *and* to enjoy the winter holidays, no doubt in the company of more well-wishers and laughing all the way, Ho, Ho, Ho! (He was Jewish, yes, but he knew from Ho, Ho, Ho, okay?)

"People told me," Buchwald wrote in *Too Soon to Say Goodbye*, "they loved talking to someone who wasn't afraid to discuss death." He died in January 2007, almost a year after stopping dialysis.

Seasons Don't Fear the Reaper

Fear. *Bingo!* It's fear that makes death out to be such a bad thing. In cultures that embrace the body's demise as an essential part of life's endless cycle, fear of death is not that much of an issue. But around here — yikes! We avert our eyes and pray the shadow will pass as quickly as possible.

"Seasons don't fear the reaper," sang Blue Oyster Cult, and I'll add: Nor do the lions, tigers, and bears. Even humans — even Westerners! — can learn to "get over it" about death, especially if ever they come very close to "crossing over." (See Dr. Peg's fascinating summary of near-death experiences in Way 33.) Survivors of life-threatening illness, too, tend to get their heads on pretty straight about The Inevitable.

"You realize all the platitudes are true," said Lynne, the marathoning leukemia survivor I introduced earlier. "Life *is* precious! Every day *is* a gift."

Instead of averting their eyes, the seriously ill are forced to fix death with a steady, penetrating gaze, and as a result, their lives, however long they last, almost invariably grow more meaningful.

Can we be like they are? Come on, baby! Confront the fear. Look death right in the eye. And if today it passes you by, then — by all that you hold dear — live, live, live! Like there's no tomorrow.

SCRIBBLES & DOODLES
Death-Gazer's Choice — Obituary, Eulogy, or Full Funeral Plan

There is nothing like the well-imagined view from one's own coffin to spur a person to truly live! Read the newspaper's obits section for inspiration, then write the story you'd love to have printed after *you* go. Or imagine that you could stand up at your own funeral and address the dearly beloved gathered there. What would you say? Either way, obituary or eulogy, do not hold back. This is a celebration of *your whole life,* so go for all the gusto. (P.S. It never hurts to plan ahead, should you get a wild hair to plan your actual funeral. Me? I've gotten as far as listing a few of the songs I'd like played at my wake. Just be sure to keep next of kin in the loop, since you really won't be able to take care of the very last steps yourself.)

COOL MOVES

Play Dead (Hatha Yoga's Corpse Pose)

Savasana, yoga-speak for "resting comfortably on your back," is best done after full-body stretching. Lie on a carpeted floor or mat, with legs straight (or with a pillow beneath your knees) and feet together.

Align your spine and hips for optimal relaxation. Roll your head from side to side a few times, then bring it back to center. Tuck the chin slightly. Relax your arms, with elbows straight but soft, and palms upward, well out from the hips. Allow your feet and knees to roll apart. Quiet your thoughts, breathe evenly, and let your weight sink into the floor. Stay for five to ten minutes (or until your snoring wakes you up!). Come out of the position slowly: wiggle fingers and toes, flutter your eyelashes, stretch lightly, then bend your knees, turn on to your left side, and sit up.

 DOC IN THE BOX: *Just in Case (Advance Directives)*

Fifty may be the new thirty, but not a one of us is going to live forever. Now, before you get old and decrepit, is a good time to be thinking about how you want to make your grand exit. Of course, you don't get to dictate every detail of the last act, but you do have some say. I'm talking about advance directives, which are your written answers to some important end-of-life questions.

How do you want to spend your last hours or days on earth? What kind of care do you want if you are near death or in a coma? At what point might you want your medical team to provide comfort rather than to prolong life? These questions and others are answered by you, in writing, in a living will.

Signing a "power of attorney for healthcare" means designating someone who will make your healthcare decisions for you if you can't do it for yourself. If you don't do this, some long-lost loudmouth of a relative might end up taking the reins, and trust me, you do not want this.

Thinking and talking about death can be difficult, but you are a veritable grown-up now, which means you can wrestle with tough questions. And no, it's not too soon. You may be healthy today, but tomorrow you could get hit by a truck.

If you balk at doing this for yourself, then do it for your loved ones. It will make it far easier on them if you have made some decisions and put them in writing.

Check out www.agingwithdignity.org, which publishes a wonderful user-friendly guide called Five Wishes; the National Cancer Institute at www.cancer.gov; and www.familydoctor.org for good general information and links.

〰️ THINGS TO TRY AT LEAST ONCE

❑ *Befriend the dying.* This is one of the most courageous gifts a human being can give. Volunteer at a hospice, attend closely to a seriously ill friend, or become a pen pal with someone on death row. The experience will change your life and ease the end of his or hers.

❑ *Contemplate impermanence.* Attend a Tibetan sand-painting event, in which Buddhist monks spend all day creating an intricate mandala of brightly colored sand, after which they ritualistically offer it to the wind, rain, or river for destruction. Their beautiful, painstaking creation — just like each of us — was never meant to last.

❑ *Practice corpse meditation.* May sound creepy to non-Buddhists, but another (profound!) contemplation of impermanence (described in Thich Nhat Hanh's *The Miracle of Mindfulness: An Introduction to the Practice of Meditation*) calls on you to visualize a dead body decomposing, from its beautiful, lifelike slumber in an open casket all the way to dry bones in the earth.

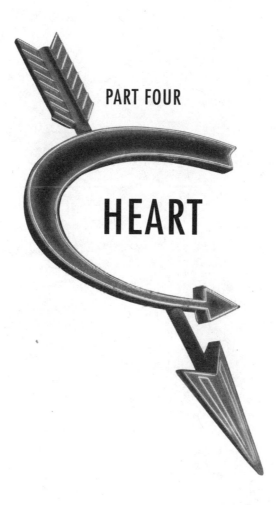

PART FOUR

HEART

39 # Okay, Have a Crisis Already!

Close scrutiny will show that most "crisis situations" are opportunities to either advance, or stay where you are.
— Dr. Maxwell Maltz

There cannot be a crisis next week. My schedule is already full.
— Henry Kissinger

*W*ith this Way, we move into the emotional Heart section, and where better to begin than with the classic: the emotional state so often associated with people our age that it's called the "midlife crisis."

The first one I ever witnessed (though I was clueless at the time) happened around 1975, when I was fifteen. My best friend's dad, a jolly-big fellow and friend to my whole family, suffered a heart attack, went off to some big-city hospital for what seemed like forever, and came back a trim, tanned Mr. Groovy. I'm sure I gaped to see this "old" family friend, a guy no cooler than my own dad, decked out like all the young dudes, in turtleneck, bell-bottoms, even a goatee. Suddenly I understood what people meant when they said, "You look like a million bucks!"

But what really screamed midlife crisis (especially as I look back on it now) was his sweet new ride. Surprised? Of course you're not. It was one of those souped-up custom vans, all shiny chrome on the outside and plush burgundy accoutrements within. Tongues did wag, of course, but who really cared? Certainly not the guy behind the wheel. He was alive, by God, and he was going to live it up while he still could.

Make Mine the Classic, with Everything, Please

Believe it or not, the midlife crisis was originally the domain of creative geniuses. At least, that's who social scientist Dr. Elliott Jaques was writing about when he coined the phrase, in a 1965 research paper. A decade later, about the time Mr. Groovy wheeled into my hometown, Gail Sheehy recast the phrase more broadly in her bestselling book *Passages*.

A generation later, midlife crises are so common as to be cliché, but, come on! That's no reason not to have one. Could be you're long overdue for a complete makeover, replete with wardrobe revolution, your first tattoo, and a much sportier ride. This Way is like a get-out-of-jail-free card, a hall pass for grown-ups, stamped "Why not? *Everybody's* doing it!" Should you prefer to buck the trend, stay the course, and do nothing rash, I respect you for that. But the midlife crisis is your ticket to ride, my friend, not just new wheels, but entirely new vistas, new spiritual paths, possibly even new career paths. So take the card, already!

Time Is Flying, Friends Are Dying

Midlife crises are an easy target for parody, but let me be clear: true crisis is no synonym for fun. What with the fear and the pain that come with crises, any one of us would be a plumb-fool idiot to go looking for one. And yet! When a big, bad *something* barges into your life un-bidden, what other choice do you have but to deal with it?

I took in a lecture by theologian and author Matthew Fox in the early 1990s, shortly after his silencing by the Vatican ended, and he drew a word image that stays with me still: "Too many of us want to tiptoe *around* the Valley of the Shadow of Death," he said, to a big, knowing laugh. Of course! Who *wouldn't* rather sneak along a narrow (but not too narrow), rocky (but not too rocky) ledge, high above the fray, and never, ever have to experience the pain, the sorrow, the gnash-ing of teeth? Of course, life's not like that. Some-times there's no ledge whatsoever. Or what tiny ledge there is, you can't get there from here, at least not before total chaos reigns.

SCRIBBLES & DOODLES
Cathartic Writing

Talk about the classic! What better use for a journal than to get it all out, what's in your head, your heart, your *spleen*. Any writing implement will do, but consider inks of bile green or raging red. Waste not one moment on how to begin; just hit the page running, and don't stop until the fury passes. *Vaya con Dios, my darling.* May the Force be with you.

The best advice I can offer is to just keep breathing, to take good care of yourself, and to accept people's offers of help. A crisis moment is no time to go hide yourself away, whether in fear or with prideful stoicism; it's a time to reach out, to connect, to take advantage of the fact that *you are not alone.*

Oh, and keep telling yourself, with the wisdom of Friedrich Nietz-sche: "This is bound to make me stronger."

DOC IN THE BOX: *Hang On, Help Is on the Way (Verbal First Aid)*

You come upon a car accident. You're the first one on the scene. What should you do?

You don't have to be a paramedic to help. Simply by offering your calm, supportive presence, you can clear the path to healing. Judith Acosta and Judith Simon Prager, in their book *The Worst Is Over*, offer some simple and powerful techniques, what they call "verbal first aid":

1. Administer physical first aid first. Call 911, apply pressure to bleeding, and so on.
2. Identify yourself and your purpose. "My name is Peggy, and I am here to help you."
3. Touch the victim, if possible. Maintain physical contact if you can.
4. Engage the victim in the process. "Will you give me your hand?"
5. Be realistic and encouraging: "The worst is over. Help is on the way."
6. Distract the victim from pain by helping him or her with visualization. "What is your favorite place? The beach? Okay, imagine you are there now."

These are the basics of a training program for first responders (EMTs and paramedics). But you don't need to go through a formal program. Simply being there, willing to help, *does* help. And remember that the Good Samaritan law is there to protect you from being sued for trying. Take a deep breath, then step up. You *will* make a positive difference.

THINGS TO TRY AT LEAST ONCE

❏ *Quit your job.* Drastic, yes, but sometimes it's the only answer.

❏ *Do some primal screeeeeeeeeeeaming!* (Into a pillow, please, lest your neighbors call the cops.) It's tough on the vocal cords, but some folks swear by it. Others just swear. Loudly.

❏ *Walk off a cliff.* Take a ropes course, and learn to rappel. Once you've descended a sheer mountain face and emerged unscathed, life's little stresses will pale in comparison.

Lose It or *Lose It!*

Nothing is more desirable than to be released from an affliction, but nothing is more frightening than to be divested of a crutch.

— James Baldwin (1924–1987)

I'm just off the phone with my mom. She marked the Big *Eight-oh* last year. "Mother's Day was lovely," she was saying. "You may not believe it, but we didn't drink so much as a bottle of wine!" I do believe it, I told her, though such temperance is still a fairly new development in my once hard-drinking family. Mom comments on it after every holiday nowadays. My guess is that she never thought she'd live to see the day.

Quit Drinking, or Die

This topic is about as funny as a crutch, but let's face it: the "hard stuff" gets harder on us now. Our livers are not as young as they once were, nor are our lungs, coronary arteries, colons, yada, yada. When my brother Sean needed a new liver last year, it wasn't because of alcohol consumption. Nevertheless, his doctors' orders left not a jigger's worth of wiggle room: his drinking days were over.

My husband, Richard, faced a similar ultimatum as he underwent surgery for bladder cancer just a few months later. No one actually uttered the words "Stop smoking, or die!" But they uttered other words that added up the same way. In both cases, these men I love did the hard work of tossing away the crutch. I would gush about how proud I am of them (and grateful!), but it would only make them blush.

Let "It" Equal "Ex"

As a nonsmoking teetotaler, you may be thinking that this Way is not for you. Could be. It depends on what your definition of "it" is. This Way asks you to rid yourself of *whatever* might be stunting your personal growth, lest you lose out on realizing just how great you could be.

Maybe your stumbling block is unrelenting perfectionism, or impatience. Maybe it's a potty mouth or constant sarcasm. Maybe it's a tendency to underestimate yourself. Maybe it's a weakness for gossip or the compulsion to correct people when they're wrong. Hey! Maybe it's that "friend" of yours, the one who treats you so badly.

Whatever "it" is, *lose it*, lest it drive you mad — or worse, into an early grave!

Jack Be Kindled, Jack Be Lit

When I say "drive you mad," I'm not simply being dramatic. Road rage, school shootings: you don't have to look far in our society for evidence of people "losing it." In every case, I suspect a stopped-up energy system. If the chi can't flow, sooner or later, something's got to give, which is why I consider energy blockage a culprit — or at least an unnamed coconspirator — in problems ranging from migraines to murder.

Robert Scaer, MD, in his book *The Body Bears the Burden*, uses the word *kindled* to describe the nervous system that is so overloaded, it's ready to blow. In extreme cases, said blowup could result in catatonia or dissociation. The more common response is rage. The least little spark of annoyance touches off a total conflagration: zero to forest fire in the space of a few quickening heartbeats!

If this sounds at all familiar, if you suspect your own nervous system might be a bit kindled, clear away the combustibles. Take down the stress level. If you possibly can, *lose* (at least for a while) one or two of your life's ongoing to-dos (a volunteer obligation, say, or a weekly social get-together). Accept that the people around you *are* the way they are. Accept, too, that while you are free to make suggestions — even frequent ones — as to how they could improve themselves, *you can never, ever change them*. They've got to do that for themselves.

SCRIBBLES & DOODLES
Resolve and Release
(Rehabituation Ritual)

Keep a "lose it" pad handy for this empowering little ritual: any time you catch yourself "doing it again" (or even *craving* it again) — *It* being whatever substance, behavior, or thought pattern you're in the process of losing — dash off a quick note affirming your resolve to quit, then tear it out and lose it. Scribble, rip, crumple, toss. Just like that. Repeat as necessary — and watch "as necessary" become less frequent!

Don't Lose It — Invest It

Most of all, don't waste your fabulously seismic energy merely blowing your top. What a waste! Channel it into a dynamic work of art or a societal improvement. Pound the earth (garden) or the pavement (run!). Scrub your house till it shines. Take up *cardio kickboxing* — I'm not kidding! You can take out every last one of your frustrations on that 150-pound bag (your perfectly safe, unfeeling, uncaring "opponent"), build your muscles and cardiovascular system in the bargain, and go home feeling as peaceful and benevolent as Mother Teresa.

 DOC IN THE BOX: *What If You Can't Dance the 12-Step?* *(Addiction Recovery Alternatives)*

Twelve-step programs such as Alcoholics Anonymous help tons of people get clean and sober and stay that way. AA alone has over 2 million members worldwide. But many addicts find the first few steps — essentially "I am powerless" and "I surrender my will to a Higher Power" — to be such big stumbling blocks that they'd rather not even try to "do the 12-step."

Luckily, AA and its offshoots are no longer the only choices on the dance card. Here are some other resources to get you started:

- Rational Recovery (www.rational.org) asserts that self-recovery is the most effective path and uses a technique called AVRT® (Addictive Voice Recognition Technique). You can take their course online.
- *The Diseasing of America*, by Stanton Peele, is one of the first books to challenge the concept of alcoholism as a disease and to propose individual responsibility and capability as tools for recovery.
- *The Heart of Addiction*, by Lance Dodes, decries the prevailing view of the addict or alcoholic as weak, shameful, and diseased. He advocates a psychological approach to discovering *why* you gravitate toward an addiction and learning alternative methods for handling helplessness in your life.
- *Mindful Recovery: A Spiritual Path to Healing from Addiction*, by Thomas and Beverly Bien, proposes that addicted people use drugs (or other addictions) rather than explore what hurts, and offers mindfulness as a gentle method for beginning to face the pain.
- Your local community resources. Look to family, friends, counselors, healers, and groups for support. For some people, a familiar, intimate, supportive setting is just the ticket.

Whatever method you choose, once you make the decision to let go of your addiction and move on, you have taken the biggest step, and I salute you.

COOL MOVES
New Moves

"The hardest part about quitting cigarettes" — I've heard this a million times — "is what to do with my hands? What to do with my mouth?" Whether you're quitting cigs, booze, fast food, shopping sprees, or any other "addictive" behavior, identify the physical moves associated with the habit and consciously create different ones. Chew a toothpick. Walk around while on the phone. As you exit buildings, pull out a piece of gum. Challenge yourself to find regular driving routes that lead you nowhere near temptation.

THINGS TO TRY AT LEAST ONCE

❑ *Keep fighting that "losing" battle.* Health benefits accrue even from cutting back. If you fall off the wagon, first congratulate yourself for how long you stayed clean. Then get back on.

❑ *Find your tribe.* Whether it's a 12-step program or some other type of support group, you need not go it alone. Google "addiction support," or talk with your doctor or therapist. And keep searching until you find the group in which you feel at home.

❑ *Lean on your pen instead of your crutch.* Whether you write as part of your recovery work or simply to spew the occasional mean, nasty, ugly, rude, sarcastic, hurtful thing you're just *dying* to say (but can't because you gave all that up), let 'er rip. Your journal can take it.

Paint It Black

Middle age went by while I was mourning for my lost youth.
— Mason Cooley (1927–2002)

*T*here, there, darling, you just go ahead and cry. Let it all out. If it is any comfort whatsoever, you are not alone in your grief. *Lots* of people consider their fiftieth birthday a major bummer. So do what you've got to do, love — here's a tissue. I'll go put on a little music. Maybe lighten the mood?

"It's My Party, and I'll Cry If I Want To"

It's no use, is it? There's just no cheering you up. All right then, let's call this a pity party and really *lean into* the sorrow. Pass the tea and sympathy. Misery loves company. I'm glad you're here. Sit! Sit! Forget the mess. We'll speed-walk later and get our endorphins to give us a lift.

But first, talk. And tears.

Grief *is* the appropriate response in times of loss, and what can I say? Aging brings with it plenty of loss. Others may wonder at your grief, or not even notice it. No matter. If no "company" calls to share in your misery, just pull the door shut and engage in whatever private rituals of mourning feel right to you. Play dirges. Dress in black. Wallow among old photographs. Weep. Wail. Take to your bed.

In Defense of Hibernation

You might think I'm joking about the weeping and wailing, and the taking to your bed. No way! Especially not the bed part. A little hibernating is an excellent way for the body to integrate all the wonderful new habits you're developing in midlife. Besides, if grief has you down, then you may be really, truly, genuinely pooped!

As to weeping and wailing, *well!* Crying Exercise was about the last thing I would've expected to learn in Dahn yoga, steeped as it is in a culture that values (teaches, expects) self-discipline, regimentation, and daily practice, *no matter what*. Nor did Crying Exercise square, in my mind, with Dahn's emphasis on laughter and play. Did I tell you? A common instruction to the Dahnhak newbie is to pretend you're five years old, so as to free yourself to move with childlike enthusiasm, if not quite reckless abandon.

SCRIBBLES & DOODLES
Lay Your Ghosts to Rest

Light a candle, open your journal, and hold a little "writing séance" for your Lost Youth — all of them! The child, the teen, the new college grad, you at thirty, you at forty. Imagine you could sit at a table with the whole gang. Ask each, in turn, about unfinished business. Write quickly. Be the scribe (the court reporter, if you will), and just try to keep up, until each voice subsides. Let them all speak, then — this is important — *let them all go*. Sing a sad song. Blow out the candle.

When You Cry, Make Sound

Oh, but how does a five-year-old behave when life feels miserable? By indulging in a big, fat cry, that's how. And not a quiet one, either.

Indeed, many times they even fake it till they make it — which, incidentally, is the how-to of Crying Exercise, in a nutshell.

Crying is a uniquely human capability and one of nature's greatest gifts to our kind, yet too many of us stuff the gift away, unopened. Don't box up your grief. Don't stick it on the top shelf of a dark closet in a room you never go into. Unpack it! Let it out. No, you don't have to sob loud enough to wake the dead, but do at least give voice to your exhalations. Let them become like soft, little chuckles of grief. And tears! Let them pour down like rain, a real gully washer to carry away the accumulated "vuggum" (as my husband likes to say) from your hibernation within.

There, now! Breathe. S-t-r-e-t-c-h. Have another tissue. There is nothing like a good cry. *Hey!* You about ready for that speed walk to get our endorphins pumping, or what?

COOL MOVES

Statue of Grief

This prayerful pose engages the acupressure points for "letting go." Sit up tall, or stand. Cross your wrists in front of your heart, and bow your head slightly. Spread your fingers, and feel for the nooks where your collarbone meets your shoulders. Apply firm pressure in those nooks with your curved middle fingers. Breathe slowly and deeply for at least one minute. Mindfully release all tight muscles and any sensations of being bottled up. Open, open, open. If tears come, let them. *Behold the crying statue!* You are a miracle.

DOC IN THE BOX: *No Colors Anymore (Depression)*

Are you depressed? Before you say no, consider these questions. Have your sleep patterns changed? Are you sleeping more or less than usual? What about your appetite? Are you eating more, or maybe less? Are you having persistent headaches, stomach problems, or chronic pain? Do you feel tired and slow? Are you drinking more alcohol than usual?

Any yesses in there? You could be depressed. These physical symptoms of depression might be combined with feelings of sadness, emptiness, worthlessness, or guilt. *Or they might not.* Lots of people experience just the physical stuff, at least at first glance.

Midlife is a time of change, change that may include losses. But while loss and grief are normal at this time, depression is not. Common, yes. Up to an estimated 37 percent of people in midlife suffer from depression. But that does not mean it should be accepted as normal. It's no good to feel bad. I urge you, again: if you're suffering, don't settle.

Depression comes in lots of flavors, as does its treatment. Acknowledging symptoms of depression does not commit you to a lifetime of pill popping, unless you choose that. There are numerous nonmedical ways to manage depression. Making changes to your exercise and diet regimens might be enough. Aerobic exercise increases endorphins, the body's natural-high chemicals, and for some people, that's all it takes. Certain foods (see *Potatoes, Not Prozac* by Kathleen Desmaisons) are better for sustaining your mood than others. Staying well hydrated helps, too. Some herbal supplements, such as St. John's Wort, have been shown to improve depression symptoms. And, of course, there are prescription medications, and science has come a long way toward making these effective and user friendly.

Or maybe you just need someone to talk to. A good therapist, counselor, or life coach will listen to your troubles and help you find solutions to your problems. Ask around, or look in the phone book.

It's also possible that your symptoms are due to some medical problem and not to depression at all. Thyroid disorders, for example, are famous for masquerading as depression.

The bottom line here is, if you think you might be depressed, please don't ignore it. Take care of yourself. You deserve to feel good!

∿ THINGS TO TRY AT LEAST ONCE

- [ ] *Pull a Johnny Cash.* Dress in black from head to toe.

- [ ] *Write an "unsent letter."* Write several! A big part of grief can be the things left unsaid, but it's never too late to say them. You can even "send" these letters if you want. Cast them into a fire (safely!), or bury them. All jokes about the "dead-letter office" aside, I don't recommend actually dropping them in the mail.

❏ *Visit a loved one's grave.* How long has it been? Pack some tissues, and pick up fresh flowers on the way. Linger. Speak aloud, if you want. Wander among the gravestones. Do a charcoal-on-paper rubbing of your loved one's gravestone or any inscription you find arresting.

❏ *Throw an ancestor party.* The Pagans call theirs Samhain ("SOW-in," don't ask). Latinos call theirs Día de los Muertos, the Day of the Dead. The Chinese call theirs Qing Ming Jie, Tomb-Sweeping Day. Whatever *your* tradition, celebrate your ancestors!

WAY 42   Make the Call

If you are not already dead, forgive. Rancor is heavy, it is worldly; leave it on earth: die light.

— Jean-Paul Sartre (1905–1980)

To err is human; to forgive, infrequent.

— Franklin P. Adams (1881–1960)

*A*sk any winemaker. The greatest thing about the passage of time is its mellowing effect, and it can work as well on people as it does on fermented grapes. Hotheadedness cools. Opinions, once hard and fast, soften. You come to see that, sometimes, even you can be wrong. No? Well . . .

The Troubles of Two People vs. a Hill of Beans — Who Wins?

Even if you still feel quite certain you were in the right all those years ago, what does it matter now? You're so over it, you tell yourself, yet thoughts of the Other just won't stay buried. Well, with all due respect, *What did you expect*, burying them alive like that?

Pick up the phone, already! In healing rifts, as in making wine, time can only do so much. Until *someone* uncorks the bottle, nothing comes of the magic. Dare to make the first move.

Disconnected or No Longer in Service

It's hard, I know. After all these years, you can't help but wonder: has the other person mellowed, too, or just turned to vinegar?

SCRIBBLES & DOODLES
Take Tough Talks "Out the Front Door"

"Oh, but what to *say*? How to even *begin*?" The dread is pretty universal. Here's a mnemonic device to help you sort through the jumble in your head and move toward active resolution. Let "Out the Front Door" be code for Observe, Think, Feel, Do. Think back on what happened, and answer the following questions. Later, when you make the actual call, think O.T.F.D., and you'll say what you want to say *straight out*, no sweat!

O — "What did I *observe?*" Tell the story from your point of view. (Let *observe* encompass all your senses.)

T — "What did I *think* of what I observed?" What did it mean to you? What conclusion did you reach?

F — "How did I *feel* about it?" What emotions were stirred up?

D — "Now, here's what I'd like you (or us) to *do.*" What needs to happen to set things right, as far as you're concerned?

Either way, take heart! Your very attempt at reconciliation sets healing in motion. Even if the conversation crashes and burns, given today's telecom technologies and a tiny bit of luck, it's a good bet "the party to whom you were speaking" at least snagged your call-back number. This is progress.

Success! The Call Goes Through!

Maybe there wasn't even a fight. It could be you have entirely different reasons for feeling reluctant to make the call. That was Linda's story, decades after her parents put an end to her first serious relationship.

"This person was the one who taught me to love," Linda said of her former boyfriend, "the first person who was a true soul mate, the person I thought of daily for thirty-plus years." Cut to fiftieth-birthday time. Linda was a few months past hers, when, on *his*, she had "one of those conversations" with some girlfriends, "the kind where you tell it all, and they tell you where you went wrong and how to fix it." So Linda took her friends' advice and called her long-lost beau.

"We talked for two hours, his voice shaking, my hands shaking," Linda said. Of course they resolved to remain in contact, and they have ever since — never crossing the line of propriety, mind you, because of their current committed relationships. "It's just gratifying to know we've both made a comfortable place in each of our lives for the other," Linda concluded. "That fiftieth-birthday phone call was one of the best things I've ever done for myself."

Play "Radar Love"

You don't need a letter or call! If you're truly ready to mend a rift, and your attempt to reach out gets rebuffed, just keep beaming that sentiment "out there." Let your heart be like a beacon, sweeping the sky and pinging the depths, relentlessly pulsing its two-part message: "I forgive and seek forgiveness."

And then, dear one, move on! Leave it to time to work more of its magic. Mellow out, have some wine. *Cheers!*

COOL MOVES

The Calm before the Call

Feeling nervous? Take fifteen minutes or so to center yourself. Choose the phone location where you feel safest, and position a comfortable chair just the way you like it. Place the person's phone number next to

DOC IN THE BOX: *A Change of Heart (The Effects of Forgiveness)*

Holding on to anger is like grasping a hot coal with the intent of throwing it at someone else; you are the one who gets burned.
— The Buddha (563–483 BCE)

Forgiveness isn't always easy, but if you have been on either end of the process, you know how good it can feel. "Forgiveness has a way of cutting through anger, anxiety, and depression, and restoring emotional health," according to Robert Enright, psychologist and academic pioneer in the study of forgiveness. Forgiveness is not the same, he points out, as condoning, excusing, forgetting, or even necessarily reconciling with the offender. But by forgiving, the injured individual refuses to let anger and resentment prevail, and as a result he or she feels happier and calmer. There are whole forgiveness institutes and projects designed to foster and spread this charitable act for the betterment of individuals and society. See, for example, www.theforgivenessproject.com.

The physical effects of forgiveness are less understood, but that is shifting. Turns out a "change of heart" does exactly that. Letting go of resentment and anger lowers blood pressure and pulse, reduces physiologic stress responses, and (big surprise) increases positive emotions. Not only that; forgivers sleep better, are more energetic, have fewer physical symptoms, and use fewer medications. It's hard to argue with that kind of data.

You can even see forgiveness in action. Scientists are mapping the location of forgiving thoughts and emotions in the brain. When a person experiences forgiveness, a functional MRI, which shows changes in blood flow, lights up areas in the frontal cortex (where decisions are made), the limbic system (the seat of the emotions), and other areas identified with social cohesion.

Perhaps one day the research will expand to include such momentous concepts as forgiveness by groups of people, or even nations. In the meantime, if you do your best to let go and forgive, you'll be a happier and healthier you.

the phone. Go put a nice, full teakettle on the stove, over a low-lit burner, and toss a chamomile teabag into your favorite mug. While you wait for the water to boil, sit or stand comfortably, bow your head slightly, and make your hands into soft fists, with fingers folded loosely over thumbs. Relax your body and gently drum your "pinkies" against your lower abdomen, with alternating strokes in an easy tempo. Breathe evenly. Let your mind grow quiet. (O.T.F.D. will be there for you, don't worry.) When the kettle sings, rub your belly a few times in a clockwise direction, pour your cup of tea, and go sit comfortably in the chair by the phone. Sip your tea as you mentally rehearse your O.T.F.D. talk once through. Pick up the phone and dial. Notice that you are the very picture of calm, cool, and collected.

∿ THINGS TO TRY AT LEAST ONCE

❑ *Call a truce!* If at first you don't succeed, take to your journal and "visualize peace" in exquisite detail. Be the diplomat! Hammer out a "peace treaty" that allows everyone to save face and feel good about burying the hatchet — talking points for the next attempt.

❑ *Have a reunion for two.* And if at first you *do* succeed, by all means, celebrate! Go slowly. Smile a lot. And hug. Don't be afraid to cry, and to express your sorrow for the lost years.

❑ *Make a round of calls.* Estrangement is not the only bugaboo that keeps us apart. Use the fifty-two weekends of your fiftieth year to call friends you haven't talked to in years. Enjoy, enjoy!

Way 43 Party Hearty

W
A
Y

As for me, except for an occasional heart attack, I feel as young as I ever did.
— Robert Benchley (1889–1945)

Wheresoever you go, go with all your heart.
— Confucius (551–479 BCE)

Now we come to the tried-and-true, the time-honored tradition, the Way of all Ways. *Kick out the jams*, my friend. It's party time!

Of course, the possibilities are endless. So, what'll you have? A big bash or a table for twelve? Uptown or down-home? Catered or potluck? Live band or recorded music? Whatever you decide, make it the kind of party *you* want.

If you don't want a surprise party, say so. Emphatically. But just in case, do your Chief Loved One (and yourself!) this favor: answer just one purely hypothetical question: "If you absolutely *had* to have a birthday party — just because — what kind of party would it be?" Again, be specific. (Don't say I didn't warn you.)

Surprise!!!

Now you may well ask, "Shouldn't it be party *hardy*?" As in, "When it comes to partying" (hooking your fingers through your suspenders and talking grufflike) "*I'm* still hardy! Count me in." And naturally, in most people's minds, "party hardy" means "get really drunk!"

Now, I like to party as hardy as the next guy, but my emphasis here really is on the Heart. What say you to entering your fifties *heart* first? Party *heartily* — and not just on special occasions, either. At any given moment, on any given day, look around. There's always something to appreciate about life. Adopt "celebratory" as your personal default setting. Relate always from the heart, and see what happens!

COOL MOVES

Heart Opener Stretch

"Can you touch your elbows together behind your back?" This stretch is a great one to suggest at parties. Whether your tastes run to pecs or *pechugas*, it's a hoot to watch people try! Okay, so maybe you'd prefer to take your turn in the privacy of your own home. That's fine (though, you've got to admit, at our age, there are far worse things than having our *pechugas* ogled!).

SCRIBBLES & DOODLES
"Thank You So Much for the Lovely Gifts"

Write a cordial (if longish) thank-you note about your life at this milestone. Whether to God, your parents, or "life, the universe, and everything" doesn't matter. Take stock of your life's bountiful gifts, and express your gratitude in earnest. Can you list as many as fifty things for which you're thankful? Scrutinize your life. Really relish it.

Stand with arms straight and your hands clasped behind your back. Lift your clasped hands upward while rolling your shoulders back and tucking your shoulder blades inward. Keep your arms straight, your head up, and your chin tucked, and keep your palms together as much as possible. Hold the stretch for a slow count of ten. Repeat often throughout the day. Someone wants to ogle? Let 'em.

DOC IN THE BOX: *Gail's Story (Women and Heart Disease)*

Cresting the hill on her daily walk in the Phoenix desert, my friend Gail noticed that her chest felt a little strange. Fifty years old and fit, she attributed the spreading warm sensation to her recent bout with bronchitis. But because it happened again another day, she mentioned the symptoms to her doctor a few weeks later, at a routine checkup. He recommended some tests. Long story short, two weeks after that she was recuperating from quadruple bypass surgery, sobered by her brush with mortality.

Gail had been exercising daily for twenty years, partly because she knew her genes were stacked against her in the heart department. Good thing, too: the doctors told her if she hadn't done that she might have been dead ten years earlier. As it was, they caught it while her heart muscle was still healthy. When I met her, seven years later, she looked like a forty-five-year-old with a chest scar and was back to daily hikes with her dogs.

Heart attacks are the number-one killer of women and men in this country. But it's well known that women's symptoms tend to be different from men's. Unfortunately, there is no typical female heart attack picture. The typical male suffering a heart attack experiences crushing chest pain radiating to the jaw or left arm, sweating, nausea, and trouble breathing. Gail had none of that. Yet her heart was screaming for blood in its own way. If she hadn't paid attention and gotten it checked out, I never would have had the pleasure of that green-eyed grin. That was my take-home message, a variation on my "listen to your body" mantra: *don't ignore any unusual symptoms.*

Gail told me her take-home message from the experience was to be even more careful with her body. She declines the hollandaise sauce and chooses the fruit plate instead. She exercises daily and has lost what little extra weight she had. She is determined not to go through the ordeal of surgery again, and I believe she won't. This go-get-'em gal will still be outhiking me when she's ninety!

∿ THINGS TO TRY AT LEAST ONCE

- ❑ *Go for your heart's desire.* Obviously! Why wait?

- ❑ *Open, open, open.* If you've been an emotion-stuffer all these years, your heart may have constricted beyond mere bottleneck stage; by now it could be cinched tight, like a drawstring bag!

Work it back open. Practice generosity of spirit. Give of your time. Give of your *self*. Especially with your forgiveness, be as generous as the party host whose hospitality knows no bounds.

❑ *Party hearty*. The sharp-eyed reader will have noticed many a party idea throughout this book. Here are fifty more: birthday party (the classic, with hats and noisemakers), soiree, potluck, picnic, dinner party, dessert party, wine tasting, kegger, office party, cookout, tea party, coffee klatch, family reunion, "New Year's" party (in the sense that a birthday starts a new year), BYOB party, happy hour, cocktail party, backyard barbecue, coming-out party, bridge party, costume party, slumber party, pizza party, theme party, season-finale party, "after" party (after whatever you like), private party, dance party, Tupperware party, surprise party, ice-cream social, victory party, quilting bee, Hollywood-style "wrap" party (you are so done with your forties — that's a wrap!), Superbowl party, just-the-girls (or guys) party, street party, knitting circle, black-tie event, book-swap party, silly-hat party, manicure/pedicure party, spa party, skydiving party, block party, campout, bacchanal, sailing party, live-music extravaganza, and Croning (see the next Way).

Respect Your Elders

Sure I'm for helping the elderly. I'm going to be old myself some day.
— Lillian Carter, in her eighties

On his hundredth birthday, comedian George Burns quipped, "I was always taught to respect my elders, and I've now reached the age when I don't have anybody to respect." He may have been right, as far as that goes. But this Way calls on us to respect not just our elders but our own elderhood as well.

Congratulations, You Have *Arrived*!

Not quite ready to don the mantle of elderhood? I don't blame you. One should never be hasty about serious rites of passage, and that's what I'm talking about here. Elderhood is — or (*sigh*) should be — a highly revered status, precisely because of the connection between "older" and "wiser." If you, in your heart of hearts, do not yet feel like elder material, take your time. There's plenty in this chapter about respecting your elders in the traditional sense, too, à la good old George Burns.

One of these days, though, when you can sense it in your bones, you'll know yourself to be an elder. And when such self-recognition and acceptance dawn on you, it's time for a most auspicious rite of passage. For women, such a ceremony is commonly called a Croning. For men, the generic elderhood ceremony will do, unless of course you want to name it something fancy. In any case, while an elderhood ceremony can take any form you'd like, for it to be truly ceremonial, you'll want to go to some lengths to make it sacred.

"Hey! Who You Calling a Withered Old Hag?"

If you believed most dictionary definitions, you'd think a crone was nothing more than an ugly old woman. Not true. A crone is a *wise* older woman, and wise as she is, she has reclaimed the word for her own, transforming society's put-down into a title of honor.

I was barely thirty when I attended a Croning for the first time. The invitation was worded thus: "Bring something you've treasured for a long time but are ready to release . . . something deeply meaningful to you, that you'd like Judy to have as she journeys into her wise Crone years."

Call me kooky, but I saw that word *wise* and thought immediately of my two wisdom teeth, the ones that had been knocking around in a jewelry box for years. Why I said yes when the dentist asked if I wanted them is beyond me. I mean, show-and-tell is no place for reruns.

Remember, way back in Way 10, when I suggested that you "imbue a common thing with special meaning, and let that be part of the gift"? Well, here was my chance.

Things Handed Down

Only later did I laugh, embarrassed, at the irony of giving an "old crone" (or even a *new* crone) a couple of spare teeth! Ha! But Judy laughed, too, and still does, she says, just to think of them. Not quite a year after her Croning, as I prepared to move away from the city where we both lived, Judy opened *her* jewelry box, reached past my old teeth, and selected a beautiful necklace to bestow on me in parting.

SCRIBBLES & DOODLES
Pay Homage

Make a quick list of the most important elders you've known. Then, next to each name, write the most important thing you learned from that person. Finally, choose one name from the list, and write that person a letter, paying your respects. If he or she is "still with us," as they say, send the letter! Remember, the Internet has made it terribly easy to track down a person's current address. Good luck!

Things handed down are always a treasure, but you know what they say: the best things in life aren't *things*. Then again, neither are most of the treasures we've received from our elders.

COOL MOVES
"Roll Tape!"

Collect an oral history from an older member of your family. Get his or her permission first, of course, then fetch the video camera, the tripod, and maybe a lamp or two, and get everything set up before you start your elder talking. Be sure to test your equipment before you start, and even play a bit of tape back so you can know for sure you're getting both good picture and sound. Don't ask too many questions, and make the ones you do ask open-ended: "Tell me about..." Then just sit back and let your revered elder tell the story.

DOC IN THE BOX: *Protect Your Elders (Home Safety)*

Now or soon, you may be facing a decision about long-term housing for the elders in your life. In the meantime, at least make sure their current digs are as safe and easy as possible for them to navigate:

1. Turn the water temperature down to avoid burns.

2. Get rid of loose rugs, or put a backing under them, to avoid falls.

3. Throw away piles of magazines and newspapers. They're a tripping hazard and can completely impede paramedics with a stretcher.

4. Install night lights, and brighten up existing bulb wattage. Get a phone with large buttons and numbers, and magnifiers for reading.

5. Change the stove over to covered gas or electric. It's easy to get burned leaning across a forgotten open gas flame.

6. Go through the fridge from time to time, tossing out old food. You might want to do this when they're not around, to avoid conflict.

7. Add a seat extender to raise the toilet seat. Install bars next to the toilet and in the tub or shower. Bring in a shower chair, and replace a regular showerhead with a flexible hose head.

8. Make sure medication bottles do not have child-proof caps. Get a pill organizer, or make one using egg crates and a permanent marker.

9. Encourage your elders to get their ears cleaned regularly. If they wear hearing aids, encourage them to wear them all day long, even if they live alone. Consider voice enhancers on the phones, and flashing lights for the doorbell if needed.

10. Trim toenails regularly to avoid tripping and trauma. This is especially important if the elder is diabetic, and can be done by a podiatrist or manicurist if desired.

11. Social interaction is good for health too. Get elders a pet. From a bird in a cage to a dog to walk, an appropriate pet adds meaning, companionship, and longevity. Children and elders are a wonderful combination for all concerned, if you can find a way to make that happen. Senior centers are another good option. And of course, your visit will brighten anyone's day.

12. Prepare for emergencies. A "panic button" worn around the neck can alert local emergency services in case of fall or injury. Or sign your elders up for a daily check-in service, by button or phone. Post a short list by the phone of friends and family to call for help.

13. Reach out for helping hands. The local senior center often has a list of volunteers that will go to the home and do minor repairs, build wheelchair ramps, and so on. Or try the office of Senior Affairs, Meals on Wheels, or your local senior organizations.

∿ THINGS TO TRY AT LEAST ONCE

❑ *Share your youthful vigor with a much older friend*. Get together regularly.

❑ *Ask an older person's advice about a vexing situation*. Really listen to what he or she has to say.

❑ *Pay your respects*. Why wait until they're your *final* ones? Go see your oldest living friends and relatives. Call first, of course. Older folks tend to expect such a courtesy.

❑ *Say it loud: "I'm elder and proud!"* Celebrate by shopping antique row and selecting a beautiful relic at least twice as old as you.

❑ *Visit an old-growth forest and commune with the ancients*. Tree huggers, collectively, take a lot of ribbing. But come face-to-face with a two-thousand-year-old sequoia, and even you may feel moved to demonstrate your respect for such elder strength and beauty. Go ahead, hug that tree! Bring plenty of friends if you plan to get your hug all the way around that redwood's twenty-three-foot base. Or simply hug as much of it as you can.

❑ *Share a movie night with Mom and Dad*. Here are a few titles in the aging-folks milieu, should you care to go in that direction: *Tuesdays with Morrie*, *In the Name of the Father*, *On Golden Pond*, and *Cocoon*.

45 Respect Your Youngers

The young do not know enough to be prudent, and therefore they attempt
the impossible — and achieve it — generation after generation.
— Pearl S. Buck (1892–1973)

Behold the power of me!
— Derek S. Davidson, age 5

*L*ike many of our generation, my friend Kevin became a parent
for the first time in midlife. He'd been adopted as a baby, so
forty-nine years later, as he held his newborn daughter for the first time,
he was really blown away to realize he was meeting his first blood relative — at least the first he would ever get to know. *Kaitlyn!* Just minutes old, and already she was working gigantic wonders in the lives of
others!

Older Isn't the Only Brand of Wiser

Ten winks later — you know how it goes — Kaitlyn is out of kindergarten and, according to Kevin, still blowing her papa's mind regularly.

"On Mother's Day," Kevin exclaimed, "I couldn't believe this! I
was helping Kaitlyn to bed, and all of a sudden, she got really sad, almost teary. So I asked, 'What's wrong, honey? You look so sad.' 'I am,'

she said, 'I'm thinking of your mother. Not Grandma, but the other one. Her heart must be breaking today.' *That's* what my child said to me, on Mother's Day, about my birth mother: '*Her heart must be breaking today.*' Can you believe that? I mean, she's five!"

I believe it. I've been known to drop a jaw myself on occasion, while in the presence of pint-sized gurus. Out of the mouths of babes, ain't it the truth? We hear their take on things and glimpse the world through their eyes.

Got to Get You into My Life!

Maybe your children are older than Kevin's little Kaitlyn. It could be that the "youngers" around your house are grandkids. Or maybe there are no youngsters and never were, because you steered decidedly clear of parenthood. So it is with our generation. Offspring-wise, we're all over the map — including, notably, the brave new world of extreme maternal age, in which our sisters, helped along by medical science, give birth well into their fifties, even sixties.

But parenting, per se, is not the point. Even children are not the point. The point of this Way is to respect — that is, listen to, take seriously, maybe even mentor — those who are younger than you. Period. Become a Big Brother or Big Sister, for instance, or earn a teaching credential and go inspire the next generation of your industry's leaders! Many state universities or colleges have fast-track programs for professionals who want to take their expertise into the classroom.

Of course, you need not go through official channels to find youngers to respect. Just look around. Reach out to the new associate at work, who was hired straight out of college, the guy who's just brimming with ideas and idealism. Get to know the young couple down the street, the first-time homebuyers still paying down college loans even as they sock away a few bucks each month, into college funds for their kids — *you* remember how it was! Or how about that lonely kid shooting hoops out on the street every evening? Any of them could become pals of yours, and if they did, my guess is it would be to everybody's benefit.

(If the youngster is of minor age, please be sure to meet the parents.)

SCRIBBLES & DOODLES
Scribble. Doodle.

Feeling a little antsy? Wishing you could go outside and play, but you can't because you've got to work? Squeeze in even five minutes' worth of this colorful, tactile activity to burn off some of that playful energy. Any old collection of markers or crayons will get you by, but, *please!* Treat yourself to a set of oil pastels, those rich, almost chalklike "crayons" that rub right down to a nub if you tear off their paper wrapper and keep scribbling long enough. For paper — your "canvas" — choose the most luxurious, textured, and richly hued you can find. Shut the door. Turn off the phone. Scribble. Doodle. Enjoy.

Finnegan, Begin Again

Debbie was over forty when she took up competitive figure skating. She had not set out to do so — indeed, she had never even ice-skated before — but a gift of lessons came to her one birthday and, *boom*, she was hooked. *Boom*, she was also falling down a lot. But no matter. Soon she was flying (and falling) and spinning (and falling) and loving every minute of it. (The upside of all those spills, she reported, is that her bone density is excellent, despite her having "practically every risk factor for osteoporosis.")

DOC IN THE BOX: *Back to Basics (Feldenkrais)*

Nejem's back hurts almost all the time. Several years ago he suffered an injury that caused one of the discs between his vertebrae to get squeezed out so that it presses against a nerve root. As a doctoral candidate in economics, Nejem can't afford to be snowed on pain meds all the time, so he uses every other trick in the book. Feldenkrais is one of his favorites.

"I even get out of bed differently now," Nejem told me enthusiastically. "It's like learning how to move like a child again." In fact, that's precisely what it is.

Moshe Feldenkrais was a Russian-born physicist, engineer, and martial arts expert. After suffering crippling injuries to both knees, he applied his ample intelligence to his own rehabilitation. He studied human development and neuro-physiology in detail and watched how babies and children move when unencumbered by culture (before they start hearing "stand up straight" and "tuck that tummy in"). Feldenkrais observed that when we are all very young, we move the same way, laying down basic neural pathways to educate our nervous system. As we get older, we add extra, what he called "parasitic," movements, that give us each our unique style but also can get us injured. He went back to the beginning to retrain his body to move more efficiently, like a child's. And it worked.

Feldenkrais teaches how to "*not* do," explained Nejem. "It's all about not wasting effort. I have learned to ask myself, 'What is the *easiest* way to do this?'" The method has given him a set of tools to help prevent back spasm, as he has retrained his neuromuscular system to move with less effort. His body is more relaxed, organized, and flexible as a result of the training he received. His mind is calmer, too, partly owing to the meditative techniques involved.

The Feldenkrais method is taught in group classes and individual sessions. Most students of Feldenkrais have been previously injured in some way, but the technique has also been used by athletes and actors to improve their grace and flexibility and to help prevent injury. Learn more at www.feldenkrais.com.

"I felt like a kid on the ice that first day," Debbie, now fifty-one, re-called in an email. Almost everyone else in the rink with her really was a kid. "Many would help me here and there. I have to laugh when I re-member the time this tiny girl about six or eight years old confidently advised me on how to improve my axel — which I *still* can't do. But she gave me all these pointers and kept telling me, 'You can do it!'"

Just like a kid, isn't it, to be so sweet and encouraging?

COOL MOVES

Kid for a Day

Spend a day off pretending you're a kid (even if only in your mind), maybe the kid you used to be, maybe a different kid. Ride bike, skip rope, shoot marbles. Go see if one of the neighborhood kids can come out to play. The kid's parents, too? Sure, why not! Let the kid call the shots, and you grown-ups, please be sure to warm up and stretch before things even *begin* to get raucous, *do you hear me?* By the same token, listen to your body, and let it tell you when playtime is over.

THINGS TO TRY AT LEAST ONCE

❑ *Be always a beginner.* "In the eyes of the beginner, there are millions of options," says Wayne Dyer. "In the eyes of the expert, there are only one or two." Strive to be as open-minded as the wide-eyed child.

❑ *Party like a preschooler.* Get a moon bounce, party hats, blowers, and piñata, and invite only those young-at-heart friends you know will participate! Feeling a little out of practice at throwing kids' parties? Search online or at your local library. Better yet, ask a pint-sized partier!

❑ *Tune in to kids.* Want to hear what's *really* on the minds of some of today's young people? Google "youth radio," and listen in.

46 Touch & Glow

Touch your customer, and you're halfway there.
— Estée Lauder (1908–2004)

*W*hen I read a few years back that Japanese scientists were developing a soft, padded robot to staff nursing homes, I just about screamed. Named Riman, the prototype could lift as much as seventy-seven pounds (guess that leaves *me* out, phew!) and — get this — had a library of several dozen smells it could recognize, including urine, so they — these padded robots staffing the nursing homes of the future — would know when to change a diaper.

Hello? Earth to humankind! Come in, humankind!

If Riman is what's happening in Japan, long lauded as a culture in which the elderly are deeply honored and valued, then heaven help our species. What are we, nuts? Where's that good ol' "bar sinister" when you really need it? Because, obviously, someone should have circle-slashed that project file early on. *Bad idea! Next?*

Skin to Skin: Accept No Substitutes!

Much has been made of the fact that babies, especially fragile preemies, show "failure to thrive" without human contact. *As if they're the only ones!* Yes, we adults have grown big and strong, most of us, so you're not likely to find us literally dying from isolation. But if you've chosen a lifestyle of the touch-me-not variety, permit me to suggest that you're not fully living either. Gentle, loving, respectful touch — between friends and family, of course, but also in the larger world — is one of *the* greatest things about being human.

Don't be a crab in a shell. Reach out and touch someone! Like the song says, "ya gotta have friends," and by now there's even research to back it up: the more you stay connected with loved ones, the more likely you are to live a long, healthy, happy life. In fact, the more the merrier: the higher your number of well-in-touch friends, the greater the health benefits of friendship. It's that limbic brain of ours, don'tcha know!

"My Hands Are Healing Hands"

Your hands are healing hands, too, or can be. According to many holistic traditions (such as Dahnhak, which I practice), any of us can learn to sense the flow of chi within our bodies and even to direct our energies toward others, to assist them in their healing.

I was a brand-newbie to Dahnhak, no more than one healing lesson into my training, when an opportunity arose for me to "try my hand" at it. My daughter Maya, ten years old at the time and a healthy skeptic of all things woo-woo, came down with a tummy ache so severe she was begging me to take her to the emergency room. I tried to explain how miserable ERs are: that you can sit there all day, with no place to lie down. Still, she fixed me with a wild gaze and insisted she was dying. I had to do something!

Love or Doubt, You Choose

"Where mind goes, energy follows." My single lesson in Dahnhak-style healing taught me to begin with a choice: to heal or to doubt. Remembering this, I faced my daughter *without a doubt.* I sat right up close to her and poured my healing energy into her — or at least my love. Focusing on the "fire in my belly" (the *dahn-jon* energy center), I felt the buzz of chi flow in my hands as I rested one lightly on her belly and held one of hers in my other. Then we just breathed together for a while. A long while.

Suddenly, a doubt intruded. "I should have looked up the acupressure points for settling the stomach," I muttered.

"Don't go!" she practically wailed, as her eyes flew open and she clamped my hands in place with sudden strength. So I refocused on healing and stayed. After about half an hour, my daughter opened her eyes again — not so wild this time — and started talking about other stuff. I could tell she'd turned a corner. Her color was better, her skin no longer clammy. A few minutes more, and the episode was over. My girl popped right out of bed, and there was no more talk of tummy aches.

SCRIBBLES & DOODLES
Stressed? How Can You Tell?

When you hear yourself say that you're "sad" or "excited" or "stressed," go to your journal and ask: "What *physical sensations* am I feeling, which I have *labeled* as 'sad' (or 'excited' or 'stressed')?" This body-centered question is the starting point for Somatic Experiencing, a trauma-healing modality developed by Peter A. Levine. And the "Cool Move" that follows is the perfect next step.

For Doubting Thomas, Touching Was Believing

Skeptical? Let me read your mind: the tummy ache was nothing more than gas pain and would have resolved itself even had I done nothing. You may be right. But no one can deny that my daughter was comforted by her mama's loving touch.

Let me be clear about this: had my daughter's condition persisted, and certainly had it gotten worse, you can bet we would have sought professional medical care. As it turned out, however, all she really needed was a little hand-holding while she endured the scary pain of a bad stomachache.

Touch brings comfort. That's really all I'm saying.

Now, if we could all just allow our own touch to convey with mindful sincerity, through each moment of human contact, the intentionality of our love and concern for others — just think! What a wonderful world it would be.

 **COOL MOVES**

Shake Free of the Freeze

We all know about "fight or flight," but did you know that we mammals have a third such emergency response? It's "freeze." Playing dead out in the wild is typically a ruse of short duration, but too many of us modern-day humans seem stuck in freeze mode. We're painfully aware of our stressors but, in many cases, feel incapable of doing anything about them. Car-wise, this would be like jamming one foot on the gas pedal and the other on the brake. The hard-revving emotional energy

DOC IN THE BOX: *Healing Hands, Take Two (Therapeutic Touch)*

"Therapeutic touch" is a misnomer. Practitioners of this modality don't even touch you. Well, mostly they don't. They hold their hands two inches away from the surface of your body and move them up and down, sensing the gaps and blocks in your energy field. Then they open themselves up to the "universal energy" source. Healing energy comes pouring through them into you. Your gaps are filled, your blockages unblocked, and voilà! You're healed!

I sound like I'm poking fun, but I'm just indulging my inner drama queen. In fact, therapeutic touch is serious business. And effective, too. It comes in several variations, including Reiki, Polarity, and Healing Touch, and dates as far back as we can see into history, to ancient distance healers and layers on of hands. The modern renaissance is usually credited to Dolores Krieger, a nursing professor at New York University. She and healer Dora Kunz trained hundreds of nurses in this technique in the 1970s. Word spread rapidly. The story goes that in one hospital in the Midwest, after most of the nursing staff attended a Healing Touch workshop, their outraged boss posted a sign on the door: "There will be no Healing in this hospital!"

Therapeutic touch is used to decrease pain, speed healing, and alleviate anxiety. There are many other claims, as yet not subjected to scientific scrutiny, but with tons of anecdotal support.

One fascinating study was done with surgical wounds. Patients who thought they were having their skin's "biopotential" measured stuck their wounded arms through a hole in the wall into an adjoining room. Half of them got therapeutic touch, the other half got an empty room. The wounds were carefully measured over time, and the "touched" beat the "untouched," hands down, when it came to healing. And these test subjects didn't even know what they were receiving!

Therapeutic touch is now used in hospitals across the country, as well as in practitioners' offices. Check your local listings.

can't get away, so it too freezes in place, right there in your bodily tissues. To begin the thawing process, try this.

When you identify a bodily sensation that means (to you) "upset" or "stressed," sit quietly and focus on the feeling. Mentally follow it. Move intuitively, answering your body's urges to stretch or squirm or "shake it off." Now purposefully shift your gaze to a pleasant sight, even simply your favorite color in the room. *Stay curious* about your body's sensations. Chills, radiating warmth, and tingles are all positive signs of "thaw" and can be helped along by rhythmically tapping or sweeping down the body with your hands.

⌇ THINGS TO TRY AT LEAST ONCE

- ❑ *Get in touch.* Make time to deepen your friendships. Your health depends on it — and so does your friends'.

- ❑ *Go get touched.* Massage is not a luxury, but a health basic. Go to it as religiously as you do your annual check-up — only way more frequently! Also, tip your hairstylist handsomely for extra-long, scalp-caressing shampoos. They relax the whole body.

- ❑ *Feel your edges.* In the shower, linger over your own shampoos, too, and use a washcloth, body brush, or pair of nubby shower gloves to buff every inch of yourself. Afterward, take a l-o-o-o-n-g moment to rub oil or lotion into your hard-working feet.

47 Love, Love, Love

Love is not blind — it sees more, not less. But because it sees more, it is willing to see less.

— Rabbi Julius Gordon (1897–1954)

*A*h, love! So much has been written about this most ardent emotion — from sonnets to self-help books, from Shakespearean tragedies to situation comedies. Oh, don't get me started: love is resplendent. Love is eternal! And yet — *and yet!* Have you noticed? Seems no matter where you go, the world could always use a little more of it.

Okay, a lot more.

A Love So Nice You Have to Name It Thrice

"One love," some call it, but I prefer the repetitive and emphatic: Love, *Love*, LOVE!!! Some say it's all we need. Love, *Love*, LOVE!!! Can I put three exclamation points in a row? For *triple-strength* love, you bet I can.

Love comes in lots of flavors and colors: romantic, motherly, brotherly, you name it. While Peg and I wish you all kinds, now and forever,

I'd like to focus here on the kind of love I truly believe holds our planet's ultimate salvation. This is the love Jesus showed in communing with lepers and the Buddha showed in literally sweeping his pathway while he walked, lest he step on any *insects*, for heaven's sake. So smitten am I with this kind of love that I capitalize it: Selfless Love for the Unlovable.

"We Loved That Car!"

True story. Our car got stolen last year. At the time we bought it, fully twenty years ago, the New Car Purchase was a lifetime first for both my husband and me, so you can understand: we loved that car. Had even named "her" Stella, for her starlit, dark-as-the-night finish. She'd grown old and rusty, but wouldn't you know it? After three years spent keeping the ol' girl together with little more than sweat and duct tape, my husband had finally taken her in for some serious fix-up. Nearly $1,500 and exactly six days later, she was gone. *Stellaaa!*

Loving the Lovable: Where's the Challenge in That?

Excuse my language, but I was pissed. My life was already stressful enough without having to add my husband's commute — times two — to Mom's Daily Delivery Service. If you've ever been ripped off, you know the impulse is to curse the thief, to wish him or her ill. Well, I'm no saint, you can ask anybody, but

SCRIBBLES & DOODLES
Love Letter to Big Brother

Speak truth to power, yes, but do it ever so lovingly. Thich Nhat Hanh, the Zen Buddhist monk whose name is practically synonymous with peace education, has observed that "people in the peace movement can write very good protest letters, but they are not so skilled at writing love letters. We need to learn to write letters to the Congress and the President that they will want to read, and not just throw away." Write such a letter. Write several! Don't know your current elected officials' names and/or mailing addresses? Finding them on the Internet is a snap!

for some reason, that night as I lay in bed, I decided to do just the opposite. I imagined the sort of circumstances that could bring a person to steal a car; I allowed myself to feel compassion for the thief. Thoughts of the money we'd just sunk into the car brought a fresh flare of anger, but I did my best to quell it.

"Whoever you are, *wherever* you are," I whispered into the darkness, "you take good care of our Stella, will you?" My pillow was damp, but hey. It was just a rusty, old car. We'd live.

"It's a Sign! And There It Is Again!"

I'll admit, even I was surprised when the car was found, perfectly intact, not a scratch on it. What's even more surprising is that the car got stolen *again* — and came back to us *again*. It was waking déjà vu, and I took the cosmic one-two of it as divine proof: *Forgiving the thief was the right thing to do.*

Another epiphany: it's okay to love a car, but it's more profoundly rewarding to love a fellow living being, even one you may never meet. And yes, even one who's done you wrong.

Catch Love Fever, and Pass It On

The problems of poverty, homelessness, and discrimination demoralize all of us, not just those personally beset by such problems. Love may not be all we need to solve them, but without it, I dare say there's not a snowball's chance in hell that we ever will.

What goes around comes around, but that's just for starters. In this day and age, what goes around also has the potential to "go viral" — around the world in eighty nanoseconds! So it's more important than ever to radiate love, ever and always. Call me Pollyanna (I've been called worse). Just radiate love, would you? Triple-strength Love, *Love*, LOVE!!!

COOL MOVES
Just Beat It

Here's a real heart-pounder. I've discovered the most divine pleasure, in the unlikeliest of forms, namely, loofah on a stick. As you may know, a loofah is an especially fibrous type of gourd whose insides, once dried, make for a better shower scrub than, say, a washcloth or sponge. But on a stick? *Be still my heart!* The most divine pleasure I get from mine is from *whacking* myself on the back with it, right at heart level, right where the physics of the arms crisscross the physics of the spine. Right there! *Whack, whack, whack.* That loofah on a stick is my newest, coolest tool in a lifelong quest to untie my own personal Gordian knot. Get one for yourself, and groove to the *beat*! You will Love-*Love*-LOVE it!

THINGS TO TRY AT LEAST ONCE

- ❏ *Cut out fifty paper valentines*, mark each one with love, and give them out freely, even to people like the grocery clerk, the gals at the health club, and the UPS guy. (*Especially* the UPS guy!) Notice how good you feel. Notice how good *they* feel!

- ❏ *Be ecumenical.* Whether or not you're a churchgoer, work to bridge religious, cultural, and economic differences in your community.

DOC IN THE BOX: *True Love (Tom and Carolyn's Story)*

My cousin Tom has always been a cutup. When we were kids he'd make us laugh until our sides hurt with his silly sayings and made-up words. When he met and married Carolyn, we all knew it was a perfect match. She's as fun-loving and wacky as he is. Like a couple of puppies forever on the frolic, all those two ever do is laugh.

A couple of years ago, Carolyn got breast cancer. *Now what?* I worried. How would this loony twosome cope with a serious medical situation? An excerpt from one of Tom's reports to the family will give you a glimpse.

> Carolyn's progress is encouraging. She had "armpit surgery" on Wednesday to remove the tissue including and around the site of the tumor under her arm. As Carolyn recovers from her operation, we've been handed yet another unexpected opportunity to extract humor from what seems to be an unending series of uncomfortable realities. This time, it's the "J. P. [Jackson-Pratt] drain." (For those with weak stomachs, we don't recommend snacking as you peruse this next passage.)
>
> The J. P. drain seems to have been lifted from the pages of a nineteenth-century medical text in the same chapter as leeches and bleeding out evil humors. The device consists of a tube exiting from the wound under the arm with a clear plastic bulb on the free-swinging end designed to collect and display for your pleasure the most disgusting substances you don't want to admit were ever a part of you. Every few hours, you and your trusty spousal assistant are encouraged, nay requested, to attend to this device. As you chant in unison the mantra "in sickness and in health," and while wishing the bulb was opaque, detachable, and disposable, you squeeze its contents into a measuring cup whose gradations are so faint that they must be read with the aid of a flashlight, thereby illuminating the glory of the aforementioned contents so they shine like a neon sign blinking out the message "Cancer is not for wimps."

Too often we think of "true love" as some kind of starry-eyed fairy tale come true, with white picket fences and sugar-coated "happy-ever-afters." In my opinion, that's not even close. True love is slogging through the muck with someone, loving her when she is unlovely, holding his hand when he cries.

True love is what Tom and Carolyn have. May we all be so blessed.

❏ *Give free hugs.* Yes, I mentioned Juan Mann's video earlier (www.freehugscampaign.org), but I really, *really* don't want you to miss it. ("Juan Mann, One Love" — get it?) *Go viral with it!* Send the link to everyone you know. Oh, and don't for-get to hug someone today, someone you've never hugged before.

❑ *Check out www.gratefulness.org.* Clear your afternoon; you're going to want to dwell.

48 Launch Your Legacy

What do I have to say to the universe? A soul ought to have something to say to the universe if it's going to be immortal.

— Sheri S. Tepper

The best example of legacy thinking I've ever heard is embodied in this single sentence, from the Great Law of the Iroquois Confederacy, passed down by oral tradition since the 1100s, and first written down in the 1880s: *In our every deliberation, we must consider the impact of our decisions on the next seven generations.*

Seven! Imagine! The question is not, "How will this affect our children?" but, "How will this affect our children's children's children's children's children's children's children?" Now *that* is inspired thinking!

Madam chairperson? I move that we adopt the Iroquois Confederacy's brilliant idea as Team Human's guiding principle for the stewardship of Planet Earth, starting immediately. Do I hear a second?

One Generation Plants the Trees, Another Enjoys the Shade

This very day, on CNN.com, in the "funny news" category, come two divergent headlines that perfectly illustrate my point: "Man flies 193 miles

259

SCRIBBLES & DOODLES
Epitaph

In Way 38, I suggested you write your own obituary and/or eulogy. Now how 'bout getting down to hammer and chisel? What do you want carved on your gravestone — or in the annals of history — beneath your name? Remember: hammer-and-chisel work is hard, so keep it ultra-short.

in a lawn chair" and "Jury duty excuse: 'I'm a racist, homophobic liar.' " *Oh*, the stories these two will be able to tell their grandkids! One dreamed as a boy of flying away on a fistful of balloons — then grew up and did exactly that. The other, when a call came to give a little something back to society, decided the only thing he'd give it is the finger.

To each his own, I guess. So it is with legacy.

How Do *You* Want to Be Remembered?

Imagine the news headlines that would do you proud (not to mention your family, your community, your world). Then get busy! Have I said "tick-tock, y'all" lately?

No launch window stays open forever.

What will be your life's crowning achievement? Dream big! Set your sights on the stars and your Life's Greatest Work on the launch pad. Your fiftieth year is an auspicious moment — and could very well be the ideal time for 3, 2, 1: *blast off!*

Leave Your Mark

Deep-pocketed philanthropists sometimes create (and/or burnish) their legacies by paying huge sums in exchange for what the fund-raisers of the world call "naming opportunities." You may not recognize half the names you see spelled out on shiny, new hospital wings and the like, but I hope you'll join me in thanking the Named Ones nevertheless.

Blessed are those who share their personal wealth to improve the lives
of the masses.

... Or Don't

At the same time, let us sing for the unsung hero, the anonymous $100
donor, the helpful stranger who refuses payment. There's a creed
among nature lovers: "Take only photographs; leave only footprints."
Better yet, some say, stay on the path, lest your footfalls trample the
flora and fauna.

New hospital wings are all fine and good, but let us bless those, too,
whose idea of bettering the planet is to preserve what natural beauty
and resources it has left — for our children's children's children's chil-
dren's children's children's children.

COOL MOVES

Liftoff ... We Have Liftoff! (Chakra Chanting/Soul Launcher)

Named for the Sanskrit word for "wheel," the chakras are a progression
of seven energy vortices, arranged along the body, in front of the spinal
column. Spiritual maturation is said to proceed upward through the
chakras, from the base of the spine to the top of the head. Here's a little chanting meditation to open up your chakras and launch your spiritual energy heavenward.

Sit comfortably, with beautiful posture and eyes closed. Breathe
easily, focus inward, and feel your "root chakra" resting on the floor (or
chair). Spend about three minutes chanting the name of each chakra, in

turn, beginning at the bottom, as shown in the table below. Don't worry about proper pronunciation; just sound out the name (either Korean or Indian) as it rolls off the tongue. Vary your pitch and tempo, until it feels right. Sense the vocal vibration in your body (and, if you want, rhythmically pat yourself) at the level of the chakra whose name you're chanting. Soften. Breeeeeathe. Enjoy!

Chakra	Location (centered in body)	Dahnhak name (Korean)	Sanskrit name (Indian)	Color (vibration)
7th	Top of head (straight up from ears)	Bek-hwe	Sahasrara	White
6th	"Third eye" (between eyebrows and up a half inch)	In-dahng	Ajna	Purple
5th	Throat/thyroid glands	Chun-dol	Vishuddha	Blue
4th	Sternum/center of chest	Dahn-joong	Anahata	Green
3rd	Upper belly (midway between the navel and sternum)	Joong-wahn	Manipura	Yellow
2nd	Lower belly (two to three inches below navel)	Dahn-jon	Svadisthana	Orange
1st	Perineum (in front of anus)	Hway-um	Muladhara	Red

DOC IN THE BOX: *This Above All (Ethical Will)*

In Shakespeare's *Hamlet*, Polonius gives advice to his son, Laertes, who is boarding a ship, perhaps never to return. At the end of this famous speech, he says, "Neither a borrower nor a lender be; / For loan oft loses both itself and friend, / And borrowing dulls the edge of husbandry. / This above all: to thine own self be true, / And it must follow, as the night the day, / Thou canst not then be false to any man."

In *Tuesdays with Morrie*, Mitch Albom's favorite professor passes along his life-learned wisdom in a series of meetings at the end of the professor's life. This true story became a best-selling book and movie.

Both these stories demonstrate the concept of ethical will. Formalized, on paper, an ethical will (sometimes called a spiritual-ethical will) is a way of putting your values into words to be passed along to your descendants. Creating an ethical will is a wonderfully enriching process, for you and yours, a golden opportunity to clarify and express the very essence of you. I urge you to do it. Several books, as well as moderated workshops and study circles, can walk you through the process (see Resources, below). This is an in-depth and fascinating multistep process, involving lots of introspection and writing.

You begin with researching your ancestors and family history, most likely discovering people and stories you never knew before. You contemplate their lives and explore their connection to you. Don't know your blood ancestors? Use your adopted ones, or anyone of influence from the past. Then you turn your attention to the present, delving into your own experiences. You do lots of thinking and directed writing, detailing your thoughts and values about money, friends, family, work, and so on. Finally, you focus on the future and the message you want to pass along. When you have completed the process, you choose which of your writings to share, how, and with whom.

Now is the dawning of your life's second half. What better time to set to work on this gift of incalculable and timeless value: your spiritual legacy!

Resources

- Barry K. Baines, MD, *Ethical Wills: Putting Your Values on Paper*, 2nd ed. Cambridge, MA: Da Capo Press, 2006.
- Rachael Freed, *Women's Lives, Women's Legacies: Passing Your Beliefs and Blessings to Future Generations*. Minneapolis: Fairview Press, 2003.
- Jack Riemer and Nathaniel Stampfer, *So That Your Values Live On: Ethical Wills and How to Prepare Them*. Woodstock, VT: Jewish Lights Publishing, 1994.
- www.ethicalwill.com, www.yourethicalwill.com, www.womenslegacies.com

⌇⇢ THINGS TO TRY AT LEAST ONCE

❑ *Get your "legacy" juices flowing.* Read biographies or autobiographies of people who changed the world. Or Google a name you see on a building in your town and read up on a local benefactor.

❑ *Buy a brick* or some other relatively affordable "naming opportunity" at the nonprofit organization of your choice.

❑ *Trace your genealogy.* (Going to www.familysearch.org is a great place to start.) If you turn up something fascinating about any of your ancestors, do some more digging! Honor their legacy by finding out as much as you can. Assemble an ancestral scrapbook to share with your children and your children's children.

❑ *Troll your local toy store for stomp rockets*, rocket balloons, one of those ground-to-air/rubber-band-slingshot sorta deals — anything you can launch. Or leave the launching to the professionals and go watch an actual space launch.

Channel the Divine

> When you hold in your heart a great, righteous purpose, and you dedi-
> cate everything to achieving that dream, Heaven and Earth are moved to
> work on your behalf.
>
> — Ilchi Lee

*R*emember *Ghost*, the Hollywood weepie in which Demi Moore enjoyed one last dance with her dearly departed sweetie, Patrick Swayze (never mind that he was in the body of psychic medium Whoopi Goldberg at the time)? Okay, that is not the kind of channeling I'm talking about here. Nor am I necessarily discussing séances, speaking in tongues, drug-induced hallucinations, or, for that matter, *Invasion of the Body Snatchers*!

To me, channeling the divine simply means allowing the All Powerful to work through you. Call it God if you want. Just please don't define *divine* too narrowly, because, even capitalized, the Divine means different things to different people. And that's a beautiful thing.

Hallelujah! Hallelujah!

Messiah. Every time I hear even the least little bit of it, I marvel at the fact that George Frederic Handel wrote the *whole thing* in twenty-four

SCRIBBLES & DOODLES
Automatic Writing

Stream-of-consciousness writing is tough to do well. It's hard to keep up, and most of the words are drivel anyway. Plenty of times in this book, I've urged you to "keep your pen point moving." Paradoxically, now that we come to the Automatic Writing exercise, I will not. Instead, I ask that you *stay thy pen*, until it feels as if the thing wants to move itself!

Sitting comfortably in a darkened room, hold pen and journal at the ready, and close your eyes. Relax, let go, breathe. Strive for Silent Mind. Keeping your eyes closed, write Silent Mind across the page several times. Slowly, s-l-o-w-l-y. As thoughts barge in, allow them, but don't follow them. Note them on your page with just a word or two, as if giving them a title. Incline your mind toward that which is *beyond* words — colors, shapes, sensations — and note whatever comes, again in the sparest terms. Remain inwardly still and watchful for a good long while, jotting the occasional note, until the sitting feels complete. To return to full wakeful consciousness, count slowly to ten, out loud, while moving and stretching your body. Return to your notes, immediately and again later, and ask yourself: "What came through?" Write in your journal about it.

days flat! Forsaking food, sleep, and (I'm guessing) a fair degree of personal hygiene, he composed and wrote like a man possessed. He never once left his room, and a friend who paid him a visit during those three and a half weeks found the composer sobbing uncontrollably. But come the twenty-fifth day, Handel rested, and there in his midst lay 260 sheets of manuscript constituting nothing less than a sacred choral masterpiece for the ages.

"Whether I was in the body or out of my body when I wrote it," Handel remarked later, "I know not."

Okay, now *that's* what I'm talking about!

Don't Think You Have It in You?

Very few of us are on a par with a genius the likes of George Frederic Handel, of course. Luckily, divine intervention is not reserved exclusively for geniuses, musical or otherwise. What's more, it's available to you whether you pray to God in a church or temple, honor the Mother Goddess in a forest ritual, or go fishing alone in a boat on a river. No matter who you are or where you may be, if you open yourself up to it, the Divine will find you.

Know that you are connected to everything and everyone in all of creation and throughout all of time, and that the Divine will find you. Consciously avail yourself of That Which Is Greater Than You, and the Divine will find you. Forget whether you have it *in* you. The question is whether you can allow it *through* you.

God's Saxophone

Open. That's the best way to channel the Divine. Be open-minded, openhearted, physically unblocked, and earnestly open to serving the common good. *This is not about you!* When you channel the Divine, you are not the piper but the pipe, and the music that comes through you plays for All. So be egoless, humble, and studiously unattached to outcomes. Just keep your metaphorical instrument ready, willing, and *open*. Because you never know when the likes of God might happen by, in the mood to blow a most righteous tune.

 COOL MOVES

Channel Opener (Bowing Meditation)

Begin by warming up and stretching. The "all the way down" and "all the way back up" of this meditative form of chi manipulation will feel loads more glorious if you'll take the time to prepare your Vessel.

Stand on a mat or carpeted floor, with your feet parallel and

DOC IN THE BOX: *Crouching Turtle, Praying Mantis (Tai Chi)*

In a misty riverside park at dawn, old men in baggy Mao suits move arms and legs in solemn synchrony. Downtown in the YMCA gymnasium, kids in sweat suits do the same slow-motion dance. On a college campus, a lone dude in dreads bends and swoops as students swarm by: These are some of the many faces of tai chi, or "meditation in motion."

Originally a Chinese martial art, tai chi has become a widely popular exercise form, practiced around the world. One story has a feeding stork as the inspiration for the fluid, full-body movements, and if you've ever seen it, you can understand why. Slow and graceful, tai chi is designed to exercise the body, focus the mind, and facilitate the flow of chi.

There are many health benefits to be gained from this beautiful activity. Tai chi gently works your muscles, but enough to improve cardiovascular fitness and lower blood pressure. It loosens your joints, which can alleviate symptoms of arthritis. A degree of balance is required to perform the deliberate positions and change smoothly from one to the other, and the more you do it, the better your balance and coordination will be. Folks who practice tai chi have fewer falls, which can mean huge health savings in old age. Also, since it is a weight-bearing exercise, it puts good stress on the bones, keeping them strong and delaying osteoporosis.

The best thing about tai chi is that anyone can do it, be they old, young, stiff, or limber. Any age, any body type, any fitness level. It's safe, it's noncompetitive, and you don't need any special equipment. Like any kind of physical activity, it will improve your general health and physical functioning, reduce anxiety and depression, and improve sleep. Besides, it's fun to do and lovely to watch.

To locate a class in your community, contact your local health club, senior center, or wellness center.

hip-width apart, your hands in a prayer position at your heart, your body relaxed. Tuck the chin slightly, close your eyes, center yourself, and breathe naturally. Be of humble mind as you let your prayer hands separate, drop outward, and move in large arcs until palms meet once more overhead, then bend elbows and draw an "energy line" downward to heart level. This full-circle gesture symbolizes the gathering of yin and yang energies, from Earth and Heaven in turn, and drawing both into your body. The circle also symbolizes holism, seeing all parts of Creation as connected. Hands to heart once more, give a half-bow, right yourself, repeat the circular gesture, and begin full bows, as follows.

Bend forward at the hips until you form an angle of 90 degrees or deeper. Ease yourself down onto all fours and flatten the tops of your feet against the mat (soles upward). Shift your hips back onto the heels and touch your forehead to the earth. Plant your elbows and raise your palms heavenward. Linger a moment in the depth of your bow. Back up on all fours, reposition your toes against the mat, and use your hands as needed to regain a standing position. If you're counting your bows; that's "one." Continue bowing — slowly for meditative purposes, quickly if you'd like a more cardio-conditioning workout. Finish with Three Special Bows, taking all the time you'd like to honor (and chant one long, sustained note of the word) *Chun* (Heaven), *Ji* (Earth), and *In* (Human Being). Rest, empty-headed, in Corpse Pose afterward (see Way 38).

⁄⁊ THINGS TO TRY AT LEAST ONCE

❑ *Pull a Handel!* See what sort of masterpiece you can produce in twenty-four days flat. Whatever your medium of choice — poetry, life drawing, carpentry, culinary arts, landscaping, *whatever* — aim high! Push hard! Stay open, and let divine inspiration guide you.

❑ *Notice what channel you're tuned to.* One sure way to block the Divine from channeling through you is to have your personal antenna habitually tuned to such mundane distractions as TV. Keep an honest accounting of your screen time (computer, too) and, for extra benefit, keep notes on the programming content. Is it comedy, shoot-'em-up chase scenes, the Weather Channel, *what?* When the week is up, pore over your log, crunch some numbers, maybe even make a pie chart.

❏ *Don't channel hop — channel stop.* Next week, turn the TV off entirely. Or at least reduce your use! Then make a second pie chart, so you can see how many hours of your life you reclaimed. Continue, week by week, to redirect your personal antenna away from vapid pop culture. Tune in, instead, to... *everything else* that's out there waiting for you!

Leave 'Em Laughing

Just go up to somebody on the street and say, "You're it!" and just run away.

— Ellen DeGeneres

*I*nner jogging. That's what Norman Cousins called laughter. If his name rings a bell, it's probably issuing from wherever he is in the afterlife, the "go" bell to set him off on yet another gut-buster of a training jog — by which, of course, I mean he's stringing up his favorite Marx Brothers film on the old projector in heaven's rec room, preparing to laugh his fool head off. Again!

Still the Best Medicine, Bar None

Your parents may remember Cousins as a political essayist, but what put him on our generation's map was his medical memoir, *Anatomy of an Illness*. While coping with a debilitating form of spinal arthritis, Cousins discovered that one good hour of laughter would bring him several good hours of pain relief. In the decades since he wrote the book, scores of medical studies have borne out his findings. Indeed, by now scientists have even quantified laughter's health benefits.

Oh! And speaking of quantifying things...

"How Many Adults with ADD Does It Take to Screw in a Light Bulb?"

"I know! Let's go get a snack!"

Hoo, that's a good one! Now, before anyone with ADD writes me an angry letter, let me put big finger-gesture quotation marks around this: *I know, too,* and would be happy to jump up and go get a snack with you. Must be why I find the joke so freakin' funny.

Come *on*! It's got to be one of later life's greatest gifts — that eventually, finally, *hopefully,* even the touchiest among us learns to laugh at the bozo in the mirror. "Aw, shucks!" mopes the clown with the painted-on frown, "Fifty years old, and *still* not perfect." Care to join me in a deep, audible sigh? What else you gonna do?

Long and Loud and Clear

Laugh, dear heart, while the mornings of your life still dawn. Spaniards of yore got it exactly right when they came up with their word for smile: *sonrisa.* Isn't that almost too breathtakingly beautiful to believe? The very dawning of happiness: *sonrisa!*

Fascinating fact: even a *fake smile* has been shown to cause measurable improvements in well-being. Try it! Light up your face right now with your biggest, brightest, most convincingly happy face. Put a twinkle in your eyes. Show us your pearly whites! Now, tell me: Are You Feeling It?

This is like push-starting a car, I swear. Give a good, hard, sustained *shove* to those parts of yours that naturally "bust a move" during rollicking good times, and guess what?! The limbic brain automatically gives a little spurt of joy. Give your smiling parts regular, daily practice, practice, practice, and who knows? You might just get your happy juices to flow all the time, like milk and honey.

Tough Crowd!

In case we haven't managed to get you laughing yet, Peg and I, I'm going to throw down a gauntlet here! Shortly before you and I were born, a linguistics professor named Howard L. Chace wrote the book *Anguish Languish*, in which he recounted many familiar "furry tells" in words that *almost* sounded like the right ones. Though this 1956 book is out of print, you can read Chace's "Center Alley," "Ladle Rat Rotten Hut," and many other furry tells at www.justanyone.com/allanguish.html, and I challenge you read even one of them, out loud and in its entirety, *with a straight face*. If you can do that, dear reader, then I'm afraid your laugh muscles may have atrophied. Get help! Call a twenty-four-hour laff line. Google "jokes." Get thee to a comedy club, stat! Or go out for a "chuckle latte" with friends.

What's a chuckle latte, you ask? Listen, if you gotta ask, that's a sure sign you need one. Too much

SCRIBBLES & DOODLES
"Scrub Bull Sand Oodles"

Try your hand (and head!) at Anguish Languish. Like the crossword puzzle in Way 16, this fun word game helps keep the brain sharp, whether you're "encoding" or "decoding." Take a verse you love, or one of your most dearly held affirmations about how great it is to be alive, and rewrite it using different words, so that it *looks* totally different, but when you read it aloud, it *sounds* almost the same. Then strike up an email exchange (or several) in this "languish." You and your friends will all end up "role Incan duffle oar!"

seriousness can be toxic, you know, *seriously* downgrading your quality of life.

Do I Need to Tickle You?

Now, see, were I there in your midst, I could offer resuscitation. I can usually make enough of a singing, dancing fool of myself to get a laugh. Failing that, I could always try tickling you. With permission, of course.

Alas! You are there, I am here, and our fun together is nearly at an end. I leave you, then, to goose your own giggle-maker, by whatever methods you may choose. Just one more for the road, okay?

A shaman, a high priestess, and a secular humanist walk into a bar. Bartender says, "What *is* this, some new kind o' joke?"

Okay, that's it. Now finish up and get out of here. You've got the whole rest of your life waiting for you out there. Go live it.

Go live it *up*!

 COOL MOVES

Pick a Finger, Any Finger

This is another one to do with a friend. (Little kids love it!) You first. Extend your arms straight out in front of you. Rotate them so your thumbs point down and your palms face outward. Now cross your arms at the wrist, keeping elbows straight, and put your palms together. Clasp your hands. Then bend your elbows and pull your clasped hands down, under, and through, ending up with elbows down and hands up under your chin, still clasped, with thumbs away from you. Now ask your friend to point at (but don't touch) one of your fingers. *Raise that finger!* Did you get it on the first try? The second? Third? Go ahead and laugh at yourself. Then swap places, and laugh some more.

DOC IN THE BOX: *Laughter Heals!*

It's a medical fact: laughter is good for your health. Not only does "inner jogging" count as aerobic exercise, but those aerobically contracting abdominal muscles also serve to massage your intestines, improving digestion. When you "bust a gut," your brain releases endorphins and other neurochemicals, which dampen pain and boost immunity. And we all know that comic relief soothes tensions and improves relationships. See? With laughter, it's all good!

This is one of those things where a little is good but a lot is a *lot* better! It's impossible to overdose. In fact, just *guess* how much laughter we need? How many times a day should we laugh to maximize our health, well-being, and productivity? Five? Ten? Ha! Guess again. The answer is *two hundred* times a day! That's once every five waking minutes we should snicker and snort!

And are we getting our daily dose? Not even close! The average American fits in a paltry six to eight hoots a day. Pathetic! And when you consider that most children laugh all day long, well, you know how averaging works: some Americans must not be cracking a single smile in a day. That's worse than pathetic; it's downright health-threatening!

So, how are you going to up your chuckles? Well, you could always take after my Granddaddy Price. An avid fan of Norman Cousins, and a firm believer in the health value of laughter, Pop treated himself to a daily chortling constitutional. What a kick! There he'd be, a bent but sprightly old man, stumping down a country road all alone, white hair flying, hee-hawing at the top of his lungs. It was easy, he said. Once he got started, the cackles just kept coming. Pop lived to be ninety-six years old.

Whether you "pull a Pop," share jokes with a friend, or just make funny faces at that bozo in the mirror, please do find the humor in your life and tickle that funny bone! At least two hundred times a day. Doctor's orders!

〰 THINGS TO TRY AT LEAST ONCE

☐ *Get ready to laugh.* When you *really* need a laugh, you'll be in no mood to figure out where to find one. So write your Laugh List now. Think of the giggle-inducers that never fail you, be they snapshot, movie, website, goofy dance, or outrageous hat. Even better: make this a group exercise, sort of a "shared hilarity" brainstorming session.

☐ *Incite a laugh riot.* Mark your party invitation "gag gifts only." Then prepare for the onslaught of whoopee cushions, squirting lapel flowers, handshake buzzers, and the like. Oh, and the black balloons, the denture cream, the adult diapers, and so on. Hold your party at a comedy club. Or, if you're thick-skinned enough to take it, stage a roast, with you as the proverbial "roast beast"!

☐ *Listen to hilarious music* — not just lyrically funny, but also the kind with hilarious instrumentation: Captain Beefheart, Frank Zappa, Sun Ra, and PDQ Bach for starters.

☐ *Stage a Laughdance Film Festival: A Norman Cousins Memorial.* Plan a comedy-movie marathon fit to make a certain angel bust a gut, even as it leaves your earthly guests "role Incan duffle oar."

Acknowledgments

From Sheila

Maybe I should just go ahead and thank everyone I've ever met who has had a shaping influence on me! Every teacher, every librarian.... But as it was in the beginning, so shall it be in the end: we promised you a book you could actually lift, so let me be swift in noting the notables, with great love and deep thanks:

Martin Goldsmith, who through his own authorly example tipped the Magic into motion, on October 12, 2000.

Colleen Anderson, who the very next day brought the Answer to my doorstep, barely an hour after I'd jotted the Question, and Michael Davis, who "channeled" the Answer in the first place. I proclaim these two wild, wonderful West Virginians the godparents of *Fifty Ways to Leave Your Forties*. Blessed be!

Diane Arnold, for helping out in every pinch; Gina Pera, for early editing, when the gigantic genie was fresh out of the bottle; Lindy Gold, for such rock-solid belief in me; and the good people — all volunteers — at SouthWest Writers, whose annual contest gave this book footing, then legs.

Judy Reeves, for early raves, enduring friendship, and a foot in the door at New World Library. Further thanks to Judy, and to journal-process teachers Joan Crone, Joyce Chapman, Tristine Rainer, and Kathleen Adams, for teaching me and untold numbers of others so much about personal writing.

Georgia Hughes and Vanessa Brown — editors extraordinaire! — VB for getting us started and GH for getting us to finish! An ocean of thanks to New World Library's entire Dream-Come-True Crew, with special thanks to Mimi Kusch for her masterful copyediting; to Mary Ann Casler, for designing the coolest book cover on the planet; to Tona Pearce Myers for the gorgeous interior design; to Kim Corbin and Munro Magruder for their marketing flair; and to Kristen Cashman for dotting every *i* and crossing every *t*. A personal note of appreciation to publishers Marc Allen and Shakti Gawain, for imbuing New World Library with such a human heart. Thank you, to say the very least.

Subject-matter experts Suzanne Kryder, Bhanu Joy Harrison, and neurologist Joanna Katzman for (gently) crash-coursing me on, respectively, breath work and meditation, Somatic Experiencing, and brain plasticity. So cool to have such brainy friends! Ditto about my early Everywomen — Judith Fein, Tuko Fujisaki, and Mary Bokuniewicz.

Dawn Rose, of the Vision Re-Education Center, in San Diego, for teaching me to see properly (among so much more) and for allowing me to share some of her healthy visual habits in these pages.

Dahn master Sun Lee, for her infinite patience and good humor with me and my "lot-a-lot" of energy; and Dahnhak founder Ilchi Lee, for bestowing on the modern world a most life-enhancing and healing gift.

Peggy Spencer! Oh, my stars, talk about gifts! I wasn't even looking for a coauthor, but suddenly there she was. And not a moment too soon, since it was clear by then that the birthing of this book would require the help of a medical expert. My deep gratitude for Peg's countless contributions extend to her family, each member of which helped.

All of the authors who have taught me so much, as well as the many people who shared their midlife stories with me. In addition to individuals already mentioned, these story sharers include: Kevin Tucker, Lynne Hunt, Janine Wilkins, Stephanie Robey, Holly Finstrom, Alexa Winchell, Sue Winder, Debbie Leung, Drs. Chris and Joe Adducci, Kathy Lord, and Thomas P. Martin, as well as several people who chose to remain anonymous.

Others who helped, in one way or another: Michael Larsen, Joe Dorner, Barbara Leviton, Deborah Hoffman, Sara Otto-Diniz, Marilyn Abraham, Bill Thorness, Chandra Watkins, Jeff Katzman, Maria Stewart, Anna Ortega and Gerry Greenhouse, Leah Leyva, Michelle and Chelsea Otterness, Mes Amis Teahouse, Nancy McGough, Preston Matthews, Stephanie Freeman, Yvonne Courtenaye Brown, Peggy Hessing, Paul Ingles, Val Talento, Marianne Powers, Sue Mazzone, Sara McClure, Ginger Miles, Deborah Begel, Maria Haak, Scott Cleere, and (may they rest in peace) Lesli Pippin Fisketjon and Rick Martinez.

Mom! (aka Lorraine Key) — for my life, my sibs, my everything! *But mostly just for being there and being you, Mom.*

My siblings, Scott, Mike, Pat, Kathleen, Sean, Theresa, and Maureen, and their families — all brilliant, each unique. (Answer to the obvious question: I come between Sean and Theresa, the two who share a liver and an amazing story.) Special thanks to Kathleen Key-Imes, the very picture of hard work in the service of others; and a shout out to Dad, the late James G. Key, who had something to do with my writing chops.

My extended family — honorary sisters Susan Shepler and Connie Sass, and my in-laws, the Joan and Dick Towne family — whose love, patience, and generosity know no bounds. Either I had some awesome marriage karma coming into this life, or there's going to be hell to pay in the next one! Special thanks to Anne Towne, an angel on earth.

David and Steve Gordon, for the *Sacred Earth Drums* that kept me writing (Sequoia Records, 1994).

Napoli Coffee, for many a caffeine-fueled work session; and everyone at the Rocky Mountain Biological Laboratory, in Gothic, Colorado, for hosting us on two gloriously productive writing retreats in the high-elevation woods. Almost heaven!

Google, we'd have been lost without you — and probably *still* not finished.

Last, but most, I thank the Key-Townes, because it really did take a family to write this book. That my push to finish would coincide with my husband's cancer diagnosis and treatment, the very moment when he and our children needed me most . . . well, that just goes to show you: life is big! Maya, Sayre, and especially Richard, you absolutely amaze me. Thanks, you guys.

From Peggy

First and foremost, unending gratitude to Sheila Key, for generously inviting me to join you on this project and giving me the opportunity of a lifetime. Your skill and energy continually inspire me. Words do not suffice.

Deepest thanks to my family — Paul, Serena, and Derek — for your patience and support, and to Sheila's family for the same. To my parents and sisters for your encouragement. And posthumous gratitude to my grandfather Steven M. Spencer, longtime science writer for the *Saturday Evening Post*, for your example and your genes.

Thanks to Carolyn Spencer, Tom Spencer, Gail Newman, Nejem Raheem, and Billy Burgett for generously sharing your stories, and to geriatric nurse practitioner Deborah Anaya, for help with the Elders chapter.

Thanks to our friends at the Rocky Mountain Biological Lab. And extra special gratitude to everyone at New World Library. You are the cream of the crop!

Acknowledgments of Permissions

Grateful acknowledgment is given to the following:

Throughout the book, we have used material based on the practice of Dahn yoga with permission of BEST Life Media. For more information about Dahn yoga, please visit www.dahnyoga.com. For more information about Ilchi Lee, founder of Dahn yoga, please visit www.ilchi.com. For more books on Dahn yoga, please visit www.bestlifemedia.com.

Way 6: Portion of Kent Judkins's letter to the editor of *Time*, reprinted with permission.

Way 18: Excerpt from *Write It Down, Make It Happen: Knowing What You Want — And Getting It!* by Henriette Anne Klauser, PhD, copyright © 2000 by Henriette Anne Klauser, PhD, reprinted with the permission of Simon & Schuster Adult Publishing Group.

Way 24: From *Healing Visualizations* by Gerald Epstein, MD, reprinted with permission of Bantam Books, a division of Random House, Inc.

Notes

In the notes below, DIB stands for "Doc in the Box."

Way 2. Love Thy Body as Thyself

Enjoy your body: Mary Schmich, "Advice, Like Youth, Probably Just Wasted on the Young," *Chicago Tribune*, June 1, 1997.

I hope you're saving up for new ones: National Center for Health Statistics: www.cdc.gov/nchs/fastats/insurg.htm and American Academy of Orthopedic Surgeons: www.aaos.org/Research/stats/Hip%20Facts.pdf.

Dahn yoga (aka Dahnhak), a modernized version of an ancient Korean holistic-health program: Ilchi Lee, *Human Technology: A Toolkit for Living* (Sedona, AZ: Healing Society, 2005).

DIB: American Society of Plastic Surgeons: www.plasticsurgery.org.

Way 3. Don't Let Gravity Get You Down

Generally, we aren't aware of nerve decay as we get older: Chris Crowley and Henry S. Lodge, MD, *Younger Next Year: A Guide to Living Like 50 Until You're 80 and Beyond* (New York: Workman, 2004), 182.

283

Way 4. Get Your Motor Runnin'

Meridians consist of pathways: Ilchi Lee, *Brain Respiration: Making Your Brain Creative, Peaceful, and Productive* (Sedona, AZ: Healing Society, 2002), 51.

DIB: Harvey B. Simon, MD, FACP, "Diet and Exercise: Exercise," ACP Medicine Online 2002 (WebMD, Inc.): www.medscape.com/viewarticle/535416.

Way 5. S-t-r-e-t-c-h I-t O-u-t

DIB: Jesse C. DeLee, David Drez Jr., and Mark D. Miller, *DeLee and Drez's Orthopaedic Sports Medicine*, 2nd ed. (Philadelphia: Saunders, 2003), chap. 1.

Way 6. Run for Your life

A good set of feet can take you anywhere: Kent Judkins, letter to the editor, *Time Magazine*, September 11, 2006.

Way 7. Pause

DIB: The Boston Woman's Health Book Collective, *Our Bodies, Ourselves: Menopause* (New York: Touchstone, 2006); Christiane Northrup, *The Wisdom of Menopause: Creating Physical and Emotional Health and Healing during the Change* (New York: Bantam, 2001).

Way 8. Play Ball!

DIB: U.S. Preventive Services Task Force, *Screening for Prostate Cancer, Recommendations and Rationale* (Rockville, MD: USPSTF, 2005).

Way 9. Eat, Drink & Be Wary

DIB: Centers for Disease Control and Prevention, Division of Bacterial and Mycotic Diseases, *Escherichia coli* 0157:H7: www.cdc.gov/ncidod/dbmd/diseaseinfo/escherichiacoli_g.htm.

Ricki Lewis, "The Rise of Antibiotic-Resistant Infections," *FDA Consumer Magazine* (September 1995): www.fda.gov/fdac/features/795_antibio.html.

Way 10. Take a Load Off Fanny

DIB: Chris Crowley and Henry S. Lodge, MD, *Younger Next Year for Women: A Guide to Living Like 50 until You're 80 and Beyond* (New York: Workman, 2005).

Way 12. Take the Waters

And it doesn't take much dehydration for a body to suffer the effects: Yoram Epstein and Lawrence E. Armstrong, "Fluid-Electrolyte Balance during Labor and Exercise: Concepts and Misconceptions," *International Journal of Sport Nutrition* 9, no. 1 (1999).

Way 13. Spurn Your Bra

DIB: Center for Disease Control and Prevention, "Breast Cancer Trends" (Division of Cancer Prevention and Control, National Center for Chronic Disease Prevention, and Health Promotion, 2007): www.cdc.gov/cancer/breast/statistics/trends.htm.

Way 14. Keep on Rockin' Me, Baby

DIB: AARP, "Sexuality at Midlife and Beyond: 2004 Update of Attitudes and Behaviors": www.aarp.org/research/family/lifestyles/2004_sexuality.html.

Way 15. Please Make a Note of It

DIB: Sara M. Mariani, MD, "The Biology of Memory and Learning," *Medscape Molecular Medicine* 6, no. 1 (2004): www.medscape.com/viewarticle/469464.

Way 16. *Fuhgeddaboudit!*

We experience resistance when we try renaming: Ilchi Lee, *Brain Respiration: Making Your Brain Creative, Peaceful, and Productive* (Sedona, AZ: Healing Society, 2002), 146–47.

DIB: *Crossword Wizard 2.0 Software for Windows and Macintosh* (San Anselmo, CA: Cogix Corporation): www.cogix.com.

Way 17. Go with the Flow

In his book Flow: Mihaly Csikszentmihalyi, *Flow: The Psychology of Optimal Experience* (New York: Harper & Row, 1990), 5–8.

DIB: FamilyDoctor.org., "Urinary Incontinence: Embarrassing but Treatable": http://familydoctor.org/online/famdocen/home/women/gen-health/189.html.

"Cancer Prevention: Protecting Your Bladder," *Johns Hopkins Health Alerts* (August 31, 2006): www.johnshopkinshealthalerts.com.

Way 18. Book 'Em, Danno

At the base of the brain stem: Henriette Anne Klauser, *Write It Down, Make It Happen: Knowing What You Want — And Getting It!* (New York: Simon & Schuster, 2001), 33.

DIB: Harvard School of Public Health Nutrition Source, "Vitamins": www.hsph.harvard.edu/nutritionsource/vitamins.html.

Way 20. Say It Loud, Sing It Proud

Mantra has always been central to healing in India: Russill Paul, *The Yoga of Sound: Healing and Enlightenment through the Sacred Practice of Mantra* (Novato, CA: New World Library, 2004), xx–xxi.

DIB: Sound Healers Association: www.soundhealersassociation.org. National Center for Complementary and Alternative Medicine, "National Institutes of Health, Energy Medicine: An Overview": http://nccam.nih.gov/health/backgrounds/energymed.htm.

Way 21. Know Your Yin from Your Yang

DIB: William Collinge, *The American Holistic Health Association Complete Guide to Alternative Medicine* (New York: Warner, 1996).

Way 22. Seize the Night

DIB: Tim Simmerman, *Principles and Methods of Practice*, vol. 1 of *Medical Hypnotherapy* (Santa Fe, NM: Peaceful Planet Press, 2007). Prerelease monograph.

DIB: *Books on self-hypnosis abound*: See, for example, Forbes Robbins Blair, *Instant Self-Hypnosis: How to Hypnotize Yourself with Your Eyes Open* (Naperville, IL: Sourcebooks, 2004); and Charles Tebbetts, *Self-Hypnosis and Other Mind Expanding Techniques*, 2nd ed. (Edmonds, WA: Tebbetts Hypnotism Training Institute, 1989).

Way 23. Shake It Up Baby, Now

DIB: Max Velmans, "Defining Consciousness," online background reading for the World Wide Web "Dialogues on Consciousness" course, hosted by the Centre for Consciousness Studies, University of Arizona, Tucson, 1997. Based on extracts from chapters in Max Velmans, ed., *The Science of Consciousness: Psychological, Neuropsychological, and Clinical Research* (London: Routledge, 2006): http://cogprints.org/395/00/Definingconsciousness.html.

Way 24. Imagine All the People

Imagination needs moodling: Brenda Ueland, *If You Want to Write: A Book about Art, Independence and Spirit*, 2nd ed. (Saint Paul: Graywolf Press, 2007), chap. 4.

The individual human mind is like a computer terminal: David R. Hawkins, MD, *Power vs. Force: An Anatomy of Consciousness: The Hidden Determinants of Human Behavior* (Sedona, AZ: Veritas, 1987), 12–13.

DIB: *The second habit*: Stephen R. Covey, *Seven Habits of Highly Successful People: Powerful Lessons in Personal Change* (New York: Fireside, 1989).

DIB: Gerald Epstein, *Healing Visualizations: Creating Health through Imagery* (New York: Bantam Books, 1989).

Way 25. Believe It, or Don't

DIB: Larry Dossey, MD, *Healing Words: The Power of Prayer and the Practice of Medicine* (San Francisco: HarperCollins, 1993).

Argue for your limitations: Richard Bach, *Illusions: The Adventures of a Reluctant Messiah* (New York: Delacorte Press, 1977), 75.

Such thoughts are like bricks: Roger Mills and Elsie Spittle, *The Wisdom Within* (Renton, WA: Lone Pine Publishing, 2001), 46.

Hidden determinants of human behavior: David R. Hawkins, MD, *Power vs. Force: An Anatomy of Consciousness: The Hidden Determinants of Human Behavior* (Sedona, AZ: Veritas, 1987), 39–49.

Way 28. Go Win One for the Team

DIB: *Deaths/Mortality*: National Center for Health Statistics, Center for Disease Control and Prevention, U.S. Department of Health and Human Services: www.cdc.gov/nchs/fastats/deaths.htm.

Way 29. Sh@t or Get Off the Pot

DIB: E. Ernst, "Colonic Irrigation and the Theory of Autointoxication: A Triumph of Ignorance over Science," *Journal of Clinical Gastroenterology* 24, no. 4 (June 1997): 196–98

Stephen Barrett, MD, "Gastrointestinal Quackery: Colonics, Laxatives, and More" (Quackwatch, 2003): www.quackwatch.org/01QuackeryRelated Topics/gastro.htm.

Way 31. Get Lost

DIB: James D. Livingston, "Magnetic Therapy: Plausible Attraction?" *Skeptical Inquirer* (July 1998).

Way 32. Stop, Look & Listen

John Cage's seminal work for silent piano met with considerable scorn: "Listen Hard," *The Economist*, August 29, 2002.

My friend Gina has a different take: Meir Schneider, *Yoga for Your Eyes: Natural Vision Improvement Exercises*, DVD (Malibu, CA: Gemini Sun Records, 2004).

Way 33. Break on Through to the Other Side

If the doors of perception were cleansed: William Blake, *The Marriage of Heaven and Hell* (London, ca. 1794), plate 14, "A Memorable Fancy."

Way 36. (En)Lighten Up, Dude!

DIB: *The only thing that is ultimately real about your journey*: Eckhart Tolle, *The Power of Now: A Guide to Spiritual Enlightenment* (Novato, CA: New World Library, 1999), 88.

Way 38. Look Death Right in the Eye

Humorist Art Buchwald finally did: Art Buchwald, *Too Soon to Say Goodbye* (New York: Random House, 2006), 91.

Way 39. Okay, Have a Crisis, Already!

DIB: Judith Acosta and Judith Simon Prager, *The Worst Is Over: What to Say When Every Moment Counts* (San Diego: Jodere Group, 2002).

Way 40. Lose It or *Lose It!*

Stanton Peele, *The Diseasing of America: How We Allowed Recovery Zealots and the Treatment Industry to Convince Us We Are Out of Control* (San Francisco: Lexington Books, 1989).

Lance Dodes, *The Heart of Addiction* (New York: HarperCollins, 2002).

Thomas and Beverly Bien, *Mindful Recovery: A Spiritual Path to Healing from Addiction* (New York: Wiley, 2002).

Way 42. Make the Call

DIB: T. F. Farrow et al., "Investigating the Functional Anatomy of Empathy and Forgiveness," *Neuroreport* 12, no. 11 (Aug. 2001): 2433–38.

K. A. Lawler et al., "A Change of Heart: Cardiovascular Correlates of Forgiveness in Response to Interpersonal Conflict," *Journal of Behavioral Medicine* 26, no. 5 (Oct. 2003): 373–93.

"Enright Plants Seeds of Forgiveness in Belfast, Milwaukee," University of Wisconsin–Madison News Release, April 26, 2007: www.news.wisc.edu/releases/13724.

Way 45. Respect Your Youngers

In the eyes of the beginner: Wayne Dyer, *The Awakened Life: Beyond Success, Achievement and Performance*, CD (Niles, IL: Nightingale-Conant Corporation, 1990), disk 2, track 9.

Way 46. Touch & Glow

This body-centered question is the starting point: Peter A. Levine, with Ann Frederick, *Waking the Tiger: Healing. Trauma* (Berkeley: North Atlantic Books, 1997).

DIB: "Energy Medicine: An Overview," National Center for Complementary and Alternative Medicine. One of five background papers prepared as part of NCCAM's strategic planning efforts for 2005–2009.

Healing Touch Program: www.healingtouchprogram.com.

Way 47. Love, Love, Love

People in the peace movement: Thich Nhat Hanh, *Peace Is Every Step: The Path of Mindfulness in Everyday Life* (New York: Bantam, 1991), 110.

Way 48. Launch Your Legacy

Chakra chart based on information from Ilchi Lee, *Healing Chakra: Light to Awaken My Soul* (Sedona, AZ: Healing Society, 2002), page xx; and Caroline Myss, *Anatomy of the Spirit: The Seven Stages of Power and Healing* (New York: Harmony Books, 1996), 69.

Way 50. Leave 'Em Laughing

DIB: Bill Resnik, "Humor in the Workplace." Workshop lecture presented at the Diversity Leadership Council's Eighteenth Annual Forum on Diversity (Albuquerque, NM, April 18, 2007).

"Laughter Research Conducted at LLUMC." Loma Linda University School of Medicine News, March 11, 1999. www.llu.edu/news/today/mar99/sm.htm.

About the Authors

*S*heila Key is an award-winning writer and graphic designer who has freelanced for publications ranging from corporate business journals to New Age magazines to anthologies of poetry and art. Sheila also worked in radio for ten years, including stints as a rock DJ at commercial stations in Minnesota and Wisconsin. Most of Sheila's broadcast work was in the noncommercial realm, however, including jobs at NPR affiliates and community radio stations in North Dakota, Wisconsin, West Virginia, Tucson, and San Diego. Sheila lives with her husband and two children in Albuquerque, New Mexico, where she tends to her garden, a growing menagerie, and her blog: www.50waystoleaveyour40s.blogspot.com.

*P*eggy Spencer holds a BA from the University of California Santa Cruz and an MD from the University of Arizona. She completed a residency at the University of New Mexico, is board certified in family medicine, and is currently employed at UNM as staff physician at the Student Health Center and adjunct faculty at the School of Medicine. She writes a column for the *New Mexico Daily Lobo* newspaper answering reader-submitted health questions, contributes articles to *UNM Parent Matters* and *UNM Today*, and blogs at www.pegspot.blogspot.com. Peg is married with two children and lives in Albuquerque. Recipient of the SouthWest Writers Award for best essay in 2006, she'll be leaving her forties this year.